THE ORIGINS OF MACROECONOMICS

THE ORIGINS OF MACROECONOMICS

Edited by
Robert W. Dimand

Volume V
Kalecki and the Marxian Tradition

London and New York

First published 2002
by Routledge
2 Park Square, Milton Park, Abingdon, Oxon, OX14 4RN

Simultaneously published in the USA and Canada
by Routledge
270 Madison Ave, New York NY 10016

Routledge is an imprint of the Taylor & Francis Group

Transferred to Digital Printing 2009

Typeset in Times by
Keystroke, Jacaranda Lodge, Wolverhampton

British Library Cataloguing in Publication Data
A catalogue record for this book is available from the British Library

Library of Congress Cataloging in Publication Data
A catalog record for this book has been requested

ISBN 0–415–24929–5 (set)
ISBN 0–415–24934–1 (volume V)

Publisher's Notes

The publishers have made every effort to contact authors/copyright holders of works reprinted in *Origins of Macroeconomics*. This has not been possible in every case, however, and we would welcome correspondence from those individuals/companies whom we have been unable to trace.

References within each chapter are as they appear in the original complete work.

KALECKI AND THE MARXIAN TRADITION

CONTENTS

VOLUME V KALECKI AND THE MARXIAN TRADITION

ACKNOWLEDGEMENTS

The publishers would like to thank the following for permission to reprint their work:

Duke University Press for permission to reprint Otto Bauer, 'The Accumulation of Capital', trans. J. E. King, *History of Political Economy*, 18, 1986, pp. 87–110. Originally Otto Bauer, 'Die Akkumulation von Kapital', *Die Neue Zeit*, 31, 1913, pp. 831–8 and 862–74. Translation copyright 1986, all rights reserved. Reprinted by permission of Duke University Press.

Polish Scientific Publishers PWN for permission to reprint Michal Kalecki, *Studies in the Theory of Business Cycles 1933–1939*, Oxford, Basil Blackwell, 1967.

Taylor and Francis Ltd for permission to reprint Michal Kalecki, *Essays in the Theory of Economic Fluctuations*, New York, Farrar & Rinehart, 1939.

Taylor and Francis Ltd for permission to reprint Michal Kalecki, *Studies in Economic Dynamics*, London, G. Allen & Unwin, 1943.

Blackwell Publishers for permission to reprint Michal Kalecki, 'Political Aspects of Full Employment', *Political Quarterly*, 4, 1943, pp. 322–31.

INTRODUCTION

The Marxian tradition provided an important strand in business cycle analysis. Building on Karl Marx's schemas of simple and expanded reproduction and on his discussion of the increasing severity of crises as the profit rate declined with the rising organic composition of capital (capital/labour ratio), Marxist economists analysed crises in terms of disproportionality between sectors and underconsumption (Howard and King 1989–92). Rosa Luxemburg (1913), Otto Bauer (1913, reprinted in this volume) and Henryk Grossman (1929) were particularly prominent in debating mathematical models of the eventual breakdown of capitalism. Luxemburg (1913) drew on the reproduction of Volume II of Marx's *Capital* to expound an (imperfect) model of capitalist breakdown due to insufficient demand, which could be staved off temporarily by finding foreign markets or such domestic equivalents of exports as military spending (Howard and King 1989, I, pp. 106–15). In the course of constructing a counterexample to Luxemburg's claim that stable equilibrium growth is impossible in a closed capitalist economy, Bauer developed a sophisticated macrodynamic model with affinities to later Harrod-Domar growth theory (Howard and King 1989, I, pp. 115–20). Grossman (1929), then at the Frankfurt Institute for Social Research and formerly at the Free University in Warsaw, showed that Bauer's numerical example would run out of sufficient surplus value to finance the required accumulation after thirty-six periods (Bauer had examined only the first four periods). However, he built upon the reproduction models of Luxemburg and Bauer to model capitalist breakdown and crisis, albeit with arbitrary rates of accumulation of constant and variable capital (Howard and King 1989, I, pp. 316–36).

Michael Howard and John King (1992, II, p. 19) conclude that 'Marxist analyses of the Depression proved deficient, and the ultimate reason is similar to that applying in the case of bourgeois economics: they lacked an adequate theory of effective demand.' Such Marxist analyses would have benefited from attention to the pioneering contributions of Michal Kalecki (1990), influenced by Luxemburg (1913). The present volume reprints Kalecki's early studies in business cycles, written in Warsaw at the Institute for the Study of Business Cycles and Prices, first published in Polish and not translated until 1966. His first two books in English, *Essays in the Theory of Economic Fluctuations* (1939) and *Studies in Economic Dynamics* (1943), are also included, together with his 1943 essay on the political business cycle.

Don Patinkin (1982) held that the central message of Kalecki's articles from 1933 to 1935 concerned investment cycles, while that of Keynes (1936) was the principle of effective demand, interpreted by Patinkin as the IS goods market equilibrium condition and its stability condition. Even Mario Sebastiani (1994, p. 61), who argues that 'unemployment equilibrium is the core of Kalecki's thought about capitalism', accepts that 'Only later – probably after the *General Theory* was published – did Kalecki seem to realize that the outstanding problem was the systematic waste of resources, and that dealing with it required separating the analysis of equilibrium from that of the dynamic process.' However, Simon Chapple (1991, 1995) argues that Kalecki determined aggregate demand in a manner consistent with Patinkin's version of the principle of effective demand, notably in a 1933 essay that Patinkin (1982, p. 69n) dismissed in a single sentence in a footnote. Whether or not one accepts Kalecki as an independent discoverer of Keynes's principle of effective demand, his work is of great interest as the culmination of a Marxian tradition of macroeconomics, and includes such stimulating insights as his 1943 essay on the political business cycle.

References

Simon Chapple (1991) 'Did Kalecki Get There First? The Race for the General Theory', *History of Political Economy* 23:2, 243–61.

—— (1995) 'The Kaleckian Origins of the Keynesian Model', *Oxford Economic Papers* 47:2, 524–37.

George R. Feiwel (1975) *The Intellectual Capital of Michal Kalecki*. Knoxville: University of Tennessee Press.

Henryk Grossman (1929) *The Law of Accumulation and Breakdown of the Capitalist System, Being Also a Theory of Crises*, trans. and abridged by Jairus Banaiji. London: Pluto Press, 1992.

M. C. Howard and J. E. King (1989–92) *A History of Marxian Economics*, 2 volumes. Princeton, NJ: Princeton University Press.

Michal Kalecki (1990) *Collected Works of Michal Kalecki. Volume I: Capitalism, Business Cycles and Full Employment*, ed. Jerzy Osiatynski, trans. Chester Adam Kisel. Oxford: Clarendon Press.

INTRODUCTION

John Maynard Keynes (1936) *The General Theory of Employment, Interest and Money*. London: Macmillan.

Rosa Luxemburg (1913) *The Accumulation of Capital*, trans. Agnes F. Schwarzchild, with intro. by Joan Robinson. London: Routledge & Kegan Paul, 1951; New York: Monthly Review Press, 1968.

Don Patinkin (1982) *Anticipations of the General Theory? And Other Essays on Keynes*. Chicago: University of Chicago Press.

Mario Sebastiani (1994) *Kalecki and Unemployment Equilibrium*. London and Basingstoke: Macmillan.

History of Political Economy 18:1

CCC 0018–2702/86/$1.50

Otto Bauer's 'Accumulation of capital' (1913)

Translated by J. E. King

Translator's introduction

Otto Bauer (1881–1938) was born in Vienna into a wealthy Jewish family with manufacturing interests in Bohemia. A brilliant student, he earned a doctorate in law with distinction and also studied economics under Böhm-Bawerk. Along with Karl Renner, Rudolf Hilferding, and Max Adler he was one of the most prominent of the Austro-Marxists (Bottomore 1978), publishing early articles on Marxian economics and a classic text on the nationality question (Bauer 1907). Between 1907 and 1914 he was secretary of the Austrian Social Democratic Party. Captured on the Eastern Front in the early months of the war, Bauer spent three years as a prisoner of war in Russia. For nine months in 1918–1919 he served as Foreign Minister of the new Austrian Republic, and from then until the Dollfuss coup he was the effective leader and principal theoretician of the SPÖ. In the Party's 1926 Linz Programme Bauer set out the centrist position characteristic of Austro-Marxism, which rejected both Bolshevism and Revisionism. Forced into exile in Czechoslovakia in 1934, he fled again, to Paris, in May 1938 and died there three months later. Further biographical detail can be found in Braunthal 1945, 70–78, Johnston, 102–5, and—for readers of German—Braunthal 1961. A selection of Bauer's writings, chiefly on political questions, is contained in Bottomore and Goode.

Bauer's article 'The accumulation of capital' was published in 1913 in *Die Neue Zeit* (31.1:831–38, 862–74), the theoretical organ of the German Social Democratic Party. Ostensibly merely a review of Rosa Luxemburg's book of that title, the article in fact presents a sophisticated two-sector Marxian growth model which, by including an increasing organic composition of capital, goes significantly further than Marx's own treatment of extended reproduction in Volume II of *Capital*. In his discussion of under- and overaccumulation Bauer also integrates growth theory, trade cycle analysis, and the problem of imperialism. The article provoked a detailed 'anti-critique' by Rosa Luxemburg (Luxemburg and Bukharin 1972) featured in Paul Sweezy's pioneering account of the 'breakdown controversy' (Sweezy, 103 n, 186–89), and inspired more than one rational reconstruction of Marxian cycle theory (see, for example, Bronfenbrenner

Correspondence may be addressed to the translator, Department of Economics, Gillow House, University of Lancaster, Lancaster, LA1 4YX, ENGLAND.

1965). Most recently three papers in *HOPE* have provided mathematical formulations of Bauer's model and compared it with Harrodian growth theory (Orzech and Groll 1983; Bronfenbrenner and Wolfson 1984; Samuelson and Wolfson 1986).

THE ACCUMULATION OF CAPITAL, BY OTTO BAUER

Accumulation and Capacity to Consume

Every year the capitalists convert part of the surplus value they have obtained into capital. They use part of the surplus value to extend existing factories and establish new ones, thereby expanding their productive capacity and increasing the labour force at their command. Marx calls this conversion of part of surplus value into capital the *accumulation of capital*. The further capitalist development progresses, the smaller becomes the part of surplus value consumed by the capitalists, and the larger the part which they accumulate. The *rate of accumulation*, the ratio of accumulated to total surplus value, rises.

While the accumulation of capital is boundless, the productive capacity of society expands, and the mass of commodities produced in the capitalists' factories increases massively, narrow limits are set to the *capacity to consume* of capitalist society. The purchasing power of the *working class* grows more slowly than capital; for, as the value of labour power falls with the development of the forces of production, the share of the working class in the value of the social product declines. But the purchasing power of the *capitalist class* also grows more slowly than capital. The more the capitalists accumulate, the less they can consume. Thus the *capacity to consume* of capitalist society falls further and further behind the boundlessly developing forces of production. This internal contradiction of the capitalist mode of production leads to the *decline in the rate of profit* that becomes apparent in disastrous crises, in which the mass of commodities thrown onto the market by the expanded productive capacity searches in vain for purchasers.

The explanation of crises in terms of disproportionality between the accumulation of capital and society's power to consume was first developed by *Sismondi*, followed by *Malthus, Chalmers*, and *Rodbertus*. For Sismondi it formed an essential component of his critique of capitalism; for Malthus and Chalmers it was an assumption behind their demonstration that capitalist society needs 'third persons' to be able to sell its commodities at all—third persons who consume without producing.

The explanation of the decline in the rate of profit in terms of disproportionality between the accumulation of capital and the growth of the work force was first provided by the 1821 *Pamphlet,*[1] *Hodgskin,* and *Ramsay.*

The defenders of capitalism have attacked this theory. They deny the possibility of general overproduction, arguing that with the growth of commodity production, the purchasing power of the producers would also increase. Crises could arise only from disproportionality between the sectors of production, not from general overproduction. And none of this could be altered by the fact that the worker has to share the value of his product with the capitalist. For the less the workers can consume, the greater becomes the purchasing power of the capitalists. The demand for commodities thus remains unchanged in total, whether the workers' share in the value of the product rises or falls. Exactly the same applies to the rate of accumulation: if it increases, proportionally fewer consumer goods are indeed purchased, but more means of production. So argued *Ricardo, MacCulloch, Say.*

No more than crises is the decline in the rate of profit to be explained by overaccumulation. The rate of profit falls only because the growing difficulties in supplying food increase the value of labour power and reduce the rate of surplus value. The decline in the rate of profit is thus attributed to inevitable natural laws: to overpopulation and the diminishing fertility of the land. So argued especially *Ricardo* and *John Stuart Mill.*

Marx finally disposed of this objection from the Ricardo-Say school, but at the same time he also gave an entirely new version of Sismondi's teaching concerning the internal contradiction of capitalist accumulation. He divided capitalist production into two parts: *the production of means of production and the production of consumer goods.* He demonstrated that the reproduction of capital can take place only if definite quantitative relations exist between the two branches of production. But in capitalist society this harmony cannot be established except as a "result of the process of dissolution of the existing disharmonies."[2] Hence crises appear not as accidental phenomena caused by chance disproportionalities in production, but as unavoidable phases in the reproduction of capital, because only through crises are the necessary quantitative relations established between the two branches of social production. The decline in the rate of profit, however, occurs even with full proportionality in production, not as a result of inevitable natural laws but as the effect of the fact that capital

1. Bauer here refers to an anonymous pamphlet entitled *The source and remedy of the national difficulties, deduced from principles of political economy, in a letter to Lord John Russell,* published in London in 1821 and praised by Marx in volume III of *Theories of surplus value* (Marx 1972, 238–41, 252–57). [*Translator*]

2. Here, as elsewhere, Bauer apparently cites Marx but does not give a source. [*Translator*]

grows faster than the labour power it sets in motion, which alone produces surplus value.

The models in the second volume of *Capital*, in which Marx presented the conditions for equilibrium between the two branches of production, powerfully influenced the *Russian economic literature*. The latter discussed the question whether capitalism was a 'transitional necessity' also for Russia; whether, as the *Zapadniki* ('Westernisers') believed, Russia too must accept the economic, social and political institutions of western and central Europe or whether, as the *Slavophiles* thought, she could preserve her national individuality and originality. Put in socialist terms: whether in Russia, too, concentration of capital, proletarianisation of the mass of the people, class conflict between bourgeoisie and proletariat are the preconditions for socialism, as the *Social Democrats* taught; or whether Russia could construct a socialist community on the basis of the *mir*, the peasant village commune, without having to go through capitalism, as the *Narodniki* ('Populists') and their followers, the *Social Revolutionaries*, supposed. Now in this controversy the question was raised as to whether capitalism could establish itself outside the area of western and central Europe; whether the development of capitalistic production in the East must not founder upon the impossibility of selling the commodities produced by its expanded productive capacity. In the battle against the Narodniki the Marxists showed, using Marx's models, that capitalism could expand further and further, that productive capacity could be increased more and more powerfully, without the capitalists lacking a market for their commodities, and thus that equilibrium between the output of means of production and of consumer goods is constantly re-created through the capitalistic mechanism itself.

The controversy between the Marxists and the Narodniki in Russia was decided by history. But now *Rosa Luxemburg* takes up the thesis of the limitedness of capitalism once more, admittedly for a quite different purpose. Her book, *The accumulation of capital: a contribution to the economic analysis of capitalism* (Berlin, Vorwärts, 1913),[3] poses a new version of the problem which has appeared, over and over again, since the days of Sismondi.

We first assume simple reproduction: the entire surplus is consumed, and none of it is accumulated. According to Marx the total production can be presented in this case as follows:

I. Means-of-production industries

Constant capital (c) + variable capital (v) + surplus value (m)

3. The English translation is Luxemburg 1951. [*Translator*]

II. Consumer-goods industries

Constant capital (c_1) + variable capital (v_1) + surplus value (m_1)

The *means-of-production industries* must buy food from the consumer-goods industries: (i) to feed their workers, amounting to v; (ii) for consumption by their capitalists, amounting to m; thus $v + m$ *in total*. On the other hand the *consumer-goods industries* have to buy c_1 means of production, from the industries which have produced them, to renew their constant capital. The exchange between the two groups takes place without disturbance if $c_1 = v + m$. This is the equilibrium condition in simple reproduction.

It is different with reproduction on an extended scale. Here the total production can be set out in the following model:

I. Means-of-production industries

Constant capital (c) + variable capital (v) + the consumed part of surplus value (k) + the accumulated part of surplus value (a) -

II. Consumer-goods industries

Constant capital (c_1) + variable capital (v_1) + the consumed part of surplus value (k_1) + the accumulated part of surplus value (a_1)

Difficulties arise here. The means-of-production industries buy food amounting to $v + k$, and the consumer-goods industries buy the same quantity of means of production to renew their constant capital. But what happens to a and a_1? First of all, a takes the form of means of production: who can buy them? And a_1 is embodied in consumer goods: where are they sold? Here Rosa Luxemburg seizes upon the old hypothesis of 'third persons.' She believes that *the part of surplus value which is to be accumulated cannot be realised at all unless capitalist production can sell its excess values outside its own sphere, to non-capitalistically producing petit-bourgeois and small peasants*. This explains the pressure of capital for the extension of its markets. Hence the effort to destroy natural economy, to transform simple commodity production everywhere into capitalist production, to make the whole earth into a market area for capitalist industry: hence *imperialism!* But once the market area can be expanded no further, capitalism can no longer sell a large part of its commodities. It suffocates in the wealth which it has produced. Its last hour approaches. This is the fundamental idea in Comrade Luxemburg's work. We must now examine whether it is correct.

Accumulation and Population Growth

Every society with a growing population must extend its productive capacity each year. This will be just as necessary for the socialist society of the future as for the capitalist society of the present, exactly as it was for the simple commodity production or the peasant economy of the past, which produced for its own needs.

Let us assume that in a socialist society the population grows at 5 per cent each year. Next year society will have 5 per cent more people to feed than this year. Thus society must (i) produce this year the consumer goods which the extra population will need next year; thus for example it must build enough houses for the total housing stock to be increased by 5 per cent, and grow enough grain for the supply of bread after the next harvest to be increased by 5 per cent, and so on; (ii) produce this year enough means of production for the necessary work places and instruments of labour to be placed at the disposal of the 5 per cent larger labour force next year. Every year society must devote a part of its labour to the production of the consumer goods and the means of production which will be needed by the extra population in the following year.

Now capitalist society must do the same. But here the extension of productive capacity and food supplies is bound up with the accumulation of capital. A part of surplus value is converted into capital, and indeed one part of the accumulated surplus value is added to variable and another part to constant capital. The capitalists carry out this accumulation in order to increase their profit; but the social consequence of accumulation is to supply the consumer goods and means of production required by the increase in population. The growth in variable capital represents the supply of food, and the growth in constant capital the provision of work places and instruments of labour for the increase in population.

But while in socialist society the social organs responsible for the planning of production ensure that the expansion of productive capacity and food supplies keeps pace with population growth, capitalist society has no such organs. Here the accumulation of capital depends upon the decisions of the capitalists. Hence accumulation can lag behind population growth or run ahead of it. We now wish to discover, first, *how the accumulation of capital must take place in order that it may remain in equilibrium with population growth*. Once we know this we will understand without any difficulty what effects the disturbance of this equilibrium condition must bring about.

We assume that the population grows at 5 per cent per annum. If equilibrium is to be maintained, variable capital must also grow at 5 per cent each year. Constant capital increases faster than variable capital; how much faster is determined by the state of technical development attained at any given time. We will assume that constant capital grows at 10 per cent per annum. Thus we obtain, for example, the series [displayed in Table 1]. To simplify the investigation we assume for the time being that the rate of surplus value remains unchanged, at 100 per cent.[4] Every year the mass of surplus value is exactly equal to that of variable capital. Which part of surplus value is accumulated, which part consumed? That part is accumulated which allows variable capital to grow at 5 per cent and constant capital at 10 per cent. For example, in the first year, surplus value amounts to 100,000. To increase constant capital (from 200,000 to 220,000) 20,000 is required; to increase variable capital (from 100,000 to 105,000) 5,000 is needed. Thus in total 25,000 is accumulated and 75,000 consumed. Over four years the process can be represented as [shown in Table 2]. First of all, 5 per cent of surplus value is withdrawn each year from capitalists' consumption and used for the expansion of variable capital. But in addition part of the surplus value must be used to increase constant capital. Since surplus value grows at the same rate as variable capital, but constant capital grows faster than variable, that part of surplus value added to constant capital must increase from year to year. The rate of accumulation (the ratio of the accumulated part of surplus value to the total surplus value)[5] is thus [that shown in Table 3].

Table 1

	Constant capital	Variable capital
Year 1	200,000	100,000
Year 2	220,000	105,000
Year 3	242,000	110,250
Year 4	266,000	115,762

Table 2

	Total surplus value	Consumed	Added to constant capital	Added to variable capital
Year 1	100,000	75,000	20,000	5,000
Year 2	105,000	77,750	22,000	5,250
Year 3	110,250	80,539	24,200	5,511
Year 4	115,762	83,374	26,600	5,788

4. This critical assumption is not in fact relaxed later in the article. A constant rate of surplus value and rising labour productivity imply increasing real wages, but it is not clear whether Bauer recognised this. [*Translator*]

5. By "rate of accumulation" Bauer thus means the capitalists' savings ratio and *not* the rate of growth of total capital, which he later defines as the "social rate of accumulation" in contrast with the "capitalist rate of accumulation" (see below, p. 00). [*Translator*]

Table 3

	Approximate rate of accumulation
Year 1	25%
Year 2	26%
Year 3	27%
Year 4	28%

[*Table 4*]

	Means-of-production industries (I)	Consumer-goods industries (II)	Total production
Constant capital (c)	120,000	80,000	200,000
Variable capital (v)	50,000	50,000	100,000
Consumed part of surplus value (k)	37,500	37,500	75,000
Accumulated part of surplus value:			
Added to constant capital (κ)	10,000	10,000	20,000
Added to variable capital (β)	2,500	2,500	5,000
Total	220,000	180,000	400,000

On the assumption of an unchanged rate of surplus value, reproduction on an extended scale with an increasing organic composition of capital is thus possible only if the rate of accumulation rises from year to year. *If accumulation and population growth are to remain in equilibrium, the growth of the rate of accumulation must bear a definite quantitative relationship to the growth of population and the increase in constant capital.* The numbers in our example show this to be the case. Anyone accustomed to thinking in terms of abstract numbers will find no difficulty with the equation which expresses this quantitative relationship in general terms.

Up to now we have looked at the growth of total capital. We will now investigate how this total capital must be divided between the two great branches of production, the output of means of production and that of consumer goods. We assume that production in the first year can be represented [as shown in Table 4].

Now, how must the capital be divided in the second year? It is impossible for the surplus value accumulated in the two departments of production to be invested productively in the same departments in the following year, for the progress to a higher organic composition of capital requires a movement of capital from the consumer-goods industries into the production of means of production. Thus we must calculate *what part of the surplus*

[*Table 5*]

Variable capital	105,000
Consumed part of surplus value	77,750
That part of surplus value added to variable capital	5,250
Total	188,000

[*Table 6*]

	Means-of-production industries (I)	Consumer-goods industries (II)	Total production
Constant capital (c)	134,666	85,334	220,000
Variable capital (v)	53,667	51,333	105,000
Consumed surplus value (k)	39,740	38,010	77,750
Accumulated surplus value:			
Added to constant capital (κ)	11,244	10,756	22,000
Added to variable capital (β)	2,683	2,567	5,250
Total	242,000	188,000	430,000

value accumulated in the consumer-goods industries must be transferred to the production of means of production to be used for their expansion.

According to Tables 1 and 2 we have, in the second year [the figures in Table 5]. In the second year the value of the products of the consumer-goods industries must thus amount to 188,000, for the consumer goods can only be exchanged against these sums of value.

In the first year in the consumer-goods industries 10,000κ (constant capital) and 2,500 β (variable capital) are accumulated. Now if the value of the products of these industries in the second year amounts to 188,000, only 5,334 κ and 1,333 β of the surplus value accumulated there in the first year can be invested in the consumer-goods industries. The remainder must be transferred to the means-of-production industries.[6] Consequently we have for the second year [the figures in Table 6]. By the same calcu-

6. [*Bauer's note*]: These numbers were calculated in the following way. In the second year the value of the products of the consumer-goods industries amounts to $c + v + m = 188{,}000$. As the rate of surplus value is 100 per cent, so that $v = m$, it follows that: $c + 2v = 188{,}000$. The growth of constant capital in the production of consumer-goods between the first and second years is $(c - 80{,}000)$, and the growth of variable capital is $(v - 50{,}000)$. If a similar proportion of κ and β are to be transferred to the means-of-production industries, we have:

$$(c - 80{,}000) : (v - 50{,}000) = 10{,}000 : 2{,}500.$$

Solving these equations we obtain

$$v = 51{,}333 \text{ and } c = 85{,}334.$$

Table [7]

	c	v	k	κ	β	Total
Year 1						
I	120,000 +	50,000 +	37,500 +	10,000 +	2,500 =	220,000
II	80,000 +	50,000 +	37,500 +	10,000 +	2,500 =	180,000
	200,000 +	100,000 +	75,000 +	20,000 +	5,000 =	400,000
Year 2						
I	134,666 +	53,667 +	39,740 +	11,244 +	2,683 =	242,000
II	85,334 +	51,333 +	38,010 +	10,756 +	2,567 =	188,000
	220,000 +	105,000 +	77,750 +	22,000 +	5,250 =	430,000
Year 3						
I	151,048 +	57,576 +	42,070 +	12,638 +	2,868 =	266,200
II	90,952 +	52,674 +	38,469 +	11,562 +	2,643 =	196,300
	242,000 +	110,250 +	80,539 +	24,200 +	5,511 =	462,500
Year 4						
I	169,124 +	61,738 +	44,465 +	14,186 +	3,087 =	292,600
II	96,876 +	54,024 +	38,909 +	12,414 +	2,701 =	204,924
	266,000 +	115,762 +	83,374 +	26,600 +	5,788 =	497,524

lations we can ascertain the quantities for the following year, obtaining the series [shown in Table 7].

The numbers which Marx uses in the second volume of *Capital* in his presentation of the reproduction process are arbitrarily selected and not without contradictions. This is easily explained by the fact that Engels found this part of Marx's work unfinished in his literary remains. But because Marx did not present his train of thought impeccably, it does not follow that this train of thought is false. Rosa Luxemburg is content to demonstrate the arbitrary nature of the Marxian models, and she seems to believe that without the arbitrariness the models would be entirely untenable. We prefer to look for a satisfactory clarification of Marx's train of thought and to conduct our own investigation with a model which is free from arbitrariness. Hence we have presented here *models which, once one accepts the assumptions, have nothing else arbitrary about them, and whose magnitudes are actually derived, one from the other, with compelling necessity.*

Only the assumptions made in the first year are arbitrary: that constant capital amounts to 200,000 and variable capital to 180,000; that variable capital is divided equally between the two departments of production; that the rate of surplus value is 100 per cent; and that the rate of accumulation is the same in both departments. Also arbitrary is the assumption that constant capital grows at an annual rate of 10 per cent, and variable capital at 5 per cent. But if these assumptions are accepted, all the magnitudes presented in the model follow from them with mathematical necessity. Development cannot proceed differently, so long as the rate of surplus value remains unchanged and the rate of accumulation stays the same in both departments. With our model we thus obtained an impeccable basis for investigating the problem posed by Comrade Luxemburg.

The Realisation of Surplus Value

From Table [7] above we now wish to discover whether the mass of commodities in which the accumulated part of surplus value (κ + β) is embodied can be sold within the capitalist world itself, or whether, as Comrade Luxemburg believes, it can find a market only outside the capitalist world.

To begin with we investigate the sale of commodities in the first year. In the means-of-production industries commodities with a value of 220,000 are produced in the first year. Who buys these commodities? First of all, the capitalists in the means-of-production industries themselves need new means of production. They meet part of this requirement by using means of production from their own factories for the renewal or extension of their factories. Thus the coal mines themselves need coal to heat their steam boilers, and the ironworks themselves require iron to renew or extend their productive capacity. Another part of the requirements is met by purchases inside the means-of-production industries. Hence ironworks buy coal from the mines, the mines buy machines from the machine factories, and the machine factories buy iron from the ironworks. Now, how large is the total requirement of the means-of-production industries for new means of production? The constant capital used up in production must first be replaced: to this end the capitalists in the means-of-production industries have to use means of production with a value of 120,000. In addition, however, the capitalists wish to use the surplus value which they accumulated in the first year to extend their existing factories or to establish new ones. If in the next year they wish to employ a capital which is 12,500 larger, they must this year build new work places, buy new machines, and increase their stocks of raw materials, so that the labour force which they will engage at the beginning of the next year will find the necessary instruments of labour ready for them. To this end they must buy from each other means of production with a value of 10,000. Thus of the means of production produced in department I (with a value of 220,000) a total of 130,000 are sold within this department itself: (i) 120,000 for the renewal of productive capacity; (ii) 10,000 for the extension of productive capacity for the next year. But what happens to the remaining means of production, with a value of 90,000?

First, the capitalists in the consumer-goods industries have to buy means of production with a value of 80,000, in order to renew the means of production used up in the first year. But in addition the capitalists in the consumer-goods industries must this year build work places, buy machines, and expand their stock of raw materials, because they wish to carry on production next year on an extended scale. To this end department II buys from department I means of production with a value of 5,334. Thus in total the capitalists in the consumer-goods industries buy means of production, for the production of consumer goods, amounting to 85,334. Hence only 4,666 worth of means of production remain unsold. Where do they find a market?

The capitalists in the consumer-goods industries transfer part of the surplus value accumulated in the first year to the means-of-production industries—either by themselves establishing factories for the production of means of production, or by transferring part of their accumulated surplus value, through the mediation of the banks, for use of the capitalists in the means-of-production industries;[7] or through buying shares in companies which produce means of production. If the productive capacity of department I is to be extended in this way in the next year, the elements of this productive capacity (workplaces, machines, raw materials) must already be purchased this year. Thus the means-of-production industries buy commodities with a value of 4,666 with that capital which was accumulated in the consumer-goods industries but is to be invested in the means-of-production industries. And so the capitalists in the consumer-goods industries buy, in addition to means of production with a value of 85,334 for use in the production of consumer goods,[8] additional means of production with a value of 4,666 destined for the production of means of production.

Thus, all in all, the means of production produced in the first year are sold in the manner [set forth in Table 8]. And so the whole mass of commodities produced in department I is sold, in its entirety.

Now, how does the sale of consumer goods take place? To simplify our investigation we first assume that the entire working class live in company houses (houses owned by the industrial capitalists) and do all their shopping in company stores (stores owned by the industrial capitalists). In this case all the consumer goods which are produced come into the hands of the industrial capitalists: one part to be consumed by them, the other to be sold by them to the workers.

In the first year the value of the commodities produced by the consumer-goods industries amounts to 180,000. A part of these commodities is used in the consumer-goods industries themselves. First, commodities with a

7. The original reads "consumer-goods industries." [*Translator*]
8. The original reads "means of production." [*Translator*]

[*Table 8*]

1. To capitalists in the means-of-production industries:	
a. For the renewal of productive capacity in I:	120,000
b. For the extension of productive capacity in I:	10,000
Total	130,000
2. To the capitalists in the consumer-goods industries:	
a. For the renewal of productive capacity in II:	80,000
b. For the extension of productive capacity in II:	5,334
c. For the extension of productive capacity in I:	4,666
Total	90,000

value of 37,500 are consumed by the capitalists of the consumer-goods industries themselves. In addition the capitalists in the consumer-goods industries must supply part of their commodities to their company stores, so that they can be sold to the workers in department II. Now, how large must this part be? The income of the workers in II amounts to 50,000 in the first year and to 51,333 in the second year. Thus the capitalists in II must supply 51,333 out of the product of the first year to their company stores, so that the necessary stock of food will be ready for the workers in the second year. Hence, from the product of department II, 37,500 + 51,333 = 88,833 are sold within this department itself.

The capitalists in the means-of-production industries must buy commodities from the consumer-goods industries. For their own needs they require consumer goods with a value of 37,500. Apart from this they need to buy commodities for their company stores. In the first year the income of the workers in department I amounts to 50,000. This will be increased to 52,500 in the second year through the addition of the accumulated surplus value. The capitalists in I must thus buy 52,500 from the first year's product of II for their company stores, so that the latter can supply the needs of the workers in the second year. Thus the total requirement of the capitalists in the means-of-production industries amounts to 37,500 + 52,500 = 90,000 consumer goods.

Finally the capitalists in II use part of the surplus value they have accumulated for the construction of new factories, in which means of production are produced. These factories too must establish company stores, which have to buy part of the consumer goods produced in the first year in order to supply the requirements of the workers employed in the new factories in the second year. They purchase consumer goods with a value of 1,167.

Consequently the consumer goods purchased in the first year are sold as [shown in Table 9]. Thus the entire mass of commodities produced in department II is sold. At the same time we see from this description that

[*Table 9.* How consumer goods bought in the first year are sold]

1. To the capitalists in the means-of-production industries	
a. For their own needs	37,500
b. For the company stores	52,500
Total	90,000
2. To the capitalists in the consumer-goods industries	
a. For their own needs	37,500
b. For the company stores in II	51,333
c. For the company stores in I	1,167
Total	90,000

the capitalists in the consumer-goods industries buy means of production with a value of 90,000 from the means-of-production industries and sell them consumer goods with the same value. The transactions between the two departments consist of the exchange of consumer goods with a value of 90,000 for means of production of 90,000. In consequence the entire value of the product of both departments, and hence also the total surplus value, is realised.

Up to now we have assumed that the sale of commodities is undertaken by the industrial capitalists themselves; that the industrial capitalists themselves accumulate stocks of commodities and sell them to the workers. But in essence nothing changes in the entire process if this function is taken over by a special capital—if *commercial capital* takes the place of the commodity capital of the industrial capitalists. In this case the following changes occur: (i) merchants rather than company stores buy the commodities, and (ii) part of commodity capital is in the hands of the merchants rather than the industrial capitalists, who share their surplus value with them; to the extent to which this occurs, the demand of the merchants replaces the demand for commodities from the industrial capitalists. The total consumer power of society remains unaffected by this. In this case too the entire surplus value is realised.

In the same way one can convince oneself, using Table [7], that not only in the first year but also in every subsequent year the entire value of the product of both departments is sold without any disturbance, and the total surplus value is realised. Comrade Luxemburg's hypothesis that the accumulated part of surplus value could not be realised is thus false. How was it possible for Comrade Luxemburg to arrive at this false hypothesis?

We have assumed *that in the first year the capitalists buy those means of production which will be set in motion by the growth of the work force in the second year, and that they buy in the first year those consumer goods which they will sell in the second year to the additional work force*. Hence

[*Table 10*]

Sales of means of production	
To renew constant capital in I	120,000
To renew constant capital in II	80,000
Total	200,000
Sales of consumer goods	
To the capitalists in I	37,500
To the workers in I	50,000
To the capitalists in II	37,500
To the workers in II	50,000
Total	175,000

a part of the product of labour in the first year will be sold for use in the second year as additional productive capital. If we do not accept this assumption, the realisation in the first year of the surplus value produced in that year would in fact be impossible, and sales would then be as shown in [Table 10]. In this case, in fact, means of production amounting to 20,000 and consumer goods amounting to 5,000 remain unsalable. It would actually be precisely that part of surplus value destined for accumulation ($\kappa + \beta$) which could not be realised.

Rosa Luxemburg believes that the accumulated part of surplus value cannot be realised. In fact it cannot be realised *in the first year,* if the material elements of additional productive capital (new workplaces, machines, raw materials, consumer goods for the increased labour force) are sold only in the second year. But they *must* finally be sold, if not in the first then certainly in the second year; for otherwise the extension of productive capacity and the productive investment of the newly formed capital is impossible. And as soon as they are sold, the hitherto only latent part of the surplus value produced in the first year will be realised.

Marx presents the circulation of capital in the following way:[9]

$$G - W \begin{cases} Pm \\ A \end{cases} \ldots P \ldots W_1 - G_1$$

9. The capitalist begins with a sum of money (*G:* Geld). He purchases commodities (*W:* Waren) of equivalent value, consisting of means of production (*Pm:* Produktionsmittel) and labour power (*A:* Arbeitskraft). In the course of the production process (*P:* Produktion) they are converted into qualitatively different commodities of greater value ($W_1 > W$). Finally, they are sold for a sum of money equivalent to their value ($G_1 > G$). The standard English notation (with *C, M* etc.) has not been adopted here, to avoid confusion with symbols used by Bauer elsewhere in the article. [*Translator*]

Now we can divide W_1 into three parts: $W_1 = W + w + w_1$, where W is equal to the cost price $(c + v)$, w to the consumed and w_1 to the accumulated part of surplus value. We then obtain the following picture:

$$G - W \begin{cases} Pm \\ A \end{cases} \ldots P \ldots \begin{pmatrix} W \\ + \\ w \\ + \\ w_1 \end{pmatrix} - \begin{pmatrix} G \\ + \\ g \\ + \\ g_1 \end{pmatrix}$$

After the conclusion of the production process, circulation is divided into three partial processes. And of course the time required for the conversion of the produced commodities into money can be divided only between these three partial processes. So long as only the process $W - G$ is concluded, absolutely no surplus value is realised, but only the cost price. Once the process $(W + w) - (G + g)$ is completed, the consumed but not the accumulated part of surplus value is realised. The accumulated part of surplus value can be realised only in the instant in which w_1 is converted into g_1; in other words, only in the instant when those commodities are sold in which the accumulated part of surplus value is embodied—those commodities, that is, which constitute the material elements of the additional productive capital for the next production period.

Thus it can actually occur that only the consumed and not the accumulated part of surplus value is realised; it will occur if $(W + w)$ has already been converted into $(G + g)$, but w_1 has not yet been converted into g_1. But this phenomenon is only a *transient phase* in the whole circulation process. To the extent to which the productive investment of newly formed capital takes place, the accumulated part of surplus value will be realised. Thus if $(W + w)$ is converted into $(G + g)$ in the first year, while w_1 produced in the first year can be changed into g_1 only in the second year, then of course only the consumed part of surplus value can be realised in the first year. That part of surplus value produced in the first year and destined for accumulation is not, however, unrealised; it too will be realised, but only in the course of the second year.

The *surplus product* which is produced in the first year consists of two parts: (i) *consumer goods* for the capitalists, and (ii) *the material elements of additional productive capital*. As soon as the first component is sold, the consumed part of surplus value is realised; as soon as the second component is sold, the accumulated part of surplus value is realised. It is impossible to realise that part of surplus value denoted by k first, and only later to supply consumer goods to the capitalists: the realisation of k takes place precisely through the sale of the first component of the surplus product. It is equally impossible to realise the $(\kappa + \beta)$ part of surplus value *first*, and only later to buy the material elements of additional productive capital: the realisation of ($\kappa + \beta$) occurs precisely in the sale of the second component of the surplus product. Thus it is not at all strange that Rosa Luxemburg cannot realise ($\kappa + \beta$) in the first year, for she assumes that capitalists buy the material elements of additional productive capital only in the second year. Realisation of ($\kappa + \beta$), and productive use of the surplus product in which ($\kappa + \beta$) is embodied, are two aspects of the same phenomenon. They can only occur *simultaneously*. The whole difficulty arises only if it is assumed that the selling period of the commodities in which the accumulated surplus value is embodied is longer than the selling period of the other commodities. In reality, of course, the circulation time of individual capitals and its division into purchase-, production-, and selling-periods varies considerably. Marx had to ignore these differences and assume the annual product to be sold within each year, so that he could set out the reproduction of capital in a simple model. But even if we disregard this assumption of the Marxian model, we obtain no other result than the unsurprising conclusion that part of the surplus value produced each year is realised only in the course of the following year.

Comrade Luxemburg believes that the commodities in which ($\kappa + \beta$) is embodied must be sold outside the capitalist world for the realisation of the surplus value contained in them to be possible. Well, what sort of commodities are they? They are the very means of production which the capitalists need to expand their productive capacity, and the very consumer goods which are required to feed the growth in the work force. If these commodities were to be ejected from the capitalist world, production on an extended scale in the following year would be altogether impossible; there would be neither the necessary means of production for the extension of productive capacity nor the food supplies required to feed an increased work force. *The withdrawal of this part of the surplus product from the capitalist market would not, as Rosa Luxemburg believes, make accumulation possible; on the contrary, it would make any accumulation impossible.*

In reality the accumulated part of surplus value is also realised within capitalist society. Of course this realisation generally comes about step by step. For example, the food used in the second year to feed the additional work force is probably as a rule produced in the first year and sold by the producers to wholesale capital; a part of the surplus value embodied in this food is thus already realised in the first year. The realisation of the other part of this surplus value then occurs only in the course of the second year, with the sale of the food by wholesalers to small shopkeepers and by the latter to the workers. Naturally the model cannot include all the details of this process. But these details alter nothing in the process as a whole. Whatever the idiosyncrasies in the circulation of individual capitals, the fact remains that the realisation of ($\kappa + \beta$) takes place simultaneously with the productive investment of the newly formed capital. Expressed more clearly, the former occurs in and through the latter. To that extent our model gives a true picture of reality. It proves that the accumulated part of surplus value can also be realised within the capitalist sphere itself.

Underaccumulation and Overaccumulation

Our model (Table [7]) assumes that (i) the work force grows at 5 per cent per annum, (ii) variable capital grows at the same rate as the work force, and (iii) constant capital grows faster than variable, to the extent required by technical progress. On these assumptions it is not surprising that no difficulty arises in realising surplus value. The workers' capacity to consume grows in this case at the same rate as their numbers. The capacity to consume of the capitalists grows equally fast, for with the number of workers the mass of surplus value also grows. Thus the capacity to consume of the whole society increases at the same rate as the value of the product. Accumulation changes nothing in this; it means only that less of consumer goods and more means of production are needed than in simple reproduction. The extension of the area of production, which is a precondition of accumulation, is here given by the growth of the population.

However, this equilibrium condition between accumulation and population growth can be maintained only if the rate of accumulation grows sufficiently rapidly that, despite the increasing organic composition of capital, variable capital increases at the same rate as the population (Table 3 above). If the increase in the rate of accumulation falls behind this requirement, the growth of variable capital will lag behind the increase in those seeking work. The condition which then arises can be termed *underaccumulation*.

The first effect of underaccumulation is the formation of an *industrial reserve army*. Part of the increased population remains unemployed. Unemployed proletarians exert pressure on wages. *Wages fall and the rate of surplus value rises*. Since in a society consisting only of capitalists and workers the unemployed proletarians can find no source of income other than wages, wages must fall and the rate of surplus value must rise, until the entire working population finds employment despite the relatively reduced variable capital. The change in the distribution of the value of the product which thus occurs is brought about by the fact that, with the increase in the organic composition of capital in which technical progress is expressed, *the value of labour power has declined*, so that *relative surplus value* has been created.

If, with an unchanged rate of accumulation, the rate of surplus value has increased, then the accumulated part of surplus value will also have risen. Thus the mass of surplus value used to increase variable capital grows too.

It must continue to increase on this course *until equilibrium between the growth of variable capital and the growth of population is restored.*

I term the ratio between the accumulated part of surplus value and the total surplus value the *capitalist rate of accumulation,* and the ratio between the accumulated part of surplus value and the value of the total product (variable capital plus surplus value) the *social rate of accumulation.*[10] We can thus present in the following way the mechanism through which underaccumulation is repeatedly generated. If the social rate of accumulation is too small, an industrial reserve army comes into existence. Wages fall and the rate of surplus value increases. Hence the social rate of accumulation also increases, even with an unchanged capitalist rate of accumulation; for, with the same capitalist rate of accumulation, the social rate of accumulation grows with the rate of surplus value. Under the pressure of the industrial reserve army the rate of surplus value increases and with it the social rate of accumulation, until the latter has become large enough for variable capital to grow at the same rate as the work force, in spite of the increasing organic composition. Once this occurs, the industrial reserve army is absorbed and equilibrium between accumulation and population growth is restored.

Thus the capitalist mode of production contains within itself the mechanism which, when accumulation lags behind population growth, adjusts it to population growth once more. But this adjustment takes place at the expense of the working class. It comes about through an increase in the rate of exploitation. Again and again the progress to a higher organic composition of capital causes underaccumulation; again and again it is overcome by the increase in the rate of surplus value. It is a *periodically recurring* but always only a *transient phase in the industrial cycle.*

Eventually the rising social rate of accumulation reaches a point at which variable capital grows faster than the population. We term the situation in which this occurs *overaccumulation.* But, like underaccumulation, overaccumulation too is always just a transient phase in the industrial cycle.

Marx describes the situation of overaccumulation in the following way: "Once capital grows so fast that neither the absolute labour time nor the relative surplus labour time performed by this population can be increased (the latter would anyway be impossible in a case where the demand for labour was so strong that wages tended to rise); thus where the increased capital can produce only the same or even a lower mass of surplus value than before, absolute overproduction will occur. In other words, the increased capital $C + \Delta C$ will produce no more profit, or even less, than before its expansion by ΔC. In both cases there will be a sharp and sudden

10. [*Bauer's note*]: Up to now when I have referred to the rate of accumulation, I have always meant the capitalist rate of accumulation.

fall in the general rate of profit, but this time because of a change in the composition of capital due not to the development of productivity but to an increase in the money value of variable capital (on account of increased wages) and the corresponding decline in the ratio of surplus to necessary labour."[11] This point indicates the *absolute limit of accumulation*. When it is reached, the adjustment of accumulation to population growth results in a devastating crisis with massive unemployment of capital, wholesale destruction of values, and a sudden fall in the rate of profit.

In reality the adjustment can take place before the absolute limit described by Marx is reached. If the rate of accumulation is too large, the reserve army is quickly absorbed, wages rise, the rate of surplus value falls, and with it the social rate of accumulation, thereby slowing down the growth of variable capital once more and achieving the adjustment of accumulation to population growth.

Moreover in a situation of overaccumulation the rate of profit falls very quickly. The rate of profit declines as a result of the progress towards a higher organic composition of capital, even if accumulation and population growth are in equilibrium. It falls even faster if the progress towards a higher organic composition of capital is accompanied by a declining rate of surplus value, as is the case with overaccumulation. In the moment "in which the above-mentioned tendencies for the rate of profit to decline assert themselves against the tendencies which, because of increasing demand, have caused a rise in prices and profits, the crisis begins."[12] In the crisis and the resulting industrial depression, the rate of accumulation is drastically reduced and the growth of variable capital once again lags behind population growth.

Like underaccumulation, overaccumulation is also generated again and again by the mechanism of the capitalist mode of production itself. There exists in the capitalist mode of production *a tendency for the adjustment of capital accumulation to the growth of population*. This adjustment has occurred as soon as variable capital grows at the same rate as the work force; but constant capital grows faster, to an extent required by the development of productivity. In a socialist society the social organs responsible for the control of production would ensure, consciously and according to a plan, that the growth of population is provided for. This adjustment must also occur in capitalist society, but here it can take place only by means of

11. Marx, *Capital* III.1, 233. (This reference is to an unspecified German edition. The passage appears, with a slightly different translation, in the 1962 Foreign Languages Publishing House, Moscow, edition, pp. 246–47; pagination differs slightly in later Moscow editions [*Translator*]).

12. Hilferding, *Finance capital*, 823. (This reference is to R. Hilferding, *Das Finanzkapital*, Vienna, 1910; an English translation with different pagination, edited by T. Bottomore, was published in London in 1981 [*Translator*]).

great crises, with unemployment, wage reductions, and increasing exploitation on the one hand, and unemployment of capital, destruction of values, and a declining rate of profit on the other.

The tendency for accumulation to adjust to population growth also dominates international relations. Each year countries with continuous overaccumulation invest a large and growing part of their accumulated surplus value overseas. Examples: France and England. Countries with continuous underaccumulation attract capital from abroad and send labour overseas. Examples: the agrarian countries of eastern Europe. *The expansion of productive capital within a country itself is always restricted by the available work force.* In the long run variable capital can grow no faster than the population, while constant capital always grows faster than variable to a degree determined by the stage of development of the forces of production. Thus one can appreciate the anxiety of the capitalists over the declining birth rate: decelerating population growth narrows the limits to the growth of their capital.

Viewing the capitalist world economy as a whole, the tendency for accumulation to adjust to population growth is apparent in the industrial cycle. Prosperity is overaccumulation, which destroys itself in the crisis. The ensuing depression is a time of underaccumulation which also brings itself to an end, inasmuch as the depression itself produces the conditions for renewed prosperity. *The periodic alternation of prosperity, crisis, and depression is the empirical expression of the fact that the mechanism of the capitalist mode of production automatically generates overaccumulation and underaccumulation, with the accumulation of capital adjusting again and again to the growth of population.*

The individual capitalist believes that it depends only on his 'abstinence' as to what part of surplus value he 'saves.' In reality capitalists are taught in every crisis that objective limits are set to their accumulation; that capital can be increased only to the extent that society is able to increase its productive capacity. Given the stage of development of the forces of production, the objective limit to accumulation is determined by the growth of the work force. Accumulation presupposes an expansion in the area of production; and the area of production is increased by population growth. "Increased population appears to be the foundation of accumulation as a continuous process."[13] If population growth were to cease altogether, variable capital could no longer be permanently increased; accumulation would then be possible only to the extent that the development of the forces of production required additional constant capital to employ an unchanged labour force.

13. Marx, *Theories of surplus value*, II.2, 244. (This reference is to the first German edition, Stuttgart, 1905–10; a one-volume English translation of Part II of *Theories of surplus value*, with different pagination, was published in London in 1969 [*Translator*].

Comrade Luxemburg knows that there are objective limits to the accumulation of capital. But she sets these limits incorrectly. Comrade Luxemburg believes that the accumulation of capital would be altogether impossible in a capitalist economy which could not sell its commodities in peasant or petit-bourgeois areas. This view is false. Every society with a growing population must extend its productive capacity. Under the capitalist mode of production the extension of productive capacity assumes the particular form of the accumulation of capital. This accumulation takes place without disturbance so long as it maintains a definite quantitative relationship on the one hand with population growth, on the other with the development of productivity which expresses itself in the progress towards a higher organic composition of capital. Of course, again and again the development of accumulation pushes ahead of these limits; but again and again accumulation is brought back within them through periodic recurrent economic crises. The result of our investigation is thus (i) that the accumulation of capital is possible even in an isolated capitalist economy, so long as it does not exceed a fixed limit at any particular time, and (ii) that it is brought back automatically to this limit through the mechanism of the capitalist mode of production itself.

This formulation cannot be interpreted as an apology for capitalism, for while the apologists for capital want to demonstrate the unbounded nature of accumulation—capacity to consume rises automatically with production!—we uncover the limit to accumulation. While the apologists wish to prove the impossibility of general crises, we show that the laws of accumulation can only operate through general crises and the consequent unemployment, wage reductions, increasing mass suffering, and growing bitterness and indignation among the mass of the workers.

The Explanation of Imperialism

Comrade Luxemburg explains imperialism in the following way. In an isolated capitalist society the conversion of surplus value into capital would be impossible. It becomes possible only if the capitalists constantly extend their market in order to sell, in areas where there is not already capitalist production, that part of the surplus product in which the accumulated part of surplus value is embodied. Imperialism serves this purpose.

As we have seen, this explanation is incorrect. Accumulation is also possible, and necessary, in an isolated capitalist society. And that part of the surplus product in which the accumulated surplus value is embodied cannot be sold to the peasants and petit-bourgeois of the colonies, because it is needed in the capitalist motherland itself to extend productive capacity.

But a kernel of truth is concealed in the false explanation. While accumulation in an isolated capitalist society is not impossible, it is nevertheless confined within limits. Imperialism does in fact serve to widen these limits.

Accumulation is limited, first, by the growth of the work force. Now imperialism greatly increases the working masses who are compelled to sell their labour power to capital. It does so by undermining the old modes of production in colonial territories, thereby forcing millions of people either to emigrate to capitalist areas or to work in their own homelands for the European or American capital invested there. Since—with a given organic composition of capital—the extent of accumulation is fixed by the growth of the available work force, imperialism is thus in fact a means of further expanding the limits of accumulation.

Besides the growth in population, the extent of accumulation is determined by the development of the forces of production, by the progress to a higher organic composition of capital. Imperialism can also stimulate this development: firstly, since it gives special encouragement to those branches of production with an above-average organic composition of capital; secondly, since it places at the disposal of capital material elements of production situated outside its homeland and thereby powerfully accelerates the development of the forces of production and the increased productivity of labour.

The adjustment of accumulation to population growth is accomplished through periodic crises. In every crisis huge masses of commodities are unsalable, and a large part of productive capital lies fallow. Crises are more easily overcome if it is possible to sell vast quantities of commodities in new sales areas. Imperialism seeks to make this, too, possible for capital.

If imperialism is not a means of making accumulation possible in the first place, it is however a means of stretching its limits and facilitating the overcoming of the crises which periodically result from overaccumulation. This effort is in fact one root of imperialism, though not the only one.

In Comrade Luxemburg's view capitalism could not exist at all without continuous expansion. If a barrier were set to the growth of its markets a large part of surplus value could not be realised, and it would break down of its own accord.

In our opinion capitalism is conceivable even without expansion. But with or without expansion, capitalism itself causes its own downfall. If its expansion is possible, it arouses indignation among the working masses through an arms race, through increasingly oppressive taxation, and through catastrophic wars. If its expansion is prevented, the limit to accumulation is narrowed and crises become more frequent, longer, more devastating. In either case a growing part of the popular masses recognise that their life interests are incompatible with the continuation of the capitalist mode of production.

Capitalism will not founder on the mechanical impossibility of realising surplus value. It will succumb to the indignation to which it drives the masses. Capitalism will break down, not when the last peasant and the last petit-bourgeois on the entire earth are converted into wage labourers, so that no extra market is open to capitalism. It will be brought down much sooner, by the growing "indignation of the working class, constantly increasing, schooled, united, and organised by the mechanism of the capitalist production process itself."

The translator is grateful for the assistance of R. Rothschild and two anonymous referees.

References

Bauer, O. 1907. *Die Nationalitätenfrage und die Sozialdemokratie*. Vienna.
Bottomore, T. 1978. "Introduction," in Bottomore and Goode 1978, 1–44.
——— and P. Goode, eds. 1978. *Austro-Marxism*. Oxford.
Braunthal, J. 1945. *In search of the millennium*. London.
——— 1961. "Otto Bauer. Ein Lebensbild," in *Otto Bauer. Eine Auswahl aus seinem Lebenswerk. Mit einem Lebensbild Otto Bauers*. Vienna.
Bronfenbrenner, M. 1965. '*Das Kapital* for the modern man.' *Science and Society* 29. 4:419–38.
——— and M. Wolfson 1984. 'Marxian macrodynamics and the Harrod growth model.' *History of Political Economy* 16. 2:175–86.
Johnston, W. M. 1972. *The Austrian mind: an intellectual and social history*. Berkeley, Calif.
Luxemburg, R. 1951. *The accumulation of capital*, with introduction by Joan Robinson. London.
——— and N. Bukharin 1972. *Imperialism and the accumulation of capital*. Edited by K. J. Tarbuck. London.
Marx, K. 1972. *Theories of surplus value, volume III*. London.
Orzech, Z., and S. Groll 1983. 'Otto Bauer's scheme of expanded reproduction: an early Harrodian growth model.' *History of Political Economy* 15. 4:529–48.
Samuelson, L., and M. Wolfson 1986. 'Expository Marxism and comparative economic dynamics.' *History of Political Economy* 18.1:65–95.
Sweezy, P. M. 1942. *The theory of capitalist development*. New York.

STUDIES IN THE THEORY OF BUSINESS CYCLES

1933–1939

by

MICHAL KALECKI

BASIL BLACKWELL

1969

631 10070 9

Translated from the first Polish edition
BY MRS. ADA KALECKA

First Polish edition 1962
English edition reprinted 1969

Published in conjunction with
PWN — Polish Scientific Publishers
Warszawa

CONTENTS

INTRODUCTION

It is difficult now to recapture the state of orthodox opinion in the early years of the great depression.

There was heavy unemployment in Britain even before the world slump set in. In 1929 Lloyd George was campaigning for a programme of public works. In reply, British officials propounded the "Treasury View" that if the Government borrowed, say, a hundred million pounds to set men to work on road building and so forth, foreign investment would be reduced by an equal sum and no overall increase in employment would occur.

In 1931 the Labour Government was led to destruction through the belief that it was necessary to balance the budget in order to save the exchange value of sterling.

Academic opinion was serenely oblivious to the problems of reality. Professor Robbins, surrounded by unemployed labour and idle plant, defined economics as "the science which studies human behaviour as a relation between ends and scarce means which have alternative uses".[1]

According to accepted theory the price level was determined by the quantity of money. But the suggestion that the depression might therefore be relieved by increasing the quantity of money was confined to cranks. In the orthodox view it would create a dangerous inflation.

The Marxists abused the academics, but they shared their belief in the principles of sound finance.

In this fog Keynes was groping for a theory of employment. He had backed up Lloyd George with a rather vague and half-baked argument that an increase in investment would generate an increase in saving (so that borrowing in one form need not be subtracted from borrowing in another)[2] and he set a young pupil, R. F. Kahn, to work it out properly. During the sessions of the Macmillan Committee on currency and banking he was coming to the view that there was a fallacy in the accepted argument that a cut in money wage rates would restore profitability to enterprise, by lowering costs relatively to prices, because prices would come

[1] *Essay on the Nature and Significance of Economic Science*, 1932.

[2] J. M. Keynes and H. D. Henderson, *Can Lloyd George Do It?*

down more or less in proportion. But in his great theoretical *Treatise* his mind was working on a different plane and it failed to produce a theory of employment, though it contained the highly significant conception that an increase of investment without (as we should now put it) a corresponding increase in the propensity to save raises profits, while an increase in propensity to save without a corresponding increase in investment reduces them.

Over the continent, no doubt including Poland, the fog of orthodoxy was even thicker than in England. Only in Sweden Wicksell's pupils were puzzling out a new line. In *Monetary Equilibrium* published in Swedish in 1931, Gunnar Myrdal twitted Keynes upon his "attractive Anglo-Saxon kind of unnecessary originality" but he was not altogether clear of the fog himself.

The *Treatise on Money* was passed for the last time to the printers in September 1930 and Kahn's article appeared in the *Economic Journal* of June 1931, setting out the analysis of the multiplier—the relation of an increase in employment in investment to the total increase in employment that it generates—and showing how the rise in incomes that accompanies an increase in investment brings about a rise in savings of an equal amount.

There followed a great bout of argument that churned over these ideas for three years.

In 1933 I published a kind of interim report, which clears the ground for the new theory but does not supply it.[3] It was not till the summer of 1934 that Keynes succeeded in getting his theory of money, his theory of wages and Kahn's multiplier into a coherent system.

In January 1935 he wrote to Bernard Shaw: "I believe myself to be writing a book on economic theory which will largely revolutionize—not, I suppose at once but in the course of the next ten years—the way the world thinks about economic problems".[4]

The main lines of that theory nowadays seem so obvious that it is hard to remember that they did indeed require a revolution in thought. They may be summarized in the propositions that the rate of saving is governed by the rate of investment, that the level

[3] "The Theory of Money and the Analysis of Output", in the first number of the *Review of Economic Studies;* reprinted in *Collected Economic Papers,* Vol. 1.

[4] R. F. Harrod, *Life of Keynes,* p. 462.

of prices is governed by the level of money wage rates, and that the level of interest rates is governed by the supply and demand of money.

The General Theory of Employment, Interest and Money was published in January 1936. Meanwhile, without contact either way, Michal Kalecki had found the same solutions. The first essay in this volume was published in 1933. Like a prelude it enunciates themes later to be elaborated.

The last few pages bring out sharply the first Keynesian proposition that an increase in investment does not require a prior decision to increase saving. Firms and governments are free to raise their rate of outlay on investment at any time, and, when they do, savings, one way or another, increase to the corresponding extent.

In the English version of the theory there was a lot of unnecessary confusion between the equality of savings and investment as an accounting identity (which requires appropriate definitions of the two quantities and the time period) and the substantive proposition that a decision to increase investment will generate a corresponding net increase in saving, while a decision to increase saving will not. The trouble arose because the careless language of Keynes and his popularisers (amongst whom I must plead guilty) gave an opening to opponents who delighted to interpret a mistaken formulation as a substantive error at the heart of the new theory.

Kalecki avoided all this pother because he started from the assumption that wage incomes are fully spent (with a negligible time-lag) on consumption, so that the gross overall surplus on the sale of consumer goods is equal to the wage bill of the investment sector *plus* the expenditure of capitalists for consumption. "The workers spend what they get; the capitalists get what they spend." An increase in investment increases profits to whatever extent is required to raise saving out of profits to the corresponding extent.

The reason for this more direct attack upon the problem arose from the different background of the two discoverers. Keynes had been brought up in the Liberal tradition of social harmony, which slurs over class differences. The preface to the *General Theory* ends thus: "The ideas which are here expressed so laboriously are extremely simple and should be obvious. The difficulty lies, not in the new ideas, but in escaping from the old ones, which ramify for those brought up as most of us have been, into every corner of our minds."

Kalecki was not brought up so. The only economics he had studied was in Marx. Keynes could never make head or tail of Marx. In the letter to Shaw, quoted above, he maintains that his new theory is going to cut the ground from under the feet of the Marxists. But starting from Marx would have saved him a lot of trouble. Kahn, at the "circus" where we discussed the *Treatise* in 1931, explained the problem of saving and investment by imaging a cordon round the capital-good industries and then studying the trade between them and the consumption-good industries; he was struggling to rediscover Marx's schema. Kalecki began at that point.

In another sense, however, Kalecki's aproach was more conventional than Keynes'. He arrived at a general theory through a model of the trade cycle. It was probably for this reason that the significance of his ideas was not recognized by readers of his French publication in 1935. The problem of the trade cycle had always been regarded in the orthodox tradition as a special kind of conundrum, apart from the main body of doctrine. Keynes, on the other hand, attacked the main body directly and never really succeeded in getting out a coherent theory of the cycle.

It is interesting to notice that the first version of Kalecki's model had the same missing link as Keynes'. In Keynes' scheme, the concept of *marginal efficiency of capital* means that, at any moment, there is in existence a schedule of possible investment projects, listed in descending order of their prospective profitability (allowing for risk). The schedule is cut off at the point where the prospective rate of net profit is equal to the rate of interest to be paid for finance. This determines the total value of investment to be undertaken. Later, Kalecki asked the pertinent question: If there are schemes which promise a rate of profit greater than the rate of interest, would not each individual enterprise be willing and anxious to carry out an indefinitely large amount of investment? It was no use to reply that a faster rate of investment would raise the cost of capital goods and so reduce the prospective rate of profit, for the rise in costs would come about as a result of actual investment, *ex post*, while the marginal efficiency of capital concerns investment plans *ex ante*.

In his later works Kalecki supplied an answer (as he tells us in the Preface, with some trouble) by introducing into the argument the obvious fact that no individual enterprise can command an indefinitely large amount of finance at a given rate of interest. He took risk over from the demand side (where it lies rather uneasily in Keynes' scheme) to the supply side, and postulated that the amount of finance that each individual enterprise will commit to investment is an increasing function of the prospective rate of profit, depending upon the ratio of borrowing to its own capital. Then, with any given distribution of capital amongst enterprises, there is a particular relation between the total amount of investment plans being drawn up at any moment and the level of prospective profits.

Whether this solution is accepted or not, it draws attention to the fact that some kind of solution is required. The re-publication of his first attempt should certainly convince Kalecki's readers that his later labours were not unnecessary.

The third theme of the Keynesian revolution—that the rate of interest is a monetary phenomenon—which raised so much controversy for us, seems to have come quite naturally to Kalecki. This also was probably due to his immunity from orthodox teaching, in which (even today) there is a strong tendency to confuse the rate of interest with the rate of profit.

The second theme of the *General Theory,* the interrelation between prices, money wages and employment, was no less important than the first. This theme is clearly sounded in the third essay in this volume and elaborated in the fifth.

Keynes' *General Theory* was worked out in terms of a closed system. It was left to me to sketch its extension into the theory of foreign trade in slump conditions. Here also Kalecki's work claims priority.

One point he raises that we had somehow overlooked. The analysis of imperfect competition was being developed side by side with the *General Theory* but they were not brought to bear on each other. Already in 1935 Kalecki had seen the connection when he showed that, if prices are sticky, a cut in money-wage rates actually reduces employment. This theme is further elaborated in the last essay in this volume, which points the way to an important element in the extension of the analysis into long-run problems that is going on today.

The publication of this volume in English provides the evidence for one of the most striking of the great coincidences of scientific discovery. But it is valuable not only in the context of the history of thought. Its sharp and concentrated statement provides a better introduction to the general theory of employment, interest and money than any that has yet been produced.

Cambridge JOAN ROBINSON

FOREWORD

This book contains my early studies in the theory of the business cycle published in Poland in the years 1933–1939 which were almost inaccessible after the war. As the reader will find, I had dealt in these essays with a number of basic issues which were in the centre of economic discussion during the subsequent twenty years[1]. The studies also reflect the most essential features of my theory of the business cycle. I modified in my later work only the factors determining investment decisions and I allowed for changes in inventories in the course of the business cycle, from which I abstracted in the first version.

Incidentally, this development of my theory (as presented in the *Theory of Economic Dynamics*[2]) which was quite laborious, hardly earned me any applause. It was frequently maintained that the first version was more lucid and elegant.[3] I myself consider that the modifications introduced meant some progress since the later version of the theory seems to me better founded and more realistic. Nevertheless this attitude of my readers is an additional inducement to re-publish my earlier studies.

The essays in this volume are put in chronological order. Some details concerning the dates of the publication of the originals and the way in which they are re-published here are given below.

The Outline of a Theory of the Business Cycle is the first (and most essential) part of my booklet *An Essay on the Theory of Business Cycle* which was published in 1933. I supplemented this study by a short passage concerning the problem of the money market taken from my *Essai d'une théorie du mouvement cyclique des affaires* published in the French quarterly *Revue d'Economie Politique,* March–April 1935. Apart from this nothing of importance has been added either to this or to other items.

The paper *On Foreign Trade and Domestic Exports* was published in *Ekonomista* in 1933 (No. 3).

[1] It is worth noticing that there is a certain affinity between these theories of mine and those of Rosa Luxemburg.

[2] George Allen and Unwin, London 1954.

[3] See, for instance, R. G. D. Allen, *Mathematical Economics,* London 1956, p. 261, and Oskar Lange, *Pisma ekonomiczne i społeczne 1930–1960* (Papers in Economics and Sociology 1930–1960), Warszawa 1961, p. 285.

The Mechanism of the Business Upswing and *The Business Upswing and the Balance of Payments* were published in the weekly *Polska Gospodarcza* in 1935. They are in a sense a popular version of the preceding two items. It may, therefore, be advisable to start reading the book from these two chapters.

Finally *Money and Real Wages* (consisting of a theoretical and a statistical part) is a complete reprint of a booklet under the same title published in Warsaw in 1939.

M. KALECKI

1. OUTLINE OF A THEORY OF THE BUSINESS CYCLE

Assumptions

We shall consider a *closed* economic system, *devoid of trends* i.e. one which returns to its original state after each cycle. In addition we shall make the following assumptions.

1. *Gross real profits.* By gross real profits P we understand the aggregate real income of capitalists including depreciation per unit of time consisting of their consumption and saving

$$P = C + A \tag{1}$$

Thus C denotes all goods which are consumed by capitalists and A includes—since we abstract from workers' savings or their "capitalist" incomes—all goods which are used in the reproduction and expansion of fixed capital as well as the increase in inventories. In the future A will be referred to as gross accumulation.[1]

The personal consumption of capitalists is relatively inelastic. Let us assume that C consists of a constant part B_0 and a part which is proportionate to gross profits:

$$C = B_0 + \lambda P \tag{2}$$

where λ is a small constant.

From equations (1) and (2) we obtain:

$$P = B_0 + \lambda P + A$$

$$P = \frac{B_0 + A}{1 - \lambda} \tag{3}$$

i.e. the gross real profits P are proportionate to the sum $B_0 + A$ of the constant part of capitalists' consumption B_0 and the gross accumulation A.

The gross accumulation A is according to the above equal to

[1] The national income is equal on the one hand to the sum of profits and wages, and on the other—to the sum of: (1) the reproduction and expansion of fixed capital and the increase in inventories A; (2) the consumption of capitalists; and (3) the consumption of workers. Since the latter is equal to wages, profits are equal to $C + A$.

the sum of the production of investment goods and the increase in inventories.[2] *For the sake of simplicity we assume that aggregate inventories remain constant throughout the trade cycle.*

It follows from the above assumptions that the real profits P are proportionate to B_0+A, where B_0 denotes the constant part of the capitalists' consumption, and A the gross accumulation which is equal to the production of investment goods.

2. *Investment.* We assume that the period of construction ϑ is the same for any investment project. This of course is not in fact the case. ϑ should be considered as the average construction period, and our assumption that the construction period is the same for all types of investment must be considered as one of the simplifications introduced in our model.

Three stages should be distinguished in the investment activity: 1) investment orders, i.e. all types of orders for investment goods for the sake of reproduction and expansion of the capital equipment the volume of which per unit of time will be denoted by I; 2) production of investment goods A which, according to the above, is equal to the gross accumulation; 3) deliveries of finished equipment per unit of time D.[3]

The relation between I and D is simple: deliveries D at the time t are equal to the investment orders I placed at the time $t-\vartheta$; thus the curve D is the curve I shifted by the time-lag ϑ (see Fig. 1).

The relation between the production of investment goods A and investment orders I is somewhat more complicated. The shaded area of the trapezium (Fig. 1) is equal to the value of orders placed during a period of the length ϑ ending at the time t, and thus equal to the portfolio of orders at the time t which we shall denote by W. Indeed, since the completing of each order takes the time ϑ all orders which come within the shaded

[2] We do not include capital under construction in inventories; a change in the volume of such capital is covered by "production of investment goods"; however, this item does not cover changes in inventories of other investment goods (e.g. in inventories of steel or cement). Changes in this type of inventory must be thus included in "the increase in inventories".

[3] A and D differ in that A is the production of investment goods in general, and D is the production of finished investment goods. It follows that the difference $A-D$ is equal to the increment of capital under construction per unit of time.

area have not yet been completed, while all equipment previously ordered has already been installed. Next, production of investment goods is equal to the portfolio of orders W divided by the period of construction:

$$A = \frac{W}{\vartheta} \tag{4}$$

Indeed, if each order is to be completed during the time ϑ then $\frac{1}{\vartheta}$ of its volume must be completed per unit of time; thus to the portfolio of orders W, there corresponds the production of investment goods $\frac{W}{\vartheta}$.

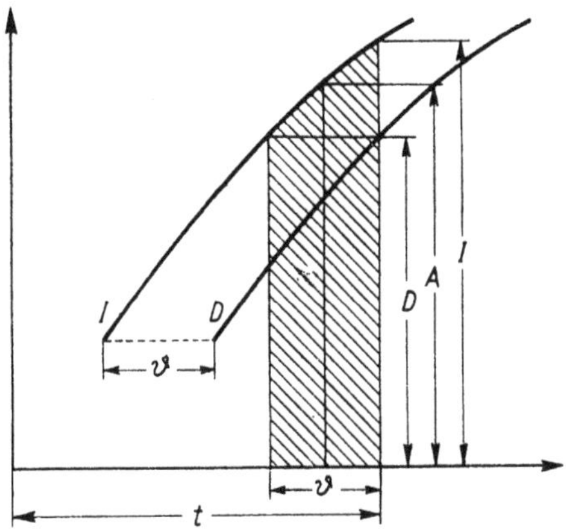

FIG. 1

It follows that A is equal to the shaded area of the trapezium divided by ϑ. If the upper side of the trapezium were rectilinear, the production of investment goods A would, at the time t, be equal to the median of the trapezium and thus to the investment orders at the time $t-\frac{\vartheta}{2}$. If the upper side of the trapezium is curvilinear, this will be only approximately true. *The production of investment goods at the time t is thus approximately equal to the investment orders at the time* $t-\frac{\vartheta}{2}$. Thus the curve A is approximately identical with the curve I shifted by $\frac{\vartheta}{2}$ (see Fig. 2).

It should be noticed that the difference $I-D$ is equal to the increase of the portfolio of orders per unit of time, while the difference $A-D$ is equal to the increase of capital under construction per unit of time. (This was already pointed out in the footnote 3 to page 4).

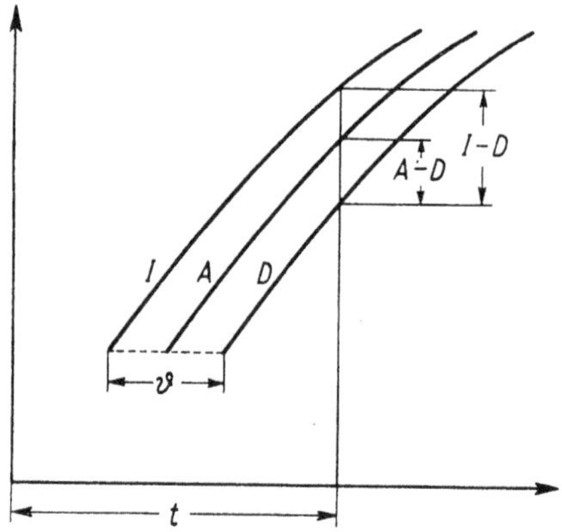

FIG. 2

3. *Changes in the volume of capital equipment.* Let the volume of capital equipment at a given time be denoted by K. Its change during a given period is equal to the difference between deliveries of new equipment and the volume of productive assets going out of use. Denoting the change of the capital equipment K per unit of time by $\frac{\Delta K}{\Delta t}$, deliveries of new equipment per unit of time—as above—by D, and the replacement requirements due to particular productive assets' going out of use per unit of time by U, we obtain:

$$\frac{\Delta K}{\Delta t} = D - U \tag{5}$$

We may assume that replacement requirements remain at a constant level in the course of the business cycle. It is true that the volume of capital equipment K shows in fact small fluctuations, and it might seem therefore that in the part I of the cycle (see Fig. 3), when K is greater than the average, the required replacements are higher than the average as well. However, it should be noticed that in part I the increase in the capital equipment consists of "young" assets of low "mortality", because the "life" of these assets is known to be considerably longer than the length of one cycle (15–30 years as compared with 8–12). Thus fluctuations of the replacement requirements can be considered negligible.

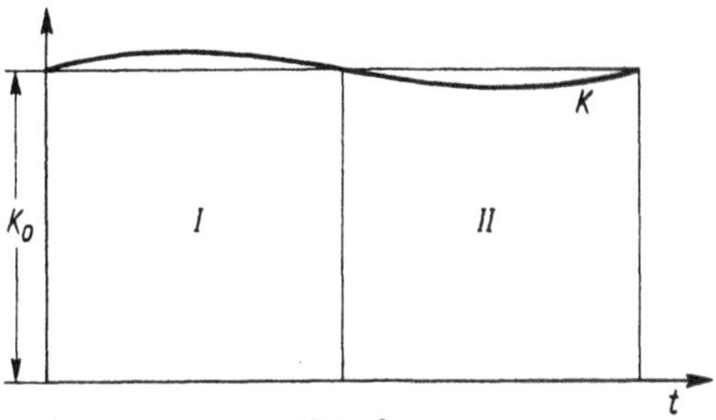

FIG. 3

The constant level of replacement requirements U is equal to the average D_0 of deliveries of new equipment D over one cycle, because we assumed that our system is devoid of trends and the volume of capital equipment returns at the end of the cycle to its original size. Furthermore, for the same reason the average over one cycle of investment orders I_0, of production of investment goods A_0 and of deliveries of new equipment D_0 are all equal. We thus obtain:

$$U = I_0 = A_0 = D_0 \tag{6}$$

4. *Investment orders as a function of gross profitability and of the rate of interest.* The volume of investment orders D at a given time depends on the anticipated net profitability. Thus if entrepreneurs consider investing a capital k in the construction of capital equipment, they will estimate in the first place the anticipated gross profit p. From this we must deduct: 1) the depreciation βk (β being the depreciation rate); 2) the interest on capital k amounting to ik (i being the rate of interest); 3) the interest on the future circulating capital which, if its relation to fixed capital k is denoted by γ, amounts to $i\gamma k$. The anticipated profitability of investment in fixed capital k will thus be

$$\frac{p - \beta k - ik - i\gamma k}{k} = \frac{p}{k} - \beta - i(1 + \gamma).$$

The coefficients β and γ may be considered to remain constant throughout the trade cycle; i is the rate of interest at a given time. The anticipated gross profitability $\frac{P}{K}$ may be estimated from the actual gross profitability of existing plant. We have already denoted the volume of capital equipment at a given time by K and the aggregate gross profit by P; consequently the gross profitability of existing plant is $\frac{P}{K}$. Thus we may conclude that $\frac{p}{k}$ is estimated on the basis of $\frac{P}{K}$, and that the investment orders at a given time depend on the gross profitability $\frac{P}{K}$ and on the rate of interest i.

It should be added that it is not the investment orders I that should be considered a function of $\frac{P}{K}$ and i, but rather the ratio of I to the volume of capital equipment K, i.e. $\frac{I}{K}$; indeed, if P and K increase in the same proportion, $\frac{P}{K}$ will remain unchanged, while I is likely to increase in the same proportion as P and K. Thus we arrive finally at the relation:

$$\frac{I}{K} = f\left(\frac{P}{K}, i\right) \tag{7}$$

where f is an increasing function of $\frac{P}{K}$ and a diminishing function of i.

It is known that in the course of the trade cycle the rate of interest rises in the upswing and falls in the downswing. When we come to develop our theory, we shall try to explain this connection (see page 15). At the moment we shall accept it *a priori*, and on this basis we shall make the following simplifying assumption. *The rate of interest i is an increasing function of the gross profitability* $\frac{P}{K}$.

From this assumption and the equation (7) it follows that $\frac{I}{K}$ is a function of $\frac{P}{K}$:

$$\frac{I}{K} = F\left(\frac{P}{K}\right) \tag{8}$$

Let us also assume that *the rate of interest increases sufficiently slowly in relation to the gross profitability* $\frac{P}{K}$ *for F to be an increasing function.*

Since, as was shown above, the gross profit P is proportionate to B_0+A where B is the constant part of capitalists' consumption and the gross accumulation A is equal to the production of investment goods, $\frac{P}{K}$ is proportionate to $\frac{B_0+A}{K}$ and the equation (8) may be written as follows:

$$\frac{I}{K} = \varphi\left(\frac{B_0+A}{K}\right) \tag{9}$$

where φ is an increasing function.

Moreover, we assume that φ is a linear function i.e.

$$\frac{I}{K} = m\frac{B_0+A}{K} - n \tag{10}$$

The constant m must be positive since φ is an increasing function. Equation (10) may be written in the form:

$$I = m(B_0+A) - nK \tag{10a}$$

We shall now show that n must be positive. From the equation (10a) it follows that

$$n = \frac{m(B_0+A)-I}{K}$$

I representing the orders for goods used for the reproduction and expansion of capital equipment remains always positive; it may, however, possibly approach the zero level. Let us imagine that I falls below the positive value mB_0. For values of I less than mB_0 the expression $\frac{m(B_0+A)-I}{K}$ is greater than $\frac{mA}{K}$ i.e. $\frac{mA}{K}$

will be then less than n. Since, however, the coefficient m is positive, as shown above, and since A (production of investment goods) and K (volume of capital equipment) are also positive, it follows that the coefficient n must be positive.

According to equation (10a), in which the coefficient m and n are positive, the volume of investment orders I is an increasing function of the gross accumulation A and a diminishing function of the volume of capital equipment K.

The Mechanism of the Trade Cycle

1. The main conclusions of the argument in the preceding chapter may be stated as follows:

a) The time-lag between the placing of investment orders and deliveries of new equipment is ϑ; the curve of deliveries D is shifted from the curve of investment orders I by the time ϑ. The curve of the production of investment goods A is shifted from the curve of investment orders approximately by $\frac{\vartheta}{2}$.

b) In our system the production of investment goods A is equal to the gross accumulation (since inventories remain at a constant level).

c) Deliveries of new fixed assets D lead to an increase in the volume of the capital equipment by $D - U$, where U denotes the replacement requirements. U remains constant throughout the trade cycle and its value is equal to the average D_0 of deliveries D over a full cycle. D_0 is also equal to the average of investment orders I_0 and the average production of investment goods A_0.

d) Investment orders I are an increasing function of the gross accumulation A and a decreasing function of the volume of capital equipment:

$$I = m(B_0 + A) - nK$$

where m and n are positive coefficients, and B_0 is the constant part of capitalists' consumption.

2. These points already enable us to say something about the mechanism of the trade cycle. An increase in investment orders calls forth an increase in the production of investment goods which is equal to the gross accumulation. This in turn causes a further increase in investment activity, as indicated by equation (10a).

However, after an interval of time ϑ has elapsed from the time when investment orders have exceeded the level of replacement requirements, the volume of capital equipment starts to increase. Initially this restrains the rate at which investment activity is increasing, and at a later stage causes a decline in investment orders.

In particular it is impossible to stabilize investment activity at a level exceeding the replacement requirements. Indeed, if investment orders remain at a constant level the production of investment goods, which is equal to the gross accumulation, will remain unchanged as well, while capital equipment expands investment being greater than replacement requirements. Under such conditions, however, investment orders will begin to decrease as indicated by the equation $I = m(B_0 + A) - nK$ and the stability of investment activity will be disturbed.

During the depression the process described here is reversed. Investment orders are not sufficient to cover the replacement requirements; this leads to a decrease in the volume of capital equipment and eventually to a resumption of the increase in investment orders. To stabilize investment activity at a level lower than that which provides adequate replacement is as impossible as to stabilize it at a level which exceeds the replacement requirements.

3. We shall now make a detailed examination of the way in which the mechanism of the trade cycle functions. Fig. 4 shows deviations from the average for: investment orders I, the production of investment goods equal to the gross accumulation A, deliveries of new equipment D, i.e. the values: $I - I_0$, $A - A_0$, $D - D_0$. It should be remembered that the averages I_0, A_0, and D_0 are all equal and that they are also equal to the replacement requirements U.

Conclusion (a) at the beginning of this section shows that the curve A is shifted approximately by $\frac{\vartheta}{2}$ and the curve D by ϑ from the curve I.

The ordinate of the curve D is equal to $D - D_0$ which, as shown by conclusion (c), is also equal to the change per unit of time in the volume of capital equipment K. On this basis the curve K can be drawn. The curve K will rise during the period when the ordinate of the curve D is positive and it will decline when the ordinate of the curve D is negative. (Also in this case the abscissa axis is taken to correspond to the average value of K which is denoted by K_0, i.e. deviations from the average $K - K_0$ are again presented here).

By *recovery* we understand here the phase of the cycle of the length ϑ during which investment orders exceed the level of replacement requirements; capital equipment, however, has not yet begun to expand because deliveries of new equipment are as yet lower than the replacement requirements.

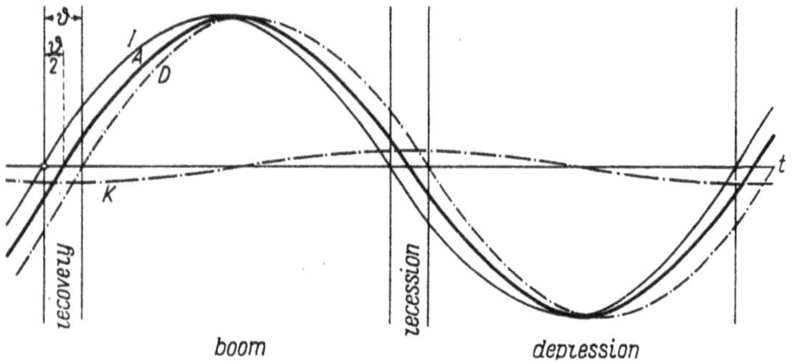

FIG. 4

The production of investment goods A, which is equal to the gross accumulation, increases; but the volume of equipment K is still shrinking, as a result of which investment orders I which are equal to $m(B_0 + A) - nK$ rise steeply.

During the *boom* deliveries of new equipment already exceed the replacement requirements and consequently capital equipment K begins to expand. The increase of K initially restrains the rate of growth of investment orders and subsequently causes their decline. This is followed in the second half of the boom by a decline in the production of investment goods.

During the *recession* investment orders are below the level of replacement requirements. The volume of capital equipment, however, is still expanding because deliveries of new equipment are higher than this level.

The production of investment goods which is equal to the gross accumulation A continues to fall, and this together with the increase of K, produces a steep fall in investment orders.

During the *depression* deliveries of new equipment are already below the level of replacement requirements, and consequently the volume of capital equipment K shrinks. This decrease in K initially slows down the fall in investment orders and subsequently causes their increase. This is followed by a rise in the production of investment goods in the second half of the depression.

4. We considered here the interrelated changes of investment orders, the gross accumulation, and the volume of capital equipment which produce the business cycle. The fluctuations of the gross accumulation which result from this mechanism must also be reflected in the fluctuations of the aggregate production. The gross real profits P are, on the one hand, an increasing function of the gross accumulation A (P is proportionate to $B_0 + A$, where B_0 is the constant part of capitalists' consumption), and on the other hand, they can be expressed as the product of the volume of the aggregate production and of the profit per unit of output.[4]

The relation between changes in the gross accumulation which is equal to the production of investment goods, and those of the aggregate production materialises in the following way. When production of investment goods rises the aggregate production increases directly *pro tanto,* but in addition there is an increase due to the demand for consumer goods on the part of the workers newly engaged in the investment good industries. The consequent increase in employment in the consumer-good industries leads to a further rise in the demand for consumer goods. The levels of aggregate production and of the profit per unit of output will ultimately rise to such an extent that the increment in real profits is equated to the increment of the production of investment goods.

The account of the process is not yet complete because changes in capitalists' consumption have not been taken into consideration. This consumption C is dependent to a certain degree on the aggregate profits P and will increase together with the gross accumulation A since from equation (2) and (3) it follows that $C = \frac{B_0 + \lambda A}{1 - \lambda}$. The increase in capitalists' consumption exerts the same influence as that in the production of investment goods: the production of consumer goods for capitalists expands; this leads to an increase in employment and this raises again the demand for consumer

[4] We assume here that aggregate production and profit per unit of output rise or fall together, which is actually the case. This results at least to some extent from the fact that a part of wages are overheads.

goods for the workers which causes a further rise in production. *The aggregate production and the profit per unit of output will ultimately rise to such an extent as to assure an increment in real profits equal to that of production of investment goods and capitalists' consumption.*

5. Some doubts may be raised by the final part of the preceding paragraph. The conclusion that the increase in capitalists' consumption increases in turn their profits, contradicts the common conviction, that the more is consumed the less is saved. This approach which is correct with regard to a single capitalist, does not apply to the capitalist class as a whole. If some capitalists spend money, either on investment or consumer goods, their money passes to other capitalists in the form of profits. Investment or consumption of some capitalists creates profits for others. Capitalists as a class gain exactly as much as they invest or consume, and if—in a closed system—they ceased to construct and consume they could not make any money at all.

Thus capitalists, as a whole, determine their own profits by the extent of their investment and personal consumption. In a way they are "masters of their fate"; but how they "master" it is determined by objective factors, so that fluctuations of profits appear after all to be unavoidable. Capitalists' consumption is a function of the gross accumulation. The gross accumulation which is equal to the production of investment goods is determined by investment orders which in turn were undertaken in a past period on the basis of the profitability in that period, i.e. on the basis of the gross accumulation and the volume of capital equipment in that period.

The question may still arise, where the capitalists find the "means" to increase the production of investment goods or their personal consumption. If we abstract from the "technical" elements of the money market, we may say that the capitalists as a whole do not need money in order to achieve this since, as shown above, the expenditure of some capitalists is converted into profits for others; the outlay on construction of a fixed asset is by no means "frozen", as some people think, and "released" only as the capital invested is gradually written off—but it is already returned in the course of construction in the form of profits accruing to the firms whose sales (either of investment or consumer goods) are directly or indirectly connected with this construction. If during a particular period more money is spent, e.g. out of bank deposits, then *pro tanto* more money flows back into the banks in the form of realised profits, so that the sum of deposits remains unchanged. In actual fact, however, credit inflation is inevitable owing to the "technical" elements of the money market mentioned above. This is connected with the fact discussed above that the increase in production of investment goods or in the capitalists' consumption, i.e. in real profits must be reflected in the increase in aggregate production. This increase (together with the usual rise of prices which accompanies it) engenders a higher demand for money in circulation, i.e. cash and current accounts, which is met by credit inflation.

Thus the demand for money in circulation increases during the upswing and falls during the downswing. The rise and fall in the rate of interest follows suit. This is the basis of our assumption that the rate of interest i is an increasing function of the gross profitability $\frac{P}{K}$ (which is only a crude approximation). This assumption enables us to pass from equation (7):

$$\frac{I}{K} = f\left(\frac{P}{K}, i\right) \tag{7}$$

where f is an increasing function of $\frac{P}{K}$ and a decreasing function of i, to the equation (8):

$$\frac{I}{K} = F\left(\frac{P}{K}\right). \tag{8}$$

Moreover, we assumed that i rises sufficiently slowly in relation to the gross profitability $\frac{P}{K}$ for the stimulating effect of the increase in the latter upon investment to outweigh the restraining influence of the rise in the rate of interest i. If this rate were to increase sufficiently fast for the influence of the increase in gross profitability to be fully offset, an upswing would prove impossible. There is thus a close connection between the phenomenon of the business cycle, and the response of the banking system to the increase in demand for money in circulation at a rate of interest which is not prohibitive to the rise in investment.

2. ON FOREIGN TRADE AND "DOMESTIC EXPORTS"

1. Capturing of new foreign markets is frequently mentioned as a way out of depression. But it is usually not added that what is essential in this context is an increase in the export surplus rather than in absolute exports.

In fact, aggregate profits are equal to capitalists' consumption *plus* investment *plus* the balance of foreign trade.[1] Profits of a given year were either consumed, invested in construction of capital equipment and in increase in inventories or, finally, were used for repayment of foreign debts or granting of foreign credits.[2] In the course of a "normal" upswing the increase in profits is due to the rise of the component "investment". Let us suppose that 8 factories are built each year instead of 5. The real income of the capitalists—if other components of profits remain constant—increases by the value of these three "additional" factories.[3] The expansion of investment activity must therefore lead to such a rise in aggregate production and in the profit per unit of output that this increase in aggregate profits would materialize. The consequent higher profitability of existing establishments induces a further rise in investment activity which thus enhances the upswing.

In order to stimulate the upswing by means of foreign trade, the balance of trade component of profits must increase, i.e. new surplus of exports over imports must be achieved.

This surplus, like a boom in investment activity, leads to such a general increase in production and in the profit per unit of output that aggregate profits rise by an amount equal to the increment of the balance of trade. The higher profitability of existing establishments, which results from this, acts as a stimulus

[1] We abstract from workers' savings here.

[2] In addition to the increase of foreign claims or the payments of foreign debts the influx of gold may also be an equivalent of the surplus of exports over imports. Gold influx, however, may be treated in the same way as that of foreign currency, i.e. as an increase in foreign claims.

[3] We assume—as is actually the case—that increased investment is carried out by means of creation of purchasing power rather than at the expense of capitalists' consumption.

to investment activity; the upswing resulting from a new surplus in foreign trade thus leads to a "normal" boom.

But if exports increase and at the same time there is an equal increase in imports, overall profits remain unchanged; international trade is boosted, but production in the country considered does not increase, nor will there be any inducement for expansion of investment activity. If e.g. Great Britain increases its exports to China this would lead to an improvement in the British economic situation if China pays for these imports in gold or if she receives a loan from British capitalists which will be ultimately used for the purchase of British goods. The profits of British capitalists will then be increased by the amount equal to the new surplus in trade with China. But if more machines were exported to China, and *pro tanto* more cotton cloth were imported from China, then the situation in the British machine industry would improve, and the situation in the British cotton industry would deteriorate, while the general economic situation would remain unchanged since the aggregate profits would not have increased.

2. Let us assume that increased exports from a given country do involve a rise in the surplus of foreign trade. The condition for stimulating the upswing is thus fulfilled—an increase in the balance of trade is followed by a rise in production. The latter, however, leads, *inter alia,* to a greater demand for foreign commodities, especially raw materials, which are an indispensable element of domestic production—and thus to an increase in imports.[4]

Let us denote the increase in the balance of trade by s, the corresponding increase in imports and exports by i and e respectively. Thus we obtain:

$$e = i + s \tag{1}$$

This means that exports must increase not only by the increment of the balance of trade but also by an additional amount which would warrant a rise in imports, indispensable for the expansion of production. In other words: only a part of the total

[4] As a result of the price increase accompanying the upswing imports will increase and exports will slacken, owing to a weakening in the competitive position of the country's products. This factor plays a considerably lesser role than the increased demand for foreign goods resulting from the rise in production. Thus, for the sake of simplicity, we shall not take it into account here.

increase in exports contributes to the increase in the balance of trade and consequently in aggregate profits. The remainder is used for additional imports necessary for the higher output.

We shall now establish the relation between the increments i and s. As was shown above, the increase in the balance of trade by s raises aggregate profits *pro tanto*. Let the relative share of profits in the aggregate value of production be α[5]: thus production will increase by $\frac{s}{\alpha}$. Moreover let the ratio of imports to the value of aggregate production be β[6]; then the increase in imports will be $i = \beta\frac{s}{\alpha}$; thus we obtain:

$$\frac{s}{i} = \frac{e-i}{i} = \frac{\alpha}{\beta} \tag{2}$$

We shall illustrate this process by an example. If some country manages to increase the balance of trade and its total exports increase by 70 mil. zl, only a part of this sum raises the balance of trade, while another part is used to cover the imports of goods indispensable for the expansion of production. The proportion between these two parts is the same as that between the relative share of profits in the value of aggregate production (equal, say, to 0.5), and the ratio of imports to this value (equal, say, to 0.2). It follows that the increase of the balance of trade amounts to $\frac{0.5}{0.5+0.2}70 = 50$ mil. zl.

Exports rise additionally by 20 mil. zl. but imports increase by the same amount, or exports increase by 70 mil. zl., imports by 20 mil. zl., and the balance rises by 50 mil. zl., and the aggregate profits by just as much.

3. If a government borrows from the capitalists at home, spending the proceeds of the loan, e.g. on armaments, payment of doles, or public works, the result is very similar to that of securing a surplus in foreign trade. To the surplus of exports over

[5] This relative share changes in the course of the business cycle, increasing during the upswing and declining during the downswing. However, the changes are rather small, and for the sake of simplicity it will be treated as constant here.

[6] This ratio is of course, subject to changes which, however, are not of great importance and for the sake of simplicity it will be treated as constant here.

imports there corresponds here the sale of commodities, used for the purposes mentioned above: armaments, consumer goods for the unemployed; construction materials for public works and consumer goods for the workers employed in these works. The equivalent of these sales of commodities is the increase in the claims of the capitalists on their government, just as the equivalent of the surplus achieved in foreign trade was the increase of foreign claims or the reduction of foreign debts. And obviously this increase in government debts may absorb profits in the same way as an increase in foreign claims (or a fall in foreign debts). Consequently the formula for profits must be modified: in addition to capitalists' consumption, investment and the balance of trade, they also include "domestic exports", equal to the increase of government indebtedness to capitalists. The starting of "domestic exports" thus stimulates the upswing in the same way as a surplus secured in foreign trade. It is followed by such an increase in production and in the profit per unit of output that a rise in aggregate profits takes place which is equal to these "exports". This in turn acts as a stimulus for the expansion of investment activity. Financial processes connected with securing a surplus in foreign trade and with "domestic exports" are also very similar in character.

The analogy is obvious in the case when the capitalists of a given country grant a foreign loan or a loan to their government which is used for purchase of commodities in that country. The capitalists lend money abroad or to their government in return for bonds. Funds obtained by a foreign country or by the government flow back through the purchases of commodities to the capitalists, if we abstract from workers' savings (though, of course, not necessarily to the same capitalists). As a result, the profits of the capitalist class in a given period increase by an amount equal to the value of the government or foreign bonds received, which is equal in turn to the surplus secured in foreign trade or to "domestic exports" respectively.

A surplus in foreign trade may also be covered by the influx to the country considered of foreign currency or gold rather than by its granting foreign loans. In the case of "domestic exports" the analogous process is, as will be shown below, the financing of government expenditure by the Central Bank.

Gold and foreign currency which are the equivalent of the

surplus in foreign trade will be ultimately exchanged by capitalists for national currency at the Central Bank or used to repay credits extended to them by this bank. The profits of capitalists will rise in a given period by the amount of the increase in the circulation of notes and of the repayment of credits to the Central Bank which is equal to the surplus secured in foreign trade.

If "domestic exports" are financed by discounting treasury bills in the Central Bank, the notes acquired by the government pass into the hands of capitalists. These notes either remain in circulation or are ultimately used for repayment of credits to the Central Bank. The profits of capitalists increase in a given period by the sum of the increase in the quantity of money in circulation and of the repayment of credits to the Central Bank which sum is equal to the "domestic exports".

In either case the profits of capitalists are raised by the sum of the increase in the quantity of money in circulation and of the reduction in the Central Bank credits.

The foreign claims of the Central Bank in the form of gold or foreign currency or its claims on the government in the form of treasury bills increase by the same amount. In this way foreign countries or the government become indebted to the capitalists of a given country through the medium of the Central Bank to the extent of the surplus secured in foreign trade or of the "domestic exports".

4. As a result of the stimulation of the upswing through "domestic exports"—just as in the case of the application of any other device for this purpose—a rise in imports will take place due to the increased demand for foreign goods which are indispensable for home production (see section 2). Since there was no reason for a simultaneous increase in exports, "domestic exports" are accompanied by a decrease of the balance of trade. Let us examine the problem in detail with reference to the argument of section 2.

We shall denote the increase in imports by i, as above, and the increase in the balance of trade by s. Since exports are assumed to be unchanged

$$i = -s \tag{3}$$

which means that the rise in imports equals the decrease in the balance of trade. We shall denote "domestic exports" per unit of time by e_1. It was shown in the preceding section that as a result of stimulating the upswing by means of "domestic exports", the profits of capitalists increase by e_1. However, we did not take into account how this affects the balance of foreign trade. If this balance changes by s, then according to the argument in section 1, profits change by s as well. Thus the total increase in profits is $e_1 + s$. And since $s = -i$ here, the increase in profits will amount to $e_1 - i$, i.e. they will be equal to the difference between "domestic exports" and the rise in imports as a result of the stimulating effect of "domestic exports" upon aggregate production.

As in section 2, we shall now denote the share of profits in the value of aggregate production by α; thus the value of production will increase by $\frac{e_1 - i}{\alpha}$. If, moreover, we denote the ratio of imports to the value of aggregate production by β, the corresponding rise in imports will amount to $i = \frac{e_1 - i}{\alpha}\beta$. It follows that

$$\frac{e_1 - i}{i} = \frac{\alpha}{\beta} \quad (4)$$

This equation is identical with the equation (2) except that instead of the increase in exports e, we have here the "domestic exports" e_1. Like the equation (2) the equation (4) indicates that "domestic exports" are divided into two parts $e_1 - i$ and i bearing the same relation as α to β (where α is the relative share of profits in the value of aggregate production, and β the ratio of imports to the value of aggregate production). The part $e_1 - i$ is equal to the increase in profits and the part i to the rise in imports. But it is here that a fundamental difference arises: both the increase in "foreign exports" and the increase in "domestic exports" lead to a rise in aggregate profits by $e - i$ or $e_1 - i$; but, while part i of the increase in "foreign exports" actually *covers* the growth of imports by means of international trade, the part i of "domestic exports" is equal to the increase in imports only in an *arithmetical* sense and, of course, is not *convertible* into imports. This brings out the fact that "domestic exports" lead to a deterioration in the balance of trade.

We can illustrate these processes by an example. Let us assume that the government borrowed in the free market or from the Central Bank 70 mil. zl. and spent it on public works. As a result of the increase in production, imports increase by i, which—the level of exports remaining unchanged—means a reduction in the balance of trade by the same amount. Profits rise by $70 - i$. This item bears the same proportion to i as the relative share of profits in the value of aggregate production (say 0.5) to the ratio of imports to the aggregate production (say 0.2). It follows that the rise in imports, and thus the fall in the balance of trade, amounts to 20 mil. zl. This rise in imports will have two results: 1) profits will increase not by 70, but only by 50 mil. zl.; 2) there will be a deterioration of 20 mil. zl. in the balance of trade.

5. It was shown in the preceding section that the starting of "domestic exports" leads to a fall in the balance of trade. In the balance of payments this can be covered by: 1) the influx of foreign capital; 2) the suspension of the servicing of foreign debts; 3) outflow of gold and foreign currency. Since "domestic exports" raise the average profitability, there will be a tendency for the influx of foreign capital into the country which, however, is usually offset by the anxieties as to the solvency of the country raised among foreign capitalists by the deterioration of the balance of trade. As foreign investment is not forthcoming, gold and foreign currency begin in fact to flow out of the country.

This can still be prevented (in the case of a debtor's country) by suspending the servicing of foreign debts. If however, "domestic exports" exceed a certain level, the balance of foreign trade—as a result of a substantial rise in production and imports—becomes nevertheless negative, and gold or foreign currency start again to flow out of the country. Finally reserves of foreign currency and gold decline to such an extent that the only way to maintain imports is to try to increase exports through currency depreciation.

As a result of depreciation the prices of domestic products in terms of foreign exchange are reduced which leads to such an increase in their exports that, despite the unfavourable terms of trade, it is possible to purchase for the proceeds from exports a higher volume of foreign goods. In this way the imports required for the production, increased as a result of starting the "domestic exports", are secured. There is, however, a limit to securing imports in this way. First of all the reduction of domestic prices in terms of foreign currency is limited, both as to the magnitude and the time it lasts, by a tendency of these prices to rise in terms of the domestic currency. But even if we abstract from this tendency—which can be prevented, e.g. in such a way that no formal depreciation of currency is undertaken but only a general export premium is established—the capacity to secure imports is, nevertheless, limited. Let us suppose that the prices for the products of a given country are reduced n times by currency depreciation, and that, as a result, the volume of exports increases m times: the imports of foreign goods, acquired in exchange for these exports, will thus change in the proportion $\frac{m}{n}$. It is obvious that for sufficiently large values of n the ratio $\frac{m}{n}$ will become less than one, i.e. for a larger quantity of domestic products a smaller quantity of foreign goods than before the currency depreciation will be obtained. Thus, there is a certain maximum level of imports which can be secured through depreciation. The depreciation of currency beyond this point will lead, not to a rise, but to a fall in the capacity of a given country to import. This also shows that stimulating the upswing by means of "domestic exports" has a limit: the aggregate production cannot reach such a level that indispensable imports would be greater than the maximum imports obtainable through depreciation. This may, and often will result in a situation in which the upswing caused by "domestic exports" will not lead to the full utilization of idle capital equipment because of the deficiency of foreign goods (especially raw materials) which are an indispensable complementary factor. The more a given economy depends on imports, and the more difficult it is for this economy to expand its exports through depreciation (e.g. in view of the raising of custom duties by other countries), the sooner will the upswing engendered by "domestic exports" reach its peak.

It should be added that with progressing depreciation the real income reaches its maximum at an earlier point than production; for a decreasing amount of real income is yielded by a unit of aggregate production, a part of this production being exchanged for foreign goods at deteriorating terms of trade.

6. We concentrated above on the phase of stimulating the upswing by a surplus secured in foreign trade or by "domestic exports". The resulting increase in profits induces an expansion of investment activity and in this way the phase of the "natural" boom is reached.

Thus it is possible then to reduce gradually the "domestic exports" slowing down the progress of the upswing without, however, causing a collapse of the boom. If the upswing is stimulated through a rise in the balance of trade this influence is automatically halted in the period of increasing investment. Indeed, the latter leads to an expansion of production and thus to a rise in imports which is not counterbalanced by an increase in exports (investment activity has much the same effect here as "domestic exports"). This leads to a deterioration in the balance of trade whose increase had previously stimulated the upswing, and at a certain level of production the difficulties which were discussed in the preceding section may appear. By means of calculations similar to those in section 2 and 4 it is possible to estimate the level of investment at which a tension in the balance of trade may arise.

Let us denote by s the increase in the balance of trade which caused the upswing. Let us suppose that in the next phase of the upswing investment increased by k, and the previous increase in the balance of trade got "lost" owing to the increase in imports, i.e. it dropped by s thus returning to its initial level. Therefore in the period of expansion of investment, aggregate profits increased because of the rise in the item "investment" by k, but fell by s as a result of the decline in the item "balance of trade". On balance the increase in profits amounted to $k-s$. As in section 2 and 4, let us denote the relative share of profits in the value of aggregate production by α and the ratio of imports to this value by β. The increase in the value of production corresponding to the increase in profits by $k-s$ is equal to $\frac{k-s}{\alpha}$, and the corresponding rise in imports to $\frac{k-s}{\alpha}\beta$. Since imports increased by the same amount as the decline in the balance of trade, i.e. by s, we obtain:

$$\frac{k-s}{\alpha}\beta = s$$

It follows directly that

$$k = s\left(1+\frac{\alpha}{\beta}\right) \tag{5}$$

As in sections 2 and 4, let $\alpha=0.5$ and $\beta=0.2$; k will then amount to 3.5 s. It will be seen that the tension in the balance of payments, which accompanied "domestic exports" from the start, in the case of an upswing stimulated by securing a surplus in foreign trade arises only at the point when investment has reached a level several times greater than this surplus, i.e. at an advanced stage of the boom. Moreover, it is probable that prior to this a considerable improvement in the economic situation which does not involve balance of payment difficulties will lead to an influx of foreign capital. If this flow of foreign capital is lasting in character there may be no tension in the balance of payments at a later stage as well. It is now clear what are the advantages of an upswing stimulated by means of securing a surplus in foreign trade. It is worth mentioning that the "natural" upswing based on the automatic increase in investment activity does not enjoy these advantages, and if there is no influx of foreign capital, it will be confronted with the same balance of payments difficulties as the upswing based on "domestic exports".

3. THE MECHANISM OF THE BUSINESS UPSWING

1. Mass unemployment seems to be the most obvious symptom of depression. Is this unemployment due to the shortage of capital equipment, i.e. to inadequate accumulation of fixed capital in relation to the increase of population? Certainly not. The position is rather the reverse. During the depression the existing capital equipment is utilized to a small degree: the idle capital equipment is the counterpart of the unemployed labour force. To what should be attributed the fact that the owner of unutilized equipment who encounters a lasting supply of idle labour does not embark upon production? Any single entrepreneur would certainly answer that this would be an unprofitable proposition: the prices at which he could sell would not even cover his current costs, i.e., the outlay on raw materials, labour, taxes etc. Thus a reduction of wages is being recommended as a way to overcome the depression. Now, one of the main features of the capitalist system is the fact that what is to the advantage of a single entrepreneur does not necessarily benefit all entrepreneurs as a class. If one entrepreneur reduces wages he is able *ceteris paribus* to expand production; but once all entrepreneurs do the same thing—the result will be entirely different.

Let us assume that wages have been in fact generally reduced, and likewise taxes as a counterpart of cuts in civil servants' salaries. Now the entrepreneurs owing to the "improved" price–wage relation utilize their equipment to capacity and in consequence unemployment vanishes. Has depression been thus overcome? By no means, as the goods produced have still to be sold. Now, production has risen considerably and as a result of an increase in the price-wage relation the part of production equivalent to profits (including depreciation) of the capitalists (entrepreneurs and rentiers) has grown even more. A precondition for an equilibrium at this new higher level is that this part of production which is not consumed by workers or by civil servants should be acquired by capitalists for their increased profits; in other words, the capitalists must spend immediately all their additional profits on consumption or investment. It is, however, most unlikely that this should in fact happen. Capitalists' consumption changes in general but little in the course of the business cycle. It is true that increased profitability stimulates investment but this stimulus will not work right away since the entrepreneurs will temporise until they are convinced that the higher profitability is going to last. Therefore the immediate effect of increased profits will be an accumulation of money reserves in the hands of entrepreneurs and in the banks. Then, however, the goods which are the equivalent of the increased profits will remain unsold. The accumulating stocks will sound the alarm for a new price reduction of goods which do not find any outlet. Thus the effect of the cost reduction will be cancelled. On balance only a price reduction will have occured, offsetting the advantage of the cost reduction to the entrepreneurs since unemployment going hand in hand with under-utilization of equipment will reappear.

In fact wage reduction does not, as a rule, result even in the temporary increase in production described above. Indeed, not only investment but even utilization of existing equipment will not respond immediately to an improvement in profitability. For immediately after the reduction of wages and before the entrepreneurs manage to increase production within the existing capital equipment a fall in prices makes its appearance. As the entrepreneurs do not at once make use of the means taken away from the workers for buying consumption or investment goods, the revenue of industry is reduced *pro tanto*. What the entrepreneurs gain on wage reductions is soon dissipated through price declines. All this could be noticed in all countries during the world depression in the period 1931–32, when the wave of wage reductions brought about a rapid fall in prices rather than an increase in production.

2. The doctrine of wage cuts as the way out of depression is sometimes supplemented by a remedy against the price fall. Creation of cartels is recommended to stop the "cut throat competition". Let us assume that in all industries cartels have been formed, that wages have been duly reduced, but that the diminished demand of the workers could not have any repercussions on prices since they are maintained by cartels at a stable level. Will the "improved" price-wage relation be of any help in overcoming the depression? Now, it is rather unlikely that cartels would invest profits derived by wage reductions more promptly than the entrepreneurs under conditions of "free competition". The opposite is rather the case. Thus in a totally cartelized system, just as under "free competition",

the proceeds of industry will diminish as much as their costs, and as prices remain unchanged the sales of goods will drop in the same proportion as the proceeds have shrunk. Thus while wage reductions do not cause any increase in production in the case of a competitive economy, in a fully cartelized system they lead, as a result of rigidity of prices, to a shrinkage of production and a rise in unemployment.

In a "mixed" system, consisting of a cartelized and a competitive sector, the result of wage cuts will be something intermediate: a fall of production will ensue but it will be weaker than in a fully cartelized system.

3. It follows from the above argument that a reduction of wages does not constitute a way out of depression, because the gains are not used immediately by the capitalists for purchase of investment goods. Now we shall try to prove that the opposite is the case: the increase in investment *per se* unaccompanied by a wage reduction causes a rise in output.

Let us assume that as a result of some important invention there is an increase in investment associated with its spreading. Now, is it possible for the capitalists to step up their investment, even though their profits have not increased (there was no reduction in wages) nor have they curtailed their consumption *ad hoc* (this, indeed, is most unlikely). The financing of additional investment is effected by the so called creation of purchasing power. The demand for bank credits increases and these are granted by the banks drawing on their reserves. The means used by the entrepreneurs for construction of new establishments reach the industries of investment goods. This additional demand makes for setting to work idle equipment and unemployed labour. The increased employment is a source of additional demand for consumer goods and thus results in turn in higher employment in the respective industries. Finally the additional investment outlay finds its way directly and through the workers' spending into the pockets of capitalists (we assume that workers do not save). The additional profits flow back as deposits to the banks, whose reserves are thus restored. This makes it possible to draw on them again in order to grant credits for the continuation of investment associated with the new invention. As a result of this accelerated money circulation bank credits increase by the amount additionally invested and deposits by the amount of additional profits.

The entrepreneurs who engage in additional investment are "propelling" into the pockets of other capitalists profits which are equal to their investment, and they are becoming indebted to these capitalists to the same extent *via* banks.

In the preceding sections we were faced with the problem whether the profits resulting from the reduction of costs are invested. In the case presently considered, the profits, to put it paradoxically, are invested even before they have come into being. Profits that are not invested cannot be retained because they are annihilated by the ensuing fall in production and prices. The creation of the purchasing power for financing additional investment increases the output from the low level reached in the depression and thus creates profits equal to this investment.

It should be pointed out that the increase in output will result in an increased demand for money in circulation, and thus will call for a rise in credits of the Central Bank. Should the Bank respond to it by raising the rate of interest to a level at which total investment would decline by the amount equal to the additional investment caused by the new invention, no increase in investment would ensue and the economic situation would not improve. Therefore the precondition for the upswing is that the rate of interest should not increase too much in response to an increased demand for cash.

What will happen, however, when the new invention has been spread and the original source of the business upswing has dried up and thus the stimulus for investment vanishes? Is the downswing unavoidable then? No, because in the meantime the increased profitability prevailing in the economy as a whole will have resulted in a rise in investment. It is this investment caused by higher profitability which will step in when the effect of the new invention will have petered out.

4. We described in the preceding section a business upswing resulting from the investment stimulated by an important invention, which to some extent is a matter of chance. Without such an external stimulus, would the depression last for ever? Is it not inherent in the depression to breed forces that put an end to it by causing an increase in investment?

Let us assume that the economy became stabilized at the bottom of the depression at a very low level of economic activity; that investment in particular has shrunk to such a degree that it does not cover the necessary replacement of the ageing capital equipment. Let us suppose that this equipment consists of 2000 establishments and that every year 100 of them get out of use, but only 60 establishments are constructed. Thus the capital equipment shrinks every year by 40 establishments. However, it is this destruction of equipment that after a rather prolonged period initiates a business upswing. For owing to the shrinkage of capital equipment the same demand is met by a declining number of existing establishments which as a result improve their degree of utilization. Once the profitability of the existing capital equipment has thus increased, the level of investment will increase as well. The finance for it will be provided—as was described in the preceding section—by creation of additional purchasing power. This will result in an increase of the output of investment goods and of employment in the respective branches of industry. Moreover, the rise in demand on the part of the newly-employed workers for consumption goods will cause fuller employment in the consumer-good industries. This general increase in production brings about a further rise in profitability, followed by a new expansion of investment activity, a new creation of purchasing power etc.

This is, indeed, a cumulative process causing a steady upswing. However, once investment starts to exceed the level of necessary replacement of fixed capital, i.e. once more establishments are constructed per year than the 100 establishments which are scrapped—then the factors hampering the upswing make their appearance. Just as during the depression the shrinkage of capital equipment was the inception of the upswing, so now the expansion of this equipment finally brings the boom to a stop and starts the downswing.

The process of collapse of the boom is the reverse of that starting the upswing from the bottom of depression. Let us assume that at the top of the boom investment is stabilized at the level of 140 establishments and, as 100 establishments are scrapped p.a., the capital equipment is expanding by 40 establishments p.a. Now the demand will be met by an increasing number of establishments and as a result the degree of utilization of each of them will diminish. The resulting lower profitability will be followed by a decline in investment. And just as the increase in investment at the bottom of depression meant the start of the upswing of production and of a decline in unemployment—a fall in production and an increase in unemployment will ensue here. And this downward movement will gather momentum as in the period of the upswing the upward tendencies were cumulative in character.

It is not, of course, the purpose of this essay to present a complete theory of business fluctuations. An attempt is made to give a general idea of the mechanism of a "natural" upswing, and in particular to clarify one of its aspects. It now becomes apparent that investment has a favourable effect upon the economic situation only at the time when it is executed and provides an outlet for additional purchasing power. On the other hand the productive character of investment contributes to the slackening of the upswing and finally brings it to an end. For it is the expansion of capital equipment that in the light of the above analysis causes the collapse of the boom. We face here one of the most remarkable paradoxes of the capitalist system. The expansion of the capital equipment, i.e. the increase in the national wealth contains the seed of a depression in the course of which the additional wealth proves to be only potential in character. For a considerable part of capital equipment is idle then and becomes useful only in the next upswing.

This statement sheds some light on the problem of government anti-slump intervention by means of public investment, with which we shall deal now.

5. After we have studied the mechanism of the business cycle let us turn again to the case where the upswing is started by a new invention which stimulates some entrepreneurs to embark upon "extra investment". By making use for this purpose of additional purchasing power, they set in motion the mechanism of the upswing. This case is very close to that of government anti-slump intervention. In order to pass from the former to the latter it suffices to substitute for the entrepreneurs induced to invest by the new invention the government taking up investment which is financed likewise by means of additional purchasing power in order to break the deadlock of the slump.

Let us assume that the government issues treasury bills and sells them to the banks which draw on their cash reserves to buy the issue. The government spends the money, e.g. on construction of railways. As in the cases described above, employment in investment-good industries increases and subsequently, as a result of the higher purchasing power of the workers, in consumption-good industries as well. The amounts spent by the government flow as profits directly or through spending of the workers into the pockets of capitalists, and return to the banks as their deposits. In this way the money lent to the government is restored to the banks which enables them to discount the next issue of treasury bills, and thus to continue the financing of railway construction. On the side of bank assets, the government debt accrues in the form of discounted bills, on the side of liabilities there is an increase in deposits equal to the additional profits. Thus the government gets indebted via banks to the private capitalists by an amount equal to the value of the investment effected. It will be seen that a complete analogy exists between the case now being considered and that of an upswing resulting from a new invention. And in both instances increased profitability of the industry as a whole will stimulate investment and thus enhance the upswing which as a result will continue even if the government will gradually reduce its investment activity. Thus an upswing started by a new invention continues after its impact has spent itself.

It should be emphasized that the pattern of public investment taken up is not essential for the effect of government intervention; what matters is that investment should be financed by additional purchasing power. The creation of purchasing power for the sake of financing the budget deficit, whatever its reason, renders a similar effect. The divergence consists only in that the additional purchasing power flows initially into different industries. Let us assume, for instance, that the amount derived from discounting treasury bills is used for the payment of doles. In this case the direct effect of government intervention will be felt in consumer-good industries. Only after some time, when their increased profitability will induce them to invest, will prosperity be shared by investment-good industries as well. This increased investment activity financed by creation of purchasing power will enhance the upswing, so that the latter will continue even after the budget deficits will have vanished—owing to the increase in tax revenues resulting from the rise in incomes and sales.

Thus after some time private investment "takes over" from public investment: the "artificial" prosperity is replaced by a "natural" one which, by the way, sooner or later—as was proved in the preceding chapter—will come to a stop as a result of expansion of capital equipment.

It must be added that the pre-condition of successful government intervention—and of the natural upswing as well—is the possibility of meeting the increased demand for credits by the banking system without increasing the rate of interest too much. Should the rate of interest increase to such an extent that private investment is curtailed by exactly the amount of government borrowing—then obviously no purchasing power would be created, but only a shift in its structure would take place.

4. THE BUSINESS UPSWING AND THE BALANCE OF PAYMENTS

1. It is fairly obvious that the upswing tends to affect the balance of trade unfavourably. This results mainly from increasing demand for imports of goods which are not produced in the country considered. In Poland, for instance, the rise in industrial production is accompanied by an increase in imports of raw materials such as wool, cotton, hides and skins, iron ore etc.; next the expansion of investment calls for higher imports of machinery, and that of consumption for higher imports of tea, coffee and fruit.

Another factor that affects the balance of trade adversely is the increase in domestic prices in the course of upswing. This makes for an increase in imports of goods competing with the corresponding home-produced commodities and also affects adversely the competitive position of the latter in the foreign markets. It should be noticed that the influence of this increase in prices on the balance of trade is in general not so important as the rise in demand for foreign goods which are not produced at home. Indeed, in view of the existing high tariffs, the rise of domestic prices—as long as it does not exceed a certain limit—does not encourage imports of competitive goods. The adverse effect of higher home prices upon exports is more serious, but even this will not arise in the fairly frequent cases of dumping.

It is clear that should the upswing in a given country be accompanied by an improvement in the situation in the world market, the balance of trade might not deteriorate, because of an increase in exports. Let us, however, abstract from such a possibility.

In this case would not the boom which causes the deterioration in the balance of trade—mainly, as stated above, through higher demand for foreign raw materials etc.—generate forces that would tend to correct the resulting disturbance in the balance of payments? Such is no doubt the case under the conditions of free international circulation of capital. In the country where an upswing takes place the profitability of industry increases and this tends to attract foreign capital. However, the functioning of the international capital market is in general by no means

34

perfect. As a matter of fact, in one instance only is it very likely that the deterioration of the balance of trade in the course of an upswing will be automatically offset by the influx of capital. We have in mind here an upswing occurring in a country exporting capital; the higher profitability resulting from the upswing in such a country is most likely to cause a decline in the export of capital in favour of home investment. In other cases a deterioration in the foreign exchange position is rather to be expected. The decline in the balance of trade in the course of the upswing is followed by an outflow of gold and foreign exchange. If the Central Bank will not respond by raising the rate of interest, which discourages investment and thus hampers the upswing, the fall in gold and foreign exchange reserves will continue and with the progressing upswing will even gather momentum.

2. The repercussions of the upswing upon the balance of trade described above will not be affected by the upswing's being "natural" or "artificial", i.e. caused by government intervention. Whatever the reasons of the increase in production it will be followed by a rise in demand for foreign raw materials etc.: an "automatic" upswing, as well as a boom resulting e.g. from government expenditure, leads as a rule to an increase in imports.

There exists a widespread theory about a direct connection between the budget deficit and the deterioration in the foreign exchange position. It is difficult to grasp what kind of connection this might be: the foreign exchange position depends on the balance of trade and there is no direct relation between the latter and the budget deficit. There is, however, no doubt an indirect connection. If the budget deficit is covered by the creation of purchasing power, it induces an increase in production and in this way contributes to a rise in imports and thus to the deterioration in the foreign exchange position. If, however, the budget deficit were financed by credits without any creation of purchasing power being involved, i.e. at the expense of credits to private entrepreneurs, then no increase in production would follow and consequently the foreign exchange position would not deteriorate: the budget deficit will affect the foreign exchange position adversely only in the case where it affects production favourably.

There is, however, one exception to this rule. If the "public" subscribe to the "theory" of a direct connection between the budget deficit and the foreign exchange position, then the appearance of the deficit in the budget encourages them to hoard gold or foreign exchange, which indeed may upset the foreign exchange position even more seriously than the effect of the budget deficit causing an increase in production.

3. What is going to happen in a country in the course of a "natural" or "artificial" upswing if no influx of foreign capital is forthcoming? If the Central Bank, in order to prevent the outflow of gold and foreign exchange, acts according to the classical rules, i.e. if it raises the rate of interest or introduces some credit restrictions, it may—as mentioned above—re-establish the equilibrium in the balance of payments, putting a brake on the upswing, as this will tend to restrain the demand for imports. What will happen, however, if the Central Bank does not act in this way? Now, if it is the case that the country is in possession of large gold and foreign exchange reserves it is possible to disburse them until the situation in international trade or in the international capital market should improve. The position may, however, be often complicated by the fact that the continuing gold outflow might raise doubts as to the stability of the currency and thus lead to hoarding of gold or foreign exchange unless this is prevented by exchange restrictions. The question arises whether a currency depreciation, which is frequently resorted to in such a state of affairs, re-establishes the equilibrium in the balance of payments. The immediate effect of the depreciation is the return of capital that left the country just because of the anticipation that the currency might be depreciated. This is, however, a one at a time effect. We are concerned here with a different problem: whether the currency depreciation might stimulate exports to such an extent that they could cover the increased demand for foreign imports of raw materials etc. resulting from the upswing.

Let us assume that in consequence of currency depreciation the export prices of a given country measured in gold decreased by 20%. This means that pre-depreciation exports are exchanged now for only 0.8 of "old" imports. In order to obtain the same volume of imports as before the currency depreciation $\frac{1}{0.8} = 1.25$ times more has to be exported. Therefore should exports increase by less than 25% it will be impossible even to maintain the "old" level of imports.

Should exports increase by not much more than 25%, it would

be possible to increase imports somewhat, but the volume of goods at the disposal of the country would decline since production can be increased but little (because the increase in the imports of raw materials is small) and many more goods (over 25%) would have to be exported.

The shift in the structure of sales will be effected as follows: the increase in domestic prices caused by the rise in costs of imported raw materials will result in the shrinkage of home consumption.

Thus currency depreciation can solve the difficulties in foreign trade encountered in the course of the upswing only if the foreign demand for the goods of a given country is very elastic; for instance if depreciation of currency by 20% is accompanied by an increase much higher than 25% in the volume of exports. With a high tariff system in existence, however, this demand is fairly rigid.

In a free trade world the exports of the country which depreciated its currency would flood all the markets previously inaccessible to them because of the high cost of transportation and other sales costs (commissions, advertisement etc.). In a high tariff system depreciation does not work in this way because a moderate depreciation may not be sufficient for exports to "jump" the tariff barriers, and a drastic one may induce the countries affected to retaliate by raising the tariffs. In order to illustrate the rigidity of demand for goods of a given country it is useful to consider some data concerning Japan. In the period 1932–1934 the Japanese terms of trade fell by 18%. Although at that time the volume of world trade already tended to rise slowly, the quantity of goods exported from Japan increased only by 31%. Thus Japan's purchasing power for foreign goods increased in the proportion $0.82 \times 1.31 = 1.07$, i.e. only by 7%.

4. Does the above argument apply to the case where the reduction of prices of a given country in terms of gold is achieved by so called "cost deflation" rather than by currency depreciation? Let us assume that in the country considered wages and taxes (at the expense of the salaries of civil servants) are reduced and as a result the general level of prices declines. The effect is much the same as that of currency depreciation. The competitive position of exports of that country in the foreign markets is improved, but does not make sure that the means for an expansion of imports

can thus be secured. There arise here the same problems we mentioned in the discussion of the effects of depreciation. If a country sells its goods at reduced prices it receives in exchange a much greater volume of imports only if the increase in the volume of exports exceeds considerably this price reduction, i.e. if the foreign demand for the goods of a given country is elastic. The volume of exports would be highest if they were given away without charge, but no imports at all would be secured in this way. Thus, with the prevailing high tariff system, cost deflation —very much like currency depreciation—cannot solve the foreign exchange problem resulting from a business upswing.

5. The difficulties in the balance of payments accompanying the upswing—if no influx of foreign capital is forthcoming—are sometimes met by the debtor countries by a suspension of the servicing of foreign debts. In this way some surplus of foreign exchange is secured which may be used to cover the increased imports. Thus the level of the servicing of foreign debts just before its suspension circumscribes the volume of additional imports of raw materials etc. required for the expansion of production which can be secured in this way.

It must be noticed, however, that should a debtor country have a positive balance of trade with its creditor country, the latter might take hold of the surplus of the debtor country in order to cover the servicing of the debts and thus at this point no effect will be achieved.

6. What happens, however, to a country where the boom results, for instance, from government loan financed expenditure, if no influx of foreign capital is forthcoming, and the country does not suspend the servicing of foreign debts, or, having done so, cannot secure an adequate amount of foreign exchange to cover the increase in imports? The country will soon face the exhaustion of its gold and foreign exchange and it will be forced to resort to restrictions of imports of raw materials etc. Let us analyse the consequences of such a state of affairs.

The allocation of limited quantities of imported raw materials to their users results, of course, in an insufficient supply of the corresponding goods, and thus in a price increase of the latter. Consequently import restrictions have much the same effect as the emergence of cartels that would limit production in industries manufacturing imported raw materials. This is why in the course of an upswing accompanied by import restrictions a considerable rise in prices in relation to wages would take place as a result of the increase in prices of goods produced from imported raw materials. It may thus happen also that despite the higher production the workers' real income does not increase at all, because the effect of higher employment on the purchasing power of the working class is offset by a fall in real wages. Therefore in the course of such a lopsided boom the consumption of the broad masses of the population may show no increase.

It should be added that the price increase of goods with a high content of imported raw materials encourages the exploitation of inferior domestic natural resources, the utilization of salvage and byproducts, and the production of all kinds of substitutes that do not require any, or only small quantities, of imported raw materials (artificial silk replacing cotton, aluminium replacing copper and so on). All this mitigates to some extent the shortage of imported raw materials. This semi-autarky cannot, however, prevent the increase in the prices of goods produced from imported raw materials, for it is just the rise in these prices that fosters the application of the new, normally unprofitable methods of production.

5. MONEY AND REAL WAGES

PART I (THEORY)

The "Classical" Theory of Wages

1. The assumptions of the "classical" theory of wages may be subdivided into two categories:

(a) The assumption of perfect competition and of the so called "law of increasing marginal costs". The consequence of this assumption is the association of the rise in employment with a decline in real wages.

(b) The assumption of a given general price level or a given value of the aggregate demand, from which it follows that real wages change in the same direction as money wages.

Now, the cut in money wages being followed by a decline in real wages, and the latter being associated with a rise in employment, the reduction in money wages leads, according to the "classical" theory, to an increase in employment.

Before a critical appreciation of these assumptions we shall describe them in some detail.

2. Let us start from the law of increasing marginal costs and perfect competition. Imagine an establishment with a given capital equipment which produces 100 units of a certain commodity. By increasing employment slightly it may produce 101 units. Now the additional cost of producing the 101st unit, consisting mainly of the cost of raw materials and wages, is called the marginal cost at the level of production equal to 101.

According to the "law of increasing marginal costs", the marginal cost, i.e. the cost of producing the last unit, rises with the level of output obtained from a given capital equipment. This law will appear to many readers not too plausible and rightly so: whereas in agriculture a disproportionately higher input of fertilizers and labour is required in order to increase the yield, in an industrial establishment the marginal cost starts to rise spectacularly only when maximum utilization of equipment is approached, —which happens to be rather an exception.

We shall examine critically the "law of increasing marginal costs" in the subsequent sections, while at present we shall concentrate on its consequences.

Let us consider a system of perfect competition where a single entrepreneur disregards the fact of "spoiling the market" through his increasing the supply, but considers the price as given. It will be easily seen that the output of an establishment will be pushed up to the point where the marginal cost is equal to the price (on Fig. 5 this level of output is *OA*).

Indeed, once the entrepreneur increases his output, the marginal cost is higher (according to the "law of increasing marginal costs") and therefore the cost of production of the last unit exceeds the price (point *M* is above the straight line *CB*) and as a result a cut in production will ensue. If, however, the production is below the level at which the price is equal to the marginal cost, the last unit produced yields more than the additional cost involved (point *N* is situated under the horizontal line *CB*) and therefore the output will be expanded. The equilibrium is reached when the marginal cost is equal to the price.

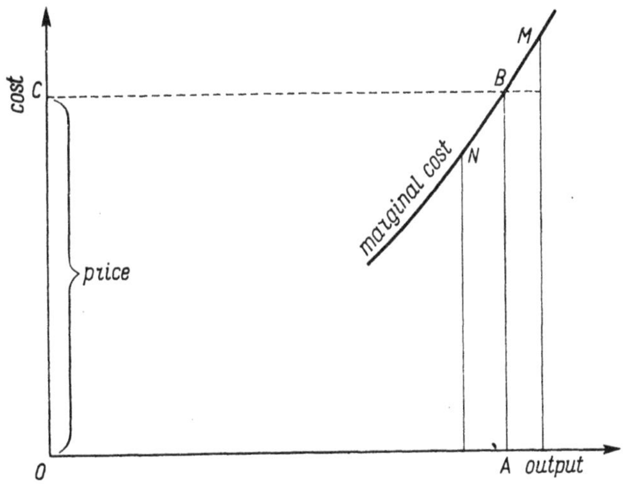

FIG. 5

3. Let us now consider a closed economic system. It may be easily shown that if we assume the "law of increasing marginal costs" the aggregate output can expand given the level of wages, only provided that the prices of the commodities produced rise. Indeed, on this assumption the increase in output is associated—

given the level of wages and prices of raw materials—with an increase in marginal costs which must be "covered" by the rise in prices. But higher prices of finished goods with given wage rates are tantamount to the fall in real wages which will thus accompany the expansion of output.

We have not taken into consideration so far a factor which will exert an additional pressure on real wages. We assumed the prices of raw materials to be given while in fact with the increase in production, and thus in the demand for raw materials, the prices of the latter will rise in accordance with the "law of increasing marginal costs". This will affect the prices of finished goods additionally and as a result the reduction in real wages associated with the increase in production will be *pro tanto* greater.[1]

On the assumption of the "law of increasing marginal costs" production can increase with a given level of money wages only on the condition that prices rise and thus real wages decline. An increase in production may also ensue if the decline in real wages is the result of a cut in money wages while prices of manufactured goods are unaltered. The marginal costs of these goods at the initial level of output will fall (the curve of marginal costs will shift downwards), and this will encourage the entrepreneurs to expand production up to the point where the marginal cost is equal to the price.

Thus from the "law of increasing marginal costs" follows the inverse relation between production and real wages.

4. From this, however, it cannot be concluded that a reduction in money wages leads to an increase in production, since no relation between the changes in money and real wages has been established yet. The "classical" theory, in order to deal with this problem, makes additional assumptions of a different type. It is sometimes assumed that the general level of prices depends on the credit policy of the banks (in particular on that of the Central Bank). Assuming, moreover, that this policy, and thus the general level of prices, is given, the conclusion is arrived at that the reduction in money wages is identical with that of real wages.

Frequently, however, a more sophisticated assumption is made

[1] As a result the curve of the marginal costs of finished goods shifts upwards, and to a given level of production then corresponds a higher marginal cost, and thus a higher price.

that it is the value of the aggregate demand or—what amounts to the same—the value of the aggregate production that is determined by the credit policy. Once we assume this value as given, the process of the reduction of money wages will be as follows. The cut in money wages results at the initial level of output in a reduction of marginal costs (the curve of which shifts downwards). However, the general price level does not change initially because the aggregate demand is assumed to be stable. Thus prices exceed the marginal costs, which leads to an increase in production. As a result the marginal costs increase and at the same time prices decline, since the same money demand is met by a larger volume of goods. The equilibrium is reached when the marginal costs are equal to the respective prices. This equilibrium is obviously reached at a higher level of production, and at a lower level of real wages than was the case in the initial position. Thus on the assumption of a given aggregate demand, a cut in money wages results in an increase in production accompanied, as follows from the above, by a reduction in real wages.

The assumption of a given general price level or a given aggregate demand is totally unfounded. We know only too well that in the course of the business cycle both magnitudes are subject to violent swings. Why then should we assume that they remain unaltered in the aftermath of a wage reduction? If, however, we reject these assumptions a quite new theoretical construction is required in order to enable us to appreciate the consequences of changes in money wages. We shall deal with this problem in the next section.

The Wage Reduction on the Assumption of Perfect Competition

1. In this section we assume for the time being rising marginal costs and perfect competition in accordance with the "classical" theory. We drop, however, the assumption of the stable general level of prices, or the stable money value of the aggregate demand. We shall assume in addition that the system is closed (we shall introduce foreign trade at a later stage), that it consists only of capitalists (entrepreneurs and rentiers) and workers, and that the workers do not save, but spend their total income on consumption. Before considering the consequences of

a wage reduction within such a framework we have to advance some argument of a more general character.

2. The national income in our system may be presented in two ways, namely from the side of incomes and expenditure:

Income	Expenditure
Income of capitalists	Investment
Wages	Consumption

or

Income of capitalists	Investment
	Capitalists' consumption
Wages	Workers' consumption

By investment is meant here the purchase of fixed capital (machinery, buildings etc.) and the increase in inventories. Since the workers are assumed to spend all their earnings on consumption, wages and salaries are equal to workers' consumption. We thus obtain:

$$\text{Capitalists' income} = \text{Investment} + \text{Capitalists' consumption}$$

This equation is of fundamental importance for our subsequent argument. It enables us to explain the fluctuations of production. Let us consider investment, capitalists' consumption and workers' consumption in a certain period. In which of these three items of national income may spontaneous changes occur? It is first obvious that workers' consumption cannot be subject to such a change. Indeed, it can neither exceed nor fall short of their earnings. But the position is quite different as far as capitalists' expenditure is concerned. In the next period they may increase their consumption or their outlay on investment above their present income, drawing on bank credits or on reserves of their own. The capitalists also may reduce their expenditure on consumption and investment below their present income, paying off credits or increasing their reserves. Once they have done it, however, the above equation shows clearly that the income of the capitalists as a body will increase or diminish precisely by as much as their expenditure was increased or diminished. The aggregate production is bound to reach the level at which the profits derived from it by the capitalists are equal to their consumption and investment. Since the workers spend on consumption goods as much as they receive in wages, the remainder of the national income, being the share of capitalists, is just equal to their expenditure on consumption and investment goods. Therefore the capitalists as a class determine by their expenditure their profits and in consequence the aggregate production.

This result is likely to appear paradoxical to many readers. Therefore it will not be out of place to shed some light on it from a somewhat different angle.

We shall represent our system schematically as composed of three departments: production of investment goods, production of capitalists' consumer goods and workers' consumer goods or wage goods. The latter are partly consumed by workers who produce them, while the surplus is bought by the workers employed in the other two departments. This surplus is the profit derived from the production of wage goods. (Indeed, the value of the remainder is equal to the wages earned in this department). If for instance the value of the production of wage goods is 10 mld. zlotys and the workers employed in their production received 6 mld. zl. in wages, then the respective profits are 4 mld. zl. But as 6 mld. zl. earned in wages in the department of wage goods are spent on these goods, the surplus equal to $10 - 6 = 4$ mld. zl. is bought by workers of the two other departments: the department of capitalists' consumer goods and the department of investment goods. Thus the wages in the two departments as well as the profits in the third department are equal to 4 mld. zlotys. If employment and aggregate wages in the capitalists' consumer goods and investment goods industries increase, the demand for wage goods increases as well and their production is bound to be stepped up to the point where the profits, i.e. the surplus of the value of production over wages in this department, would be equal to the increase of aggregate wages in the other two departments.

Next, the value of production of capitalists' consumer goods and investment goods is, of course, equal to the sum of profits and wages in the corresponding departments. However, the wages in these two departments are equal to the profits in the third one; thus the total profits are equal to the value of capitalists' consumption and investment. Let us suppose, for instance, that the value of production of these two categories is 7 mld. zl., out of which 3 mld. are profits and 4 mld. wages. As profits in the department of wage goods are equal to the wages in the other two departments, the former amount to 4 mld. Aggregate profits

3 + 4 = 7 mld. zl. are equal to the capitalists' consumption and investment.

3. As will be seen, the fluctuations in production and profits depend on the fluctuations in capitalists' consumption and investment. If at some moment, for instance, the entrepreneurs are in a more optimistic frame of mind, their investment activity will expand and employment in construction, machine industry etc. will increase. The resulting rise in the consumption of workers will in turn be followed by an increase in production of wage good industries. As was shown above, the aggregate production will expand to the point where profits will be higher by an amount equal to the value of additional investment—if it is assumed that capitalists' consumption remains unchanged.

If, however, the latter increases as well, owing to higher capitalists' incomes, the increase in profits will be correspondingly enhanced. In any case production will be finally pushed up to the point where the increase in profits will be equal to the increase in expenditure on investment and capitalists' consumption.

The question is frequently asked about the "wherewithal" for financing the increase in investment if capitalists' consumption does not decrease simultaneously and does not "release" some purchasing power for investment. It may sound paradoxical, but according to the above, investment is "financed by itself".

If, for instance, an entrepreneur is gradually drawing on his bank deposit for construction of plat, he is increasing by the same amount (on the assumption of stable capitalists' consumption) profits of other entrepreneurs (through an increase in the production), and as a result, along with the dwindling of his bank deposit the deposits of other entrepreneurs are rising *pro tanto* and therefore the banks are not forced to reduce credits. Here, however, an important reservation should be made: in line with the increased turnover the demand for cash in circulation rises. Consequently the bank deposits would diminish and thus the banks would lose a part of their cash reserves. This in its turn would cause an increase in the rate of interest which would adversely affect investment activity. For it is, indeed, the difference between the expected rate of profit and rate of interest that stimulates investment. However, the situation is relieved by the expansion of credits of the Central Bank which increases the quantity of money in circulation and in this way either prevents any rise in the rate of interest or at least limits its scope. One could, of course, envisage a banking policy which is designed to keep the aggregate demand at a constant level and, therefore, prevents production from either expanding or shrinking. (This is the assumption of the "classical" theory mentioned in the preceding chapter). In fact, however, the changes in the rate of interest are in general much too weak to halt an incipient upswing resulting from an increase in investment or to prevent a depression brought about by its collapse.

An important part is undoubtedly played here by a certain factor of a special nature. As we have just seen, an increase in the rate of interest hampers the expansion of production by discouraging investment activity. It is, however, the long-term rate of interest that is relevant to investment in fixed capital. Now, the long-term rate of interest—for reasons we cannot analyse in detail here—reacts only slightly to the changes in the short-term rate determined by banking policy. This results in the following set-up: the increase in investment activity causes a rise in the aggregate output and thus in the demand for cash; this tends to push up the short-term rate of interest which, however, is only slightly reflected in the level of the long-term rate of interest. Thus the expansion of investment is not much hampered by the reaction of the money and capital market.

4. Let us return to the problem of reduction in wages. Let us assume that money wages have been reduced in a certain proportion. How will this affect production and employment?

In the light of the preceding argument this query is reduced to the following problem: how does capitalists' consumption and investment react to a cut in money wages? For, as was shown above, it is the change in the volume of capitalists' consumption and investment that is the cause of expansion or shrinkage of production.

At the first glance it may seem that as a result of the wage reduction the capitalists increase their consumption and investment in anticipation of higher profits of their establishments. Should the capitalists act thus in fact, the reduction of wages would, indeed, be followed by an increase in production and the "classical" theory would be vindicated.

A closer analysis, however, shows that this is most unlikely to happen. It is, indeed, improbable that the investment and consumption of capitalists should increase *immediately*. First of all it is almost certain that the entrepreneurs will not step up their investment immediately after wages have been reduced, but will rather wait for an *actual* increase in profits. In addition even should they increase their orders for capital equipment, the expansion of production in the respective industries would for technical reasons materialize only with some delay.

The same is true of capitalists' consumption. Also in this case the capitalists are more likely to postpone any increase in their spending until the expected increase in incomes would materialize and even then some time-lag would probably still be involved. To sum up: *it is most likely that in the period following immediately the reduction of wages, the volume of capitalists' investment and consumption will be unchanged.*

It will be, however, easily seen that as a result both these magnitudes and in consequence the aggregate production as well will not change at a later date either. Indeed, in the period immediately following the wage-cut, capitalists' consumption and investment remain stable, as assumed, and thus aggregate production does not change either. However, as a consequence of the general reduction of wages the marginal costs and along with them the prices (equal to the respective marginal costs in the system of perfect competition) will decrease in the same proportion as wages. But in this case the only change in the economic situation is a proportionate decline in the general level of prices and wages. It is therefore obvious that the capitalists will increase neither their consumption nor investment in a later period, if they did not do so immediately.

This process may be presented by means of our scheme of three departments. According to our assumption the capitalists' consumption and investment do not change initially. Therefore there is no change either in the production of the department of capitalists' consumer goods or in the department of investment goods. The same applies to the employment in both these departments as a result of which the effective demand for wage goods produced by the third department decreases in the proportion of the wage reduction. But as the marginal costs in this department decline in the same proportion as well, there will be no change in the production of the third department either. As a result production and employment in all three departments will remain for some time unchanged, while the prices equal to the marginal costs decrease in the same proportion as wages. In this situation, however, there is no reason for the capitalists to increase their consumption and investment, as the expected increase in profitability did not materialize.

If the capitalists do not raise their consumption and investment immediately after the reduction of wages (which seems most unlikely), they are caught in a vicious circle. The profitability of enterprises does not rise, because neither investment nor capitalists' consumption has increased. But neither of these items can increase since profitability has not. Consequently the only factual result of the reduction of wages in a system of perfect competition is a decrease in the general level of prices.

5. It should, however, be noticed that a change in the general level of wages and prices may have some indirect influence upon employment. Indeed, in consequence of the decrease of the general price level with an unchanged level of production, the demand for cash diminishes and this in turn causes, as was mentioned above, a decrease in the short-term rate of interest which may favourably affect investment activity and thus cause a rise in production. However, as pointed out above, changes in the short-term rate of interest influence but slightly the long-term rate which is relevant to investment. Therefore the reduction of wages which only slightly influences the long-term rate of interest cannot stimulate investment essentially. It may even be argued that often the opposite is the case. A general reduction of prices increases the burden of indebtedness, since money incomes diminish while the "old" debts do not. This causes difficulties in servicing the debts, ending frequently in failures. As a result confidence in the solvency of firms is undermined which may lead to an increase in the long-term rate of interest even though the short-term rate declines.

This discussion points to the improbability of the effect of the reduction of wages on the level of production and employment through the medium of the rate of interest. The most likely effect of wage reduction in a system of perfect competition is a decline in the general level of prices with no change of production and employment[2].

[2] In the above consideration we omitted the effect of one more factor which may have a certain influence on the consequences of

Dropping of the Assumption of Increasing Marginal Costs and Perfect Competition

1. In the preceding section we assumed in accordance with the "classical" theory increasing marginal costs and perfect competition, while concentrating our attention on the problem of changes in effective demand and, in particular, on how it is affected by a reduction of wages. By dropping the unrealistic assumption of the stable level of prices or of the stable value of the general demand we have made the first step towards a realistic approach. Next we shall subject to a critical examination the assumption of increasing marginal costs (we have already expressed some misgivings on this account) as well as that of perfect competition.

As was stated in the preceding section, the sphere where increasing marginal costs prevail is agriculture, where an increment in yield requires a disproportionate outlay of fertilizers and labour. The position is altogether different in industry. If, for instance, in a given establishment two shifts rather than one are worked, the cost of raw materials and labour will increase more or less proportionately. Only the third shift may involve some technical problems. It is therefore reasonable to assume that in an industrial enterprise the curve of the marginal costs is horizontal over a rather long range of output and starts rising only when full capacity is approached. As experience shows, such full utiliza-

---

wage reduction. We have in mind here the shift in the distribution of profits from the entrepreneurs to the rentiers. Indeed, when prices decline in the same proportion as wages, this will be also true of profits. But the money income of rentiers consisting of the interest on "old" debts does not change and, therefore, their relative share in profits increases. If the entrepreneurs are "poorer" than the rentiers, this kind of shift will result rather in a decrease of total capitalists' consumption. Should the reverse be the case the result would be an increase in capitalists' consumption. The first pattern applies usually to societies where the concentration in industry is not too far advanced; the second—to developed capitalist economies. In the latter case, as follows from the above, capitalists' consumption is likely to increase, and this in turn will have a favourable effect on production and employment. But the final outcome is by no means certain even in this case, because quite a number of firms are in a precarious financial position, as a result of the decline in income while their "old" debts remain unchanged, and this discourages any investment activity on their part. In any case should an increase in employment at all take place, it would be on a small scale.

tion is rather exceptional and therefore the assumption of increasing marginal costs must be dropped.

Then, however, a difficult problem arises. On the assumption of increasing marginal costs the production of an establishment was pushed up to a point where the price was equal to the marginal cost (Fig. 5). Now, the price is higher than the marginal costs (Fig. 6) when the degree of utilization of the establishment is not very high. If, however, at the level of production OA the price AB_1 is higher than the marginal cost AB why does not the entrepreneur expand production even though he would in this case make additional profits? (For on each additional unit of production he would gain the difference BB_1 between the price and the marginal cost).

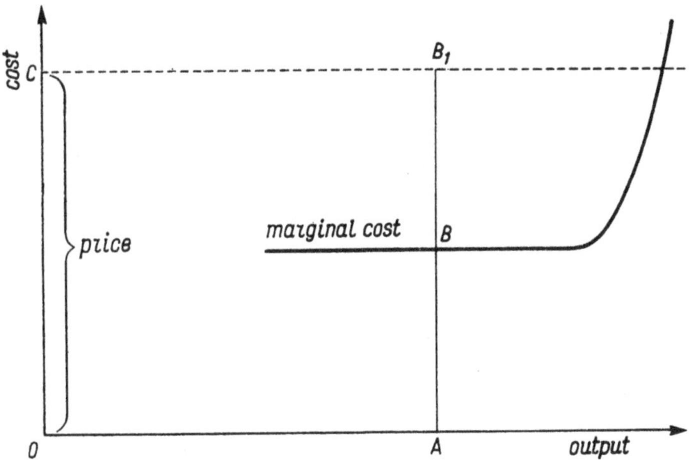

FIG. 6

The question is not difficult to explain in the case of cartels. A cartel does not expand production beyond a certain point A because the price of the commodity produced would decrease so much that in effect this would cause a loss rather than a gain. The production of a cartel does not reach the level at which the price is equal to the marginal cost but is fixed at the point at which the cartel, owing to its monopolistic position, attains the maximum profit. The price then exceeds the marginal cost.

This, however, does not solve our problem fully. It is true that the cartelized sector in a modern capitalist economy is considerable, however, in a significant part of the economy competition of one type or another is still in existence. Is it possible that in this sort of establishment the position presented in Fig. 6 may prevail?

An ingenious but simple answer to this question has been given only recently.[3]

It appears that even non-cartelized firms compete with each other in a rather *imperfect* way. Let us recall first what is actually meant by perfect competition. This is a situation in which a single entrepreneur is able to increase his sales without "spoiling the market", i.e. without affecting the market price. This is not in fact usually the case: a single entrepreneur has his "private" market, i.e. he has permanent customers, he specializes in the production of certain goods which are somewhat different from those produced by his competitors etc. Thus in order to increase his sales he must reduce his prices in order to gain new customers, to increase the demand for the specific commodities he produces etc. As a result the situation presented in Fig. 6 prevails in general in the non-cartelized industries as well. The entrepreneur expanding his sales beyond the point A would increase his profit if the price were fixed. As, however, he has to reduce it, he may make a relative loss rather than a gain. An entrepreneur when asked why he does not expand his production, hardly ever replies that the cost of additional production would be too high but rather that "he would be unable to sell more". In the light of the "classical" theory this would not make sense, but the theory of imperfect competition is in a position to interpret it quite precisely: the entrepreneur considers in fact that the extension of "his" market would require such a reduction in prices that this would not be offset by increased sales.

This is the solution of the problem in question. The establishments are in general not fully utilized since they maintain a monopolistic (cartels) or a quasi-monopolistic (imperfect competition) position in the market. This is the reason why we usually en-

---

[3] See for instance: P. Sraffa, "The Law of Returns under Competitive Conditions", *Economic Journal,* 1926; Ed. Chamberlain, *The Theory of Monopolistic Competition,* 1933; Joan Robinson, *The Economics of Imperfect Competition,* 1933.

counter the situation presented in Fig. 2, i.e. a horizontal curve of marginal costs much below the price level.

The ratio of the price to the marginal costs (higher than one) indicates how the position deviates from perfect competition and it may serve therefore to measure the "degree of monopoly".

2. The above considerations are pertinent to the problem of the changes in prices associated with those in employment. The conception of the association of a decline in real wages with the increase in production is based on the assumption of the "law of increasing marginal costs". Once we reject this assumption we have also to revise the views of the "classical" theory on the problem of real wages.

If the employment of an establishment rises but is kept within the range of stability of marginal costs (Fig. 6) then with a given "degree of monopoly" the ratio of the price of the product to the cost of wages and raw materials remains unchanged. As a result the real wages have no tendency to fall, which would be the case with increasing marginal costs. Only the increase in the prices of raw materials in relation to wages may result in a decrease in real wages since it will cause the rise in the prices of the goods produced and thus a fall in the ratio of wages to prices. From this angle the increase in employment will in fact have an adverse effect upon real wages, because in branches producing basic raw materials (in agriculture as well as mining) marginal costs are increasing, and therefore the prices of raw materials increase in relation to wages in response to a higher demand. The reduction in real wages is, however, incomparably smaller than it would be, were the marginal costs increasing in all stages of production. The price of finished commodities will increase in this case only as a result of the rise in the prices of basic raw materials which often play only a small part in costs and therefore a corresponding reduction of real wages with the increase in employment will be kept within narrow limits.

3. There is still another factor influencing the real wages in the opposite direction. In the preceding section "the degree of monopoly" measured by the ratio of prices to marginal costs was assumed to be a constant parameter. In fact, however, this ratio increases in the depression and diminishes in the boom. While the cost of raw materials and wages are reduced in the depression some prices do not fall at all or fall but little. The cartels are not

endangered by outsiders cropping up; in non-cartelized industries the entrepreneurs are rather reluctant to reduce prices, fearing to unchain cut-throat competition etc. If, however, in the course of the business cycle the prices of finished goods change less than the marginal costs, the divergence between them will increase in the depression and will shrink in prosperity. Hence real wages will be lower in the slump and higher during the boom than would be the case with a constant "degree of monopoly".[4]

Thus there are two opposite tendencies in the shaping of real wages: when production rises the prices of raw materials increase relative to wages but at the same time "the degree of monopoly" declines; when production shrinks the prices of raw materials fall in a higher proportion than wages but "the degree of monopoly" rises.

Let us imagine for instance that the ratio of the cost of raw materials to that of wages for some product is 30:70. As a result of the upswing the prices of raw materials increase by 40% and wages by 10%. The marginal cost of the commodity considered thus increases by $0.3.40\% + 0.7.10\% = 19\%$. We assume that due to the "rigidity" of the price its ratio to marginal cost decreases by 5%; as a result the price increases only in the proportion $1.19 \times 0.95 = 1.13$. Therefore the real wages decline in the proportion 1.10:1.13, i.e. approximately by 3%.

Thus the rise or decline in real wages depends on the relative weight of the two opposite tendencies. It is very likely that the resulting changes in real wages are generally rather small.[5]

4. There is still one more essential problem to consider concerning real wages. So far we have examined the question how establishments with a given equipment and a given technique respond to an increasing demand. However, when a longer period is considered it is necessary to take into account the fact that due to technical progress the cost of labour at a given level of wages is falling and hence there is a tendency for a slow but steady decline in prices in relation to wages, tantamount to a rise in real wages. Therefore the changes in real wages reflect the combined effect of cyclical fluctuations and technical progress. Our argument in the preceding section concerned rather the rela-

[4] The statistical data for Poland are quoted on p. 66.

[5] See, for instance, pp. 68–70.

tion of the cost of labour to prices than real wages. In fact real wages change in the same way as the product of this ratio and the index of productivity.

In the example considered in the preceding section the cost of labour rose by 10% and its relation to prices declined by 3%. If at the same time productivity increases, say, by 2% this means that the money wages rose in fact by 12% and the real wages declined by 1%.

Reduction of Wages under Imperfect Competition

1. We shall now examine the problem of the reduction of wages after dropping the assumptions of the increasing marginal costs and perfect competition. In order to do that we shall only have to repeat our argument in the section *Reduction of Wages on the Assumption of Perfect Competition* (pages 43–49) modifying it in accordance with the change in assumptions introduced in the preceding section.

Our argument was based on the fact that the volume of investment and capitalists' consumption is the basic determinant of production and employment, which are pushed up to the point where the income of capitalists is equal to their expenditure on consumption and investment. Moreover, we assumed that immediately after the reduction of wages the capitalists do not increase the volume of their consumption or investment. As a result the employment in the industries producing capitalists' consumer goods or investment goods does not increase and the purchasing power of the workers shrinks in the proportion of the wage reduction. This line of argument applies *in toto* to the case considered. Modifications are introduced only in its next stage. Under the assumption of perfect competition prices were equal to marginal costs and thus they fell in the same proportion as wages. Now there is a divergence between the prices and the marginal costs due to the cartelization or imperfect competition. Moreover, the reduction of wages will tend to cause a rise in this divergence because most likely some prices will prove to be "rigid" and thus will fail to decline in the same proportion as wages. Consequently the real purchasing power of the workers will decline: initially it decreases in money terms proportionately to wages while the decline in prices is less. As a result the demand for wage goods will fall and in consequence the employment in the corresponding department as well. Thus the decline in real wages (the prices are reduced to a lesser extent than wages) is associated here with the *fall* in employment.

Is this the end of the process? Will not investment and capitalists' consumption—which according to our assumption did not change immediately after the reduction of wages—increase after some delay as a result of the "improved" relation of prices to wages? It may easily be shown that this is not the case. The volume of capitalists' consumption and investment has, for the time being, not risen. Since capitalists' income is equal to the value of this volume, it declined in the same proportion as prices. Therefore the relation of the income of capitalists to the prices of investment goods has not changed. Consequently the profitability of new investment has not increased: this profitability is nothing else but the ratio of its yield to its value. Also the capitalists' consumption does not tend to increase, as their real income (money income corrected for price changes) has not changed. Thus we are faced here with the same position as in the case of the reduction of wages under conditions of perfect competition: if capitalists' consumption and investment do not increase immediately after the reduction of wages there arises such a situation that these items will not increase at a later date either.

We may summarize the above analysis as follows: *A reduction in money wages is usually accompanied as a result of price "rigidity" by an increase in "the degree of monopoly" and consequently leads to a reduction in real wages as well. However, this decline is accompanied by a fall rather than by a rise in employment. The slump in employment in question affects the wage good industries while employment in industries producing investment goods and capitalists' consumer goods remains unchanged. The real income of the capitalists does not rise but the real income of the workers declines.*

The Reduction of Wages in an Open System

1. The problem of wages was discussed above under the assumption of a closed system. We will inquire now into the influence of foreign trade on the processes considered. A reduction in wages and the consequent fall in prices will obviously improve

the competitive position of the goods produced by a given country in the world market and thus will contribute to an expansion in the volume of exports. This would affect production and employment favourably. However, the reduction of wages, as will be seen below, exerts an opposite influence as well so that the final outcome is by no means certain.

Indeed, the reduction of wages in a given country has obviously no influence on the prices of imported raw materials. Therefore the prices of goods manufactured from them decline *pro tanto* more slowly. As a result real wages decline (in addition to their decrease caused by the "rigidity" of prices discussed in the preceding section). Consequently the purchasing power of the workers is correspondingly lower and has an adverse effect on the industries producing wage goods.

The final outcome of the reduction of wages depends on the extent to which the reduction of wages and prices will increase the volume of exports. For instance, should the resulting increase in employment just balance the reduction in real wages, the purchasing power of the workers as a whole would not change and therefore the reduction of wages would not influence adversely the production of wage goods. The production will increase in this case by the volume of additional exports; the working class, however, even as a whole, will not benefit from it, while the real income of a single worker will obviously decline. The position would be better, of course, should exports increase more than is necessary to balance the decline in real wages. If, however, they increase to a lesser degree, the real purchasing power of the workers will decline and it will be followed by a decrease in production and employment in the wage-good industries. It may even happen then that the volume of exports will increase in consequence of the reduction of wages but the aggregate production and employment will decline.

As was said above, the effect of a reduction of wages in an open system depends—as far as the aggregate production is concerned—on the extent of the expansion of exports, in other words, on the response of the foreign demand to the decline in prices of a given country. If this demand is elastic, i.e. if a small reduction in prices and wages is followed by a relatively large expansion in exports, then production and employment increase (which, however, is not necessarily tantamount to an increase in the real purchasing power of the workers). If the demand for exports of a given country is inelastic a decline in production may ensue.

It should be noticed that because of tariff barriers, import restrictions etc., the elasticity of demand for products of a given country is rather small. The tariff barriers, high though they are, grow higher still when prices of imported goods decline. Such being the position, it is rather improbable that the reduction of money wages would result in the expansion of production and employment, and in particular in the rise in aggregate purchasing power of the workers, even in an open system.

2. It is worth noticing that the effect of a reduction of wages in an open system is very much the same as that of a currency depreciation. The two cases differ only in that in the former the wages decline and the prices of imported raw materials remain unchanged, while in the latter—the wages remain unaltered (in terms of domestic currency), and the prices of imported raw materials increase in inverse proportion to the currency depreciation. The effect of depreciation as concerns production and employment depends, as in the case of the reduction of wages, on the elasticity of the foreign demand for products of a given country.

Conclusions

We shall now sum up the results of our inquiry.

We attempted to show that the reduction of wages in a closed system does not lead to an increase in production; that in conditions of perfect competition the level of production remains unchanged while prices decline in the same proportion as wages; however, under existing conditions of monopoly or imperfect competition a reduction of money wages tends to cause a decline in real wages associated with a decrease in employment. Moreover, it appears that in such a system there is in general no reason—in spite of the widespread belief—for the decline in production to be accompanied by an increase in real wages or vice versa. The analysis of the problem in an open system shows that even in such a case the reduction of wages does not necessarily lead to an increase in employment, and the prospects of raising the aggregate real income of the working class are even dimmer. In particular, under the system of high and rising tariffs it is very likely that a reduction of wages will have an adverse effect upon employment also in an open economy.

The slogan "Rigid wages as a source of unemployment"—under which title a book by Mr. Wątecki[6] has been recently published in Poland—proves in the light of the above analysis entirely unfounded. And equally hopeless is the case of the supporters of this slogan who preach that collective bargaining by making wages "rigid" causes unemployment and poverty of the working class.

[6] J. Wątecki, *Sztywne płace źródłem bezrobocia* (Rigid Wages as a Source of Unemployment), Kraków 1938.

6. MONEY AND REAL WAGES

PART II (STATISTICS)

Methodological Problems

1. Attempts were made time and again to check by means of a statistical inquiry the thesis of the "classical" theory that an increase in employment is associated with a decline in real wages. As an example the well known inquiries of the French economist Rueff may serve. He starts from the generally correct premise that when the problem of the relation between real wages and employment in industry is examined, by real wages should be meant the ratio of money wages of the industrial workers to the prices at which the respective products are sold, i.e. wholesale prices. In the realization of this approach, however, he committed gross statistical errors. Rueff simply divided the index of industrial money wages by the general index of the wholesale prices and considered the fact that the ratio increased during the slump and declined during the boom to be the proof of the "classical" theory. Now it should be recalled that the indices of wholesale prices are based mainly on raw materials and semi-manufactures. These indices thus reflect to a considerable degree the changes in the prices of domestic and imported raw materials rather than those in the prices of manufactured goods. No wonder, then, that the ratios received by Rueff increased in the slump and declined in the boom, as it is generally known that the prices of raw materials fluctuate more strongly than wages (and prices of manufactured goods). But it is also clear that the ratio of wages of the British worker to the prices of Brazilian coffee is rather irrelevant to the conditions of industrial production in Great Britain. Thus Rueff's method applied by Mr. J. Wątecki (referred to above) to Polish data is far from being a pattern worth following.

However, even apart from questions of statistical technique the posing of the problem by Rueff is not quite satisfactory. The decline in real wages associated with the increase in employment is according to the "classical" theory a conclusion from a more general principle of "increasing marginal costs". It follows from this principle that with the expansion of output the prices of finished products increase in relation to the prime costs consisting of raw materials and wages. Since, at the same time, the prices of raw materials increase in relation to wages this enhances the rise in the prices of finished products relative to wages (compare pp. 41–42). Therefore in orders to check the theorems of the "classical" theory a somewhat different approach is required. It should first be ascertained whether the prices of finished products do really increase in relation to the costs of raw materials and wages when output expands. Indeed, according to our argument (see pp. 53–54) the position should be the reverse, because the marginal costs are constant rather than increasing over the relevant range of output, while "the degree of monopoly" increases during the slump and declines during the boom. Only after the answer to this basic question has been found may we turn to another problem: how are real wages affected by the changes in the ratio of the prices of finished goods to prime costs (costs of raw materials and labour) on the one hand and by the changes of the ratio of prices of raw materials to wages on the other. Indeed, should the "classical" theory be correct real wages would fall with the increase of production. But if, as we maintain, the ratio of the prices of finished goods to prime costs diminishes in the upswing and conversely, the direction of the changes in real wages cannot be foreseen. For while the changes in prices of finished goods in relation to prime costs tend to associate the increase in real wages with the expansion of employment, the changes in the relation of prices of raw materials to wages work in the opposite direction.[1] In addition it should be recalled that real wages, apart from the cyclical fluctuations, tend to increase steadily as a result of the long-run rise in productivity due to technical progress etc.[2] It is this method that we shall follow when analysing the processes in question in the Polish economy.

Prices, Prime Costs and Real Wages in Poland

1. In the following analysis we shall treat the Polish industry as an entity. Thus as "raw materials" we shall consider only those imported or produced by domestic agriculture. As "finished industrial products" will be considered goods which after having

[1] See pp. 53–54.
[2] See pp. 54–55.

been sold do not undergo any industrial processing as contrasted to goods sold as materials by one industrial establishment to another.

For the type of inquiry envisaged here the following data are necessary: 1) The price index of "finished industrial products", i.e. finished goods in the strict sense, as well as raw materials or semi-manufactures used in this condition in other sectors of the economy (for instance, coal for households) or exported; 2) The price index of imported raw materials and home agricultural products used by industry; 3) The index of labour cost per unit of output. These data come mainly from the statistical inquiry carried out by me jointly with Ludwik Landau.[3] The indices obtained in this inquiry covered the period 1928–1934; they are extrapolated in this paper up to 1937.

2. The price index of "finished industrial products" was calculated in the inquiry quoted above in the following way.

First of all the aggregate sales of these goods were split into domestic sales and exports. Next the domestic sales were subdivided into the following groups: 1) consumer goods except food and fuel (textiles, utensils, furniture etc.); 2) sugar, beer, kerosene; 3) coal for households; 4) finished investment goods (buildings, machinery); 5) goods used in agricultural production (fertilizers, tools and agricultural machinery etc.). In Table I are presented the price indices of these groups of goods together with their weights corresponding to their domestic sales in the basic year 1928 as well as the general weighted price index of "finished industrial products" sold in the domestic market.

Next the price index of industrial exports was calculated on the basis of L. Landau: "*Polish Exports during the Depression*".[4] This index, as well as the index of "finished industrial products" sold in the domestic market, is weighted according to the proportion exports bore to the sales in the domestic market (both items valued in prices of 1928) in the single years of the period con-

[3] *Wahania cen i kosztów a wahania produkcji przemysłowej w Polsce (Changes in Price–Cost Relations and Fluctuations of Industrial Production in Poland), Papers of the Institute of Research on Business Fluctuations and Prices,* Vol. IV, No. 2. Ludwik Landau was murdered during the occupation by the Nazis.

[4] *Papers of the Institute of Research on Business Fluctuations and Prices,* Vol. III, Nos. 2–3.

TABLE I

The Price Index of "Finished Industrial Products" Sold in Domestic Market

Year	Finished consumer goods (except food and fuel)	Sugar, beer, kerosene (net of excise)	Coal for households	Finished investment goods	Goods for agricultural production	"Finished industrial products" sold in domestic market
Weights	34	12	8	36	10	100
1928	100.0	100.0	100.0	100.0	100.0	100.0
1929	98.6	105.8	113.8	103.5	101.3	102.7
1930	91.9	108.7	116.1	101.0	99.2	99.9
1931	78.9	107.3	116.1	95.5	91.5	90.7
1932	67.6	102.0	107.2	80.5	81.4	80.9
1933	61.4	90.3	96.5	70.5	75.8	72.4
1934	59.2	86.0	91.5	67.7	71.1	69.3
1935	56.8	72.7	83.9	67.0	65.6	65.4
1936	56.6	60.9	77.3	63.6	62.0	61.8
1937	58.3	60.6	77.3	66.1	64.0	63.5

sidered.[5] Thus a general index of the prices of "finished industrial products" is arrived in Table II.

TABLE II

The Price Index of "Finished Industrial Products" Sold in the Domestic Market and Exported

Year	"Finished industrial products" for the home market		Exported goods		"Finished industrial products"
	Weight	Index	Weight	Index	Index
1928	79	100.0	21	100.0	100.0
1929	78	102.7	22	99.1	101.9
1930	75	99.9	25	84.5	96.0
1931	72	90.7	28	70.3	85.0
1932	77	80.9	23	59.0	75.9
1933	79	72.4	21	54.4	68.5
1934	80	69.3	20	51.3	65.8
1935	82	65.4	18	47.6	62.2
1936	84	61.8	16	47.0	59.4
1937	84	63.5	16	53.4	62.9

[5] Variable weights are applied here because export prices deviate considerably from the home prices for the same goods.

3. Let us turn now to the price index of raw materials and semi-manufactures imported or produced by home agriculture. This index is obtained as weighted average of the indices of prices of imported raw materials and semi-manufactures, prices of wood and prices of sugar beets (weights correspond to the values of respective materials used by the industry in the basic year 1928) (Table III).

TABLE III

The Price Indices of Raw Materials for Industry (Imported or Produced by Home Agriculture)

Year	Imported raw materials and semi-manufactures	Wood	Sugar beets	Price index of raw materials imported and produced by home agriculture
Weights	66	17	17	100
1928	100.0	100.0	100.0	100.0
1929	93.3	93.3	93.1	93.1
1930	68.6	71.9	75.7	70.4
1931	51.0	49.5	58.4	52.0
1932	41.6	38.3	65.7	45.1
1933	43.8	38.7	63.1	46.2
1934	43.2	44.3	69.9	47.9
1935	41.6	44.0	62.7	45.6
1936	45.2	52.3	61.1	49.1
1937	50.9	68.3	60.8	55.7

4. The estimates of the cost of labour given in the paper quoted are corrected for changes in productivity which were not accounted for in that paper: the index of hourly wages in industry and mining is divided by the index of average productivity based on L. Landau: *Bezrobocie technologiczne w przemyśle polskim w latach 1929–1935* (Technological Unemployment in Polish Industry in the years 1929–1935)[6] (Table IV).

Now it is easy to calculate the general index of prime costs as the weighted average of the index of prices of raw materials and the index of the cost of labour. As weights we adopt: a) the value of imported raw materials and of home agricultural products used by the industry, and b) the wage bill of industry

[6] *Studies and Contributions*, published by the Institute of Social Problems, Vol. I.

TABLE IV

Indices of the Labour Cost

Year	Index of hourly wages	Index of productivity	Index of labour cost
1928	100.0	100	100.0
1929	108.4	103	105.2
1930	108.1	107	101.0
1931	100.9	110	91.8
1932	92.8	116	80.0
1933	85.5	124	68.0
1934	82.0	127	64.5
1935	80.5	130	61.9
1936	80.3	134[a]	59.9
1937	82.2	137[a]	60.0

a – Estimate

and mining in the basic year 1928. The former amounts to 1.70 mld zl.[7], the latter—to 1.67 mld zl.[8] Thus the weights bear roughly the proportion 1 : 1. The results are presented in Table V.

TABLE V

Indices of Prime Costs in Industry

Year	Cost of imported raw materials and home agricultural products	Labour costs	Prime costs
Weights	50	50	100
1928	100.0	100.0	100.0
1929	93.1	105.2	99.1
1930	70.4	101.0	85.7
1931	52.0	91.8	71.9
1932	45.1	80.0	62.5
1933	46.2	68.0	57.1
1934	47.9	64.5	56.2
1935	45.6	61.9	53.7
1936	49.1	59.9	54.5
1937	55.7	60.0	57.8

5. Having at our disposal now the index of "finished industrial products" and the index of prime costs we may calculate their

[7] *Wahania cen i kosztów* (Changes in Price–Cost Relations), p. 55, *ed. cit.*

[8] *Mały Rocznik Statystyczny, 1938* (Concise Statistical Yearbook of Poland 1938), pp. 145 and 258.

ratio which was actually our purpose. The results are presented in Table VI.

TABLE VI

Ratio of the Prices of "Finished Industrial Products" to Prime Costs

Year	Index of prices of "finished industrial products"	Index of prime costs	Ratio of prices to costs
1928	100.0	100.0	100.0
1929	101.9	99.1	102.8
1930	96.0	85.7	112.0
1931	85.0	71.9	118.2
1932	75.9	62.5	121.4
1933	68.5	57.1	120.0
1934	65.8	56.2	117.2
1935	62.2	53.7	115.8
1936	59.4	54.5	109.0
1937	62.9	57.8	108.8

We shall now compare the changes in the ratio of prices of "finished industrial products" to the respective prime costs with the changes in the indices of production[9] and employment (aggregate working hours in mining and industry)[10] (Table VII).

TABLE VII

Ratio of Prices of "Finished Industrial Products" to Prime Costs, Industrial Production and Employment

Year	Ratio of prices of "finished industrial products" to costs	Index of industrial production	Index of industrial employment
1928	100.0	100.0	100.0
1929	102.8	101.9	100.9
1930	112.0	89.7	83.5
1931	118.2	78.2	70.4
1932	121.4	63.7	55.2
1933	120.0	70.0	54.8
1934	117.2	78.8	62.0
1935	115.8	84.9	65.8
1936	109.0	94.3	71.8
1937	108.8	110.7	82.6

[9] *Monthly Statistical Tables*, published by the Institute of Research on Business Fluctuations and Prices.

[10] *Mały Rocznik Statystyczny, 1938* (Concise Statistical Yearbook 1938), p. 248.

It is immediately clear that the "classical" theory is not supported by the results of our statistical inquiry. It will be seen that the decline in production and employment is accompanied by an increase in the prices of "finished industrial products" in relation to prime costs and conversely. But this phenomenon, which is in disagreement with the law of "increasing marginal costs", can be easily explained by our hypothesis: by the constancy of marginal costs over the relevant range of output and by "the degree of monopoly" increasing in slump due to the "rigidity" of prices and decreasing in the boom. Contrary to the accepted opinion the ratio of prices to prime costs "improves" in the depression! It does not follow, of course, that profitability is high: the effect of the drop in sales outweighs by far the advantage from the increased ratio of prices to prime costs.

6. We shall calculate now the index of real wages of industrial workers. By the real wage is usually meant the ratio of the money wage rate to the cost of living. As, however, in the latter the prices of the agricultural products and the rent are included—and even weight heavily upon them—it is difficult to expect a close connection between real wages thus defined and conditions of industrial production. The counterpart of what was meant by "real wages" in our theoretical discussion is the ratio of money wages to the wholesale prices of the consumer goods sold by the industry in the domestic market. This "real wage" measures the amount of industrial consumer goods a worker could buy for his money wage. We shall first examine this series. The real wages in the usual sense are only loosely related to it. Nevertheless we shall next have a look at this series as well.

Let us construct the index of prices of the industrial consumer products for the home market. We shall use for the purpose the group indices presented in Table I of prices of: 1) finished consumer goods except food and fuel; 2) sugar, beer, kerosene; 3) coal for households—adopting the weights proportionate to those shown in this table. Next the index of money wages (taken from Table IV) is divided by the index of industrial consumer products for the home market and thus is obtained the index of "real wages" in our sense (Table VIII).

This series shows in the period considered a long-run positive trend resulting from the increasing productivity of labour due to technical progress etc. (compare pages 54–55). In order to eliminate

TABLE VIII

Index of "Real Wages" Based on Prices of Industrial Consumer Products for the Home Market

Year	The index of money wages	The index of prices of industrial consumer products for home market	"Real wages" (ratio of the money wages to prices)
1928	100.0	100.0	100.0
1929	108.4	102.4	105.8
1930	108.1	99.2	109.0
1931	100.9	90.7	111.2
1932	92.8	81.2	114.2
1933	85.5	73.0	117.1
1934	82.0	69.8	117.3
1935	80.5	64.3	125.0
1936	80.3	60.6	132.3
1937	82.2	61.6	133.3

this factor and to obtain the cyclical fluctuations of "real wages" we shall divide the cost per unit of output rather than the hourly wages by the prices of industrial consumer goods (Table IX). (This series shows the changes in the amount of industrial consumer goods a worker could buy for the wages he receives per unit of output.)

TABLE IX

Index of the Ratio of Cost of Labour to the Prices of Industrial Consumer Goods

Year	Cost of labour	Index of prices of industrial consumer goods	The ratio of cost of labour to prices
1928	100.0	100.0	100.0
1929	105.2	102.4	102.8
1930	101.0	99.2	101.8
1931	91.9	90.7	101.3
1932	80.0	81.2	98.5
1933	68.0	73.0	93.2
1934	64.5	69.8	92.4
1935	61.9	64.3	96.3
1936	59.9	60.6	98.8
1937	60.0	61.6	97.3

This series is in complete agreement with the results of the theoretical analysis on pp. 51–54. We stated there that the changes in real wages associated with business fluctuations are rather small because of two factors working in the opposite direction: in the depression the increase in the "degree of monopoly" affects real wages adversely but this is counterbalanced by the influence of the decline in the raw material prices in relation to money wages; in the boom the opposite is the case. As a result the fluctuations are slight and rather irregular. We do observe this phenomenon in the series shown in Table IX. (It is worth noticing that at the bottom of depression in 1932 "real wages"—after the elimination of the influence of the increase in productivity—remained more or less at the same level as at the top of the boom in 1928). The index of actual "real wages" shown in Table VIII is the resultant of the cyclical fluctuations and of the steady increase in productivity (compare pp. 54–55).

7. Let us have a look now at the changes in real wages in the normal sense, i.e. in the ratio of money wages to the cost of living (Table X).

TABLE X

Index of Real Wages Based on Cost of Living

Year	Money wages	Cost of living	Real wages
1928	100.0	100.0	100.0
1929	108.4	100.5	107.9
1930	108.1	92.1	117.4
1931	100.9	82.8	121.9
1932	92.8	74.8	124.2
1933	85.5	67.5	126.6
1934	82.0	62.6	131.0
1935	80.5	60.0	134.3
1936	80.3	58.0	138.5
1937	82.2	62.0	132.7

This series shows also an increasing trend. After the elimination of the rise in productivity by calculating the ratio of the cost of labour per unit of output to the cost of living we obtain in this case as well a series showing rather small and irregular fluctuations (Table XI).

Indeed these fluctuations, which, by the way, are greater than those in the ratio of the cost of labour to the prices of industrial consumer products, do not show either any clear cut positive or negative correlation with the level of production or employment.

TABLE XI

Index of Cost of Labour in Relation to Cost of Living

Year	Cost of labour	Cost of living	Ratio of cost of labour to cost of living
1928	100.0	100.0	100.0
1929	105.2	100.5	104.7
1930	101.0	92.1	109.7
1931	91.9	82.8	111.0
1932	80.0	94.8	106.9
1933	68.0	67.5	100.5
1934	64.5	62.6	103.0
1935	61.9	60.0	103.1
1936	59.9	58.0	103.3
1937	60.0	62.0	96.8

Money Wages and Employment

1. We tested above statistically the "classical" theory of the changes in the ratio of prices to prime costs and in real wages, as well as our hypothesis on the subject. It will be difficult to find as precise a method to settle the dispute between the point of view of the "classical" theory and ours on the subject of the effect of the reduction of money wages upon the level of production and employment. For the changes in production depend on many other factors of which the most important is the mechanism causing the automatic business fluctuations which bears no definite relation to the changes in money wages. We may only show that even considerable cuts of money wages could not counteract a fall in production due to the cyclical downswing.

2. In Table XII the index of money wage rates is compared with the indices of industrial production and employment.

As will be seen, a considerable reduction in wages (about 8% per year) occured in the period 1930–1933. This reduction, however, did not by any means contribute to the alleviation of the downswing which was very drastic indeed. It is true that wage cuts, although on a smaller scale, continued through the period 1933–1935 when production began to rise. Hardly anybody will, however, attribute to this factor an important part in the improvement of the business situation in the last years. It is rather generally accepted that the first stimulus was generated by the dollar

TABLE XII

Indices of Money Wage Rates and of Industrial Production and Employment

Year	Money wage rates	Industrial production	Industrial employment
1928	100.0	100.0	100.0
1929	108.4	101.9	100.9
1930	108.1	89.7	83.5
1931	100.9	78.2	70.4
1932	92.8	63.7	55.2
1933	85.5	70.0	54.8
1934	82.0	78.8	62.0
1935	80.5	84.9	65.8
1936	80.3	94.3	71.8
1937	82.2	110.7	82.6

depreciation in 1933 which caused the spending of hoarded dollars on goods (residential building especially for private use, accumulation of stocks, in particular of textiles etc.). This brought about an increase in production in 1934. The improvement in profitability of business stimulated in turn private investment in the subsequent years. In addition Government investment played an important part in the expansion of business activity.

Conclusions

The analysis of the Polish statistical data shows that the "classical" theory is wrong in maintaining that the prices of finished industrial products increase in relation to prime costs when production expands and conversely. In fact the reverse is true. This is in complete agreement with our theoretical analysis which rejects the law of the "increasing marginal costs" and assumes that the "degree of monopoly" increases in the depression and declines in the boom.

It appears also most unlikely that the considerable cuts in money wages which took place in Poland during the downswing had any mitigating effect upon it. This again is in accord with our approach to the problem of reduction of money wages.

ESSAYS IN THE THEORY OF ECONOMIC FLUCTUATIONS

by

MICHAL KALECKI

London

GEORGE ALLEN & UNWIN LTD

FOREWORD

THESE essays, though formally independent, nevertheless constitute a whole. Each of them treats a problem which is interesting in itself, but at the same time it prepares the ground for the succeeding essays. In particular the first five essays lead up to the sixth, which contains a theory of the business cycle.

The following are reprinted (all with important alterations) by permission of the editors concerned: "The Distribution of the National Income," from *Econometrica*, April 1938, "The Principle of Increasing Risk," from *Economica*, November 1937, and "A Theory of the Business Cycle," from the *Review of Economic Studies*, February 1937.

I am very much indebted to Mrs. Joan Robinson, whose comments have enabled me to make various improvements, and to Mr. Brian Tew for improving the style. I have also to thank Mr. P. Sraffa and Mr. R. F. Kahn for valuable remarks.

CAMBRIDGE,
June 1938

M. KALECKI

CONTENTS

Part One

Part Two

Part One

1

THE DISTRIBUTION OF THE NATIONAL INCOME[1]

INTRODUCTION

In this essay we investigate both statistically and analytically the relative share of manual labour in the national income. From the social point of view it would be more interesting to consider the share of labour as a whole: but it is the relative share of *manual* labour which is suitable for theoretical analysis.

For the same reason the national income is here given a slightly unorthodox meaning. First, as we are interested in the *home produced* income alone, we exclude from national income that part which is derived from foreign investments. Further, we shall deal with *gross* income, by which is meant the income before deductions for maintenance and depreciation (gross income = net income + maintenance and depreciation).[2]

It is easy to see that the gross national home-produced

[1] This essay is an altered version of the article published in *Econometrica,* April 1938. The statistical data differ from those quoted in this article owing either to the slightly altered meaning of some concepts (e.g. of the national income) or to new sources becoming available.

[2] For the sake of brevity we shall speak throughout the essay of "depreciation" instead of "maintenance and depreciation."

income is equal to the value added by all industries of an economy. Usually the Government[1] is treated as an "industry" producing public services, but we shall not adopt this procedure here. Instead we shall mean by national income *the total value added by private enterprises* which we denote below by A.

THE STATISTICAL DATA

1. The figures for Great Britain are based on Professor Bowley's *Wages and Income in the United Kingdom since 1860*, and Mr. Colin Clark's *National Income and Outlay*.

Using Professor Bowley's data on the distribution of national income (pp. 92, 139) and deducting from the total income the income from overseas (mentioned on p. 96) we obtain the relative share of manual labour[2] in home-produced income: 41·4 per cent in 1880, and 39·4 in 1913. These figures are for relative shares in *net* income; Professor Bowley does not give data on depreciation and gross income. The rate of increase of gross income in the period, 1880–1913, is, however, unlikely to differ much from that of net income; for the proportion of depreciation to net income in 1913 was only about 8 per cent, and the changes in the volume of capital equipment and in the national income between 1880 and 1913 were such that this percentage could not have undergone a great proportionate change

[1] We mean here by the Government all public authorities.

[2] Shop assistants excluded.

within this period.[1] Thus the relative share of manual labour in gross income must have altered within the period in question similarly to that in net income. Professor Bowley's figures of national income contain also the value of Governmental services, which should strictly be excluded for our present purpose, but this would for similar reasons only slightly alter the trend of the relative shares of manual labour from 1880 to 1913.[2] Thus it can be concluded from the above that the change in the relative share of manual labour in the national income in our sense (value added by private enterprises) was small.

The figures for 1911 and 1924–35 are obtained from Mr. Colin Clark's data on "Distribution of Income between Factors of Production, 1911 and 1924–35" (*National Income and Outlay*, p. 94), and on depreciation (pp. 86, 169), and expenditure on Governmental services (p. 141) in these years. The relative shares here calculated differ from those given by Mr. Clark (p. 94) in that they are taken in relation to *gross* home-produced income, from which expenditure on public services has been excluded.

[1] The real capital per head increased by about 25 per cent, the real income per head by about 40 per cent (*National Income and Outlay*, pp. 273 and 232), while the rate of depreciation was probably to some extent higher in 1913 than in 1880.

[2] The proportionate rise in expenditure on administration army, navy, etc., in Great Britain in the period considered was not much different from that in national income. See, e.g., Bernard Mallet, *British Budgets, 1887–1913*, pp. 353 and 407.

TABLE 1

Relative Share of Manual Labour[1] in the National Income of Great Britain

1911	40·7	1924	43·0	1928	43·0	1932	43·0
		1925	40·8	1929	42·4	1933	42·7
		1926	42·0	1930	41·1	1934	42·0
		1927	43·0	1931	43·7	1935	41·8

We see that the relative share of manual labour in the national income in Great Britain showed a remarkable stability both in the long run and in the short period.

2. The figures for the U.S.A. are based on Dr. King's *The National Income and Its Purchasing Power, 1909–1928*, and Dr. Kuznets' *National Income and Capital Formation, 1919–1935.*

The relative share of wages[2] in the net national income[3] was, according to Dr. King, 37·9 per cent in 1909 and 40·2 in 1925. The change in the relative share of manual labour in the gross income less "Government produced" services was probably not very different.

For the period 1919–34 Dr. Kuznets' estimates are used. It is easy here to calculate "national income" in our sense. We take "income produced" by private industries including depreciation and maintenance (pp. 14, 80). A difficulty arises, however, in connection with wages being estimated separately only in "selected

[1] Shop assistants excluded. [2] Shop assistants included.

[3] *The National Income*, p. 74. We have excluded from income the services of durable consumption goods which King treats as a part of national income (he calls this part "imputed income").

industries": agriculture, mining, manufacturing, construction, and railways; for other industries they are given jointly with salaries (pp. 62–67).

In 1925 the wage bill in the "selected industries" mentioned above was $17 milliards, while the total wage and salary bill (excluding Governmental employees) was about $44 milliards. But according to Dr. King's estimate the wage bill in trade, services, etc., amounted in 1925 to about $13 milliards, so that if we admit his figure we obtain: wages in "selected industries" 17, in other industries 13, and total salaries $14 milliards. Now as regards the amplitude of fluctuations, the wages in "other industries" keep the middle position between wages in "selected industries" and total salaries. Thus they are likely to fluctuate more or less proportionately to the total wage and salary bill. With this hypothesis it is possible to estimate roughly the wage bill in "other industries" throughout the period considered. Adding the results to the wage bill in "selected industries" as given by Dr. Kuznets, we obtain the hypothetical total wage bill in the period 1919–34 and find its relative share in the national income. The figures obtained are given in the following table.

TABLE 2

Relative Share of Manual Labour[1] in the National Income of U.S.A.

1919	34·9	1923	39·3	1927	37·0	1931	34·9
1920	37·4	1924	37·6	1928	35·8	1932	36·0
1921	35·0	1925	37·1	1929	36·1	1933	37·2
1922	37·0	1926	36·7	1930	35·0	1934	35·8

[1] Shop assistants included.

These figures represent of course only a rough estimate, but they are adequate in order to show the stability of the relative share of manual labour in the period considered.

We see that in the U.S.A., as in Great Britain, the relative share of wages in the national income shows but small variations both in the long run and in the short period. We shall now try to explain this "law," and to establish the conditions under which it is valid.

THE DEGREE OF MONOPOLY AND THE DISTRIBUTION OF THE PRODUCT OF INDUSTRY

1. Let us consider an enterprise with a given capital equipment which produces at a given moment an output x and sells it at a price p.[1]

If we denote the entrepreneurial income (inclusive of dividends) per unit of output by e_a, the average "overhead" costs (interest, depreciation, and salaries) by o_a and the average wage and raw material cost by w_a and r_a respectively, we have:

$$p = e_a + o_a + w_a + r_a$$

Further, the short-period marginal costs m (i.e. the cost of producing an additional unit of product with a given capital equipment) is made up of the sum of the short-period marginal cost of "overheads" o_m, wages w_m, and raw materials r_m.

$$m = o_m + w_m + r_m$$

[1] We mean here by p the "net price," i.e. the revenue per unit of product after deduction of advertising costs, etc.

We subtract the second equation from the first and obtain:

$$p - m = e_a + (o_a - o_m) + (w_a - w_m) + (r_a - r_m) \quad . \quad (1)$$

Following Mr. Lerner,[1] we shall call the "degree of monopoly" of the enterprise, the ratio of the difference between price and marginal cost to price, or:

$$\mu = \frac{p - m}{p}$$

If marginal cost is equal to marginal revenue, μ is equation the inverse of the elasticity of demand for the product of the enterprise. Substituting μ for $\frac{p - m}{p}$ in the equation (1), and multiplying both sides by the output x we get:

$$xp\mu = xe_a + x(o_a - o_m) + x(w_a - w_m) + x(r_a - r_m).$$

Such an equation can be written for each enterprise of an economy. Adding the equations for all enterprises we obtain:

$$\Sigma xp\mu = \Sigma xe_a + \Sigma x(o_a - o_m) \\ + \Sigma x(w_a - w_m) + \Sigma x(r_a - r_m) \quad . \quad (2)$$

The sum Σxe_a is the aggregate entrepreneurial income (inclusive of dividends). Further, the marginal "overhead" cost is in general small in comparison with the

[1] "The Concept of Monopoly and the Measurement of Monopoly Power," *Review of Economic Studies*, June 1934.

average cost; thus $\Sigma x(o_a - o_m)$ can be represented by $(1 - \beta) O$, where O is the aggregate overhead cost (interest, depreciation, and salaries), and β a small positive fraction. The average cost of raw materials can be supposed approximately constant and consequently the sum $\Sigma x(r_a - r_m)$ can be neglected. Most complicated are the problems connected with the member $\Sigma x(w_a - w_m)$; we must deal with them at some length.

2. The prevailing type of average wage-cost curve seems to have the following shape. It is more or less horizontal up to a point corresponding to the "practical capacity" of the plant, but slopes sharply upwards beyond it. This point is seldom reached—factories, e.g. only exceptionally work in more than two shifts. Thus in enterprises of this type $w_a - w_m$ is small in comparison with w_a.

Of course in some industries the situation is different. Those producing basic raw materials (agriculture and mining) are normally subject to diminishing returns, and $w_a - w_m$ is usually negative and not small as compared with w_a in the enterprises concerned. Other industries have, on the other hand, distinctly falling average wage-costs until "practical capacity" is reached (e.g. railways), and here $w_a - w_m$ is positive and not small in relation to w_a.

It is now easy to see that if wage-cost curves of the first type represent a large part of the aggregate wage bill W the sum $\Sigma x(w_a - w_m)$ is likely to be small in comparison with W. For then in most enterprises $\frac{w_u - w_m}{w_a}$

will be small while the rest will be divided between those in which $\frac{w_a - w_m}{w_a}$ is positive and those in which it is negative.

We therefore conclude that $\Sigma x(w_a - w_m)$ can be represented by γW where γ is likely to be a small (positive or negative) fraction. In other words: conditions of approximately constant returns prevail, in the short period, in the economy as a whole.

3. On the basis of the above considerations we can now write the equation (2) as follows:

$$\Sigma xp\mu = E + (1 - \beta)O + \gamma W$$

or:

$$\Sigma xp\mu = (E + O) - (\beta O - \gamma W)$$

where β and γ are small fractions.

It is obvious that βO is small in relation to $E + O$; and the same can be said of γW since, as the statistical data quoted above show, W is less than half the gross national income A and thus less than $A - W = E + O$. We can conclude that $\beta O - \gamma W$ is small in comparison with $E + O$, and therefore:

$$\Sigma xp\mu = E + O$$

can be regarded as a good approximation. Now let us divide both sides of this equation by the aggregate turnover $T = \Sigma xp$.

$$\frac{\Sigma xp\mu}{\Sigma xp} = \frac{E + O}{T}$$

The expression on the left-hand side of this equation is the weighted average of the degrees of monopoly μ, which we shall denote by $\bar{\mu}$. The sum $E + O$ is made up of profits, interest, depreciation, and salaries, and thus it is equal to gross capitalist income plus salaries.

We have thus the following proposition: *The relative share of gross capitalist income and salaries in the aggregate turnover is with great approximation equal to the average degree of monopoly:*

$$\bar{\mu} = \frac{E + O}{T} \quad . \quad . \quad . \quad . \quad . \quad . \quad (3)$$

Some remarks are still necessary on the notion of the turnover T. In our above argument by "enterprise" was really meant not the firm but a unit producing marketable goods, e.g. a spinning and weaving mill which belong to the same firm must be considered separate "enterprises." Indeed, such a weaving mill in its pricing would account the yarn from its "own" spinning mill at the market price, and consequently the formation of prices is here much as it would be if the two factories belonged to distinct firms.

Now it is important to stress that with this definition of an "enterprise" the turnover T is *not* dependent on the degree of integration of industry so long as markets for intermediate products are in existence. T is equal to the gross national income plus the aggregate cost of marketable raw materials.

HOW IS IT POSSIBLE FOR THE DEGREE OF MONOPOLY TO DETERMINE THE DISTRIBUTION OF THE PRODUCT OF INDUSTRY?

1. The results obtained in the last section may seem paradoxical. In the case of free competition the average degree of monopoly $\bar{\mu}$ is equal to zero; thus equation (3) seems to show that free competition makes it impossible not only to earn profits and interest, but even to cover depreciation and salaries—all gross income being absorbed by wages. This paradox is, however, only apparent. The formula (3) can be correct only when the assumptions on which it is based are fulfilled. According to these assumptions: (1) The short-period marginal-cost curve does not differ considerably in the majority of enterprises from the short-period average-cost curve of manual labour and raw materials up to a certain point corresponding to "practical capacity." (2) The output in these enterprises is usually below this point. These assumptions are quite realistic, but such a state of affairs is possible only with the existence of monopoly or imperfect competition. If free competition prevails, the second condition cannot be fulfilled; enterprises must close down or maintain such a degree of employment that the marginal cost is higher than the average cost of manual labour and raw materials.

In the real world an enterprise is seldom employed beyond the "practical capacity," a fact which is therefore a demonstration of general market imperfection and widespread monopolies or oligopolies. Our formula though quite realistic is not applicable in the case of free competition.

The second question which may be raised is of a more complex character. According to our formula, the distribution of the product of industry is at every moment determined by the degree of monopoly. Our formula therefore holds both for the short period and in the long run, even though it was deduced on the basis of, so to speak, pure short-period considerations. And contrary to the usual view neither inventions nor the elasticity of substitution between capital and labour have any influence on the distribution of income.

The source of the conflict between our theory and the orthodox view may be explained thus: (1) The long-period analysis of distribution is generally conducted on the basis of oversimplified representation of output as a function of only two variables—capital (taken *in abstracto*) and labour. In this way, the short-period cost curves are, as we shall see at once, excluded artificially from this analysis. (2) On the basis of our assumptions these curves have a special shape which makes for the elimination of factors other than the degree of monopoly from the mechanism of distribution. To clarify the problems concerned we shall now consider the dependence of the long-run distribution of the product of industry on the shape of the short-period cost curves.

2. A particular commodity can be produced with various types of equipment requiring more or less labour and raw materials per unit of product. (A change in the scale of plant is also considered a variation in the

type of equipment.) The conditions of production are, however, determined not only by the choice of the type of equipment, but also by the intensity with which it is used. Not only may the kind of machinery be varied, but it is also possible, for example, to work with the same machinery in either one or two shifts.

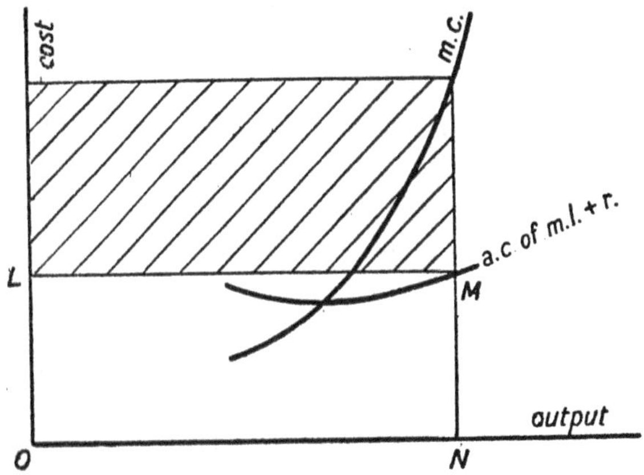

FIG. 1

Let us assume for a moment free competition and draw for each alternative type of equipment which can be applied in the production of the commodity considered, a short-period marginal-cost curve and a short-period average-cost curve of manual labour and raw materials (Fig. 1). The shaded area then represents the value of net capitalist's income, depreciation, and salaries, while the unshaded area LMNO represents the cost of manual labour and raw materials.

25

To determine the position of long-period equilibrium we define first for each type of equipment the level of prices at which the shaded area covers salaries, depreciation, interest, and normal profit (i.e., the rate of profit at which the industry in question neither expands nor contracts). We shall call this price the normal price attached to a given type of equipment, and the corresponding use of this equipment, its normal use.[1] We choose of all types of equipment that to which the lowest normal price is attached. It is easy to see that the normal use of this type of equipment represents the long-run equilibrium. It is clear now that the shape of the short-period marginal-cost curves corresponding to various types of equipment influences the formation of long-run equilibrium.

If some change in basic data takes place, e.g. the rate of interest alters or a new invention occurs, the long-run equilibrium is shifted; a new type of equipment is used in a "normal" way, and in general the relation of the shaded and unshaded areas will be different from that in the initial position. This is quite in accordance with the prevailing long-run theory of distribution. We shall see, however, that such is not the case with the peculiar shape of marginal-cost curves assumed in the deduction of formula (3), and if we admit, instead of free competition, a certain given degree of monopoly.

We take for granted that the short-period marginal-cost curve does not differ appreciably from the average-

[1] It is easy to see that with free competition the normal use coincides with the so-called "optimum" use.

cost curve of manual labour and raw materials, below the point A (Fig. 2). We represent them therefore by the same thick curve PMB.

With a given degree of monopoly the relation of price to marginal cost is a constant $\frac{1}{1-\mu}$. Thus if output remains below OA the price corresponding to it

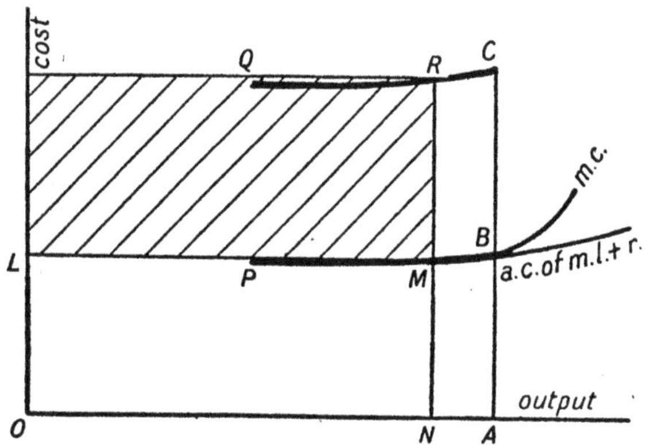

FIG. 2

is represented by the curve QRC, whose ordinates are proportionate to those of the curve PMB. The ratio of the shaded area, representing profits, interest, depreciation, and salaries, to the unshaded area, representing wages and the cost of raw materials, is equal to $\frac{1}{1-\mu}$. We define in exactly the same way as before the normal use for each type of equipment as that at which normal profit is earned. The long-run equilibrium is again represented by the normal use of such a type of equipment that, with a given degree of monopoly, it is impossible to earn profits higher than normal by employing a different type. If the basic data alter the new long-run equilibrium is represented by the normal use of a different type of equipment. The long-run equilibrium price of the product alters too, but not its relation to the average cost of manual labour and raw materials, because for all types of equipment the marginal-cost curve coincides with the average-cost curve of manual labour and raw materials, and the degree of monopoly is supposed to be given. In this way the distribution of the product among factors, as expressed by the relation of the shaded to the unshaded area, remains unaffected by changes of basic data so long as the degree of monopoly is unaltered and the use of equipment in the long-run equilibrium does not reach the point *A*.[1]

The change of basic data may of course influence the degree of monopoly. For instance, technical progress by affecting the size of enterprises influences the degree of monopoly in an industry. In this case such changes influence the distribution of income, but this is not in

[1] It may be asked how is it possible for surplus capacity to exist in the long-run equilibrium without inducing firms to curtail their plant. The answer is that large-scale economies prevent the firms from reducing their plant below a certain limit, a state of affairs described by those writers who have shown that imperfect competition must cause equipment in the long run to be used below the "optimum point." See, e.g., R. F. Harrod, "Doctrines of Imperfect Competition," *The Quarterly Journal of Economics*, May 1934.

contradiction with our results, because it is via the degree of monopoly that the influence operates.

THE DISTRIBUTION OF THE NATIONAL INCOME

1. Our aim in this essay is to investigate the changes of the relative share of the wage bill W in the national income A. The difference $A - W$ is of course equal to the sum of gross capitalist's income and salaries. Thus the equation (3) can be written as

$$\frac{A-W}{T} = \bar{\mu} \quad \ldots \ldots \quad (3a)$$

In multiplying both sides by $\frac{T}{W}$ we obtain

$$\frac{A-W}{W} = \bar{\mu} \cdot \frac{T}{W}$$

From this it follows that the relative share of manual labour in the national income is:

$$\frac{W}{A} = \frac{1}{1 + \bar{\mu} \cdot \frac{T}{W}} \quad \ldots \ldots \quad (4)$$

This formula shows at once that the increase in the degree of monopoly reduces the relative share of manual labour. The expression increases not only because of the rise in $\bar{\mu}$, but also because $\frac{T}{W}$ is increased by a rise in the degree of monopoly since this raises prices in relation to wages.

2. Changes in $\frac{T}{W}$ can, of course, be caused by influences

29

other than changes in the degree of monopoly. A change in the price of "basic raw materials," i.e. of the products of agriculture and mining, in relation to wage-costs in other industries, will clearly also have an important influence. It is easy to see that a rise in the prices of "basic raw materials" in relation to wage-cost must result in an increase of *all* prices in relation to wage-cost and consequently in an increase of $\frac{T}{W}$. On the other hand, $\frac{T}{W}$ increases in a much lesser proportion than do "basic raw materials" prices relative to wage-costs. For in each stage of production prices increase (with a given degree of monopoly) proportionately to the sum of raw material- *and wage-costs.*

It is obvious from the formula (4) that with a given degree of monopoly the relative share of manual labour falls when $\frac{T}{W}$ increases, consequently a rise in the prices of "basic raw materials" as compared with wage-costs by raising $\frac{T}{W}$ must lower the relative share of manual labour. (This may be seen also directly from formula (3*a*) according to which non-wage earners' income $A - W$ changes with a given degree of monopoly proportionately to the turnover T. Thus if the ratio of turnover to wage-bill $\frac{T}{W}$ increases owing to a rise in the prices of basic raw materials as compared with wage-costs, $\frac{A-W}{W}$ must also increase.)

It has been noticed already that a rise in the prices of "basic raw materials" relative to wage-costs causes an increase of $\frac{T}{W}$ in a *much lesser* proportion. It is easy to see from formula (4) that the proportionate fall in the relative share of manual labour in the national income is even smaller.

3. We have seen that: (1) A rise of the degree of monopoly causes a decrease in the relative share of manual labour $\frac{W}{A}$. (2) A rise of prices in "basic raw materials" in relation to wage-cost causes a fall in $\frac{W}{A}$ but in a much lesser p oportion. We thus have here some reasons for the tendency of the relative share of manual labour in the national income towards stability. For the degree of monopoly does not undergo violent changes either in the long run or in the short period. The fluctuations in the prices of "basic raw materials" in relation to wage-costs, though strong, are as stated above only slightly reflected by changes in manual labour's relative share. But of course if the most unfavourable case of joint action of these factors occurs, the change in manual labour's relative share may be appreciable. We shall see below that the remarkable stability of the relative share of manual labour which we notice in statistics is the result of these determinants working in opposite directions. This phenomenon occurred only by chance during the long period considered, and may cease in the future; but in the business cycle there seems to be a steady tendency for the conflict

of these two forces to keep the fluctuations in relative share of manual labour within narrow limits.

CHANGES IN THE DISTRIBUTION OF THE NATIONAL INCOME IN THE LONG RUN

1. The increasing concentration of industry tends undoubtedly to raise the degree of monopoly in the long run. Many branches of industry become "oligopolistic," and oligopolies are often transformed into cartels.

This tendency for the degree of monopoly to increase in the long run may, however, be offset by the diminishing imperfection of the market caused by the fall of transport costs in relation to prices, the standardization of goods, the organization of commodity exchanges, etc. In the *Spaetkapitalismus*, however, the first tendency has the upper hand, and the degree of monopoly tends to increase.

As concerns the secular trend of the relation of the prices of "basic raw materials" to wage-cost, it is difficult to say anything definite *a priori*.

2. As we have seen in the first section the relative share of manual labour in the national income in Great Britain did not change appreciably between 1880 and 1913. It can be shown that the relation of the prices of "basic raw materials" to wage-costs also did not alter in this period. For this purpose we shall compare Sauerbeck's index of wholesale prices with Mr. Clark's index for the deflation of national income.[1] It is clear

[1] *National Income and Outlay*, p. 231.

that the influence of raw material prices as compared with that of wage-costs is much greater upon the first index than upon the second. Now between 1880 and 1913 both of these indices changed in the same proportion (increased by 6 per cent), so that we can conclude that the prices of "basic raw materials" relative to wage-cost did not change. Obviously, then, the degree of monopoly could not have undergone a substantial change between 1880 and 1913 since with raw material prices unaltered as compared with wage-costs such a change would have been reflected in the relative share of manual labour in the national income.

Turning to the period 1913 to 1935, Sauerbeck's index fell during that time by 2 per cent while "income prices" rose by about 60 per cent,[1] which shows that there was a considerable fall in the prices of raw materials in relation to wage-costs. Thus since the relative share of manual labour was stationary between 1913 and 1935, this means that the degree of monopoly must have substantially increased in this period. Had a fall in the prices of basic raw materials not occurred in the last twenty-five years the relative share of manual labour would have tended to fall appreciably and the recent economic and political development of Great Britain would have been quite different.

The course of events in the U.S.A. between 1909 and 1925 was similar. The relative share of manual labour was approximately stable. The wholesale all-commodity

[1] *National Income and Outlay*, pp. 235 and 204.

index increased in this period by about 50 per cent; King's index of "income prices" by about 80 per cent.[1] Thus here again the degree of monopoly must have risen considerably, but its influence on the relative share of manual labour was counterbalanced by the fall of the prices of "basic raw materials" in relation to wage-cost. It is, of course, not at all certain that in the future the rise in the degree of monopoly will continue to be compensated by a fall in the prices of "basic raw materials." If it is not, the relative share of manual labour will tend to decline.

CHANGES IN THE DISTRIBUTION OF THE NATIONAL INCOME DURING THE BUSINESS CYCLE

1. We shall here examine first the cyclical changes in the prices of "basic raw materials" in relation to wage-cost.

The prices of the produce of agriculture and mining fluctuate much more violently than does the cost of labour in other industries. This is due to the fact that marginal-cost curves in agriculture and mining, as distinct from other sectors of the economy, slope steeply upwards. In addition, wages fluctuate much more in agriculture than in other industries during the business cycle. Consequently "basic raw material" prices rise relative to wage-cost in the boom and fall in the slump.

[1] *National Income and its Purchasing Power*, pp. 74 and 77.

Much more complicated is the question of the change of degree of monopoly during the trade cycle. It has recently been argued by Mr. Harrod that the degree of monopoly increases in the boom and falls in the slump. In the slump consumers "resent and resist the curtailment of their wonted pleasures. . . . Their efforts to find cheapness become strenuous and eager. Nor are commercial firms exempt from this influence upon their purchase policy; they, too, have received a nasty jolt and must strain every nerve to reduce costs."[1] Thus the imperfection of the market is reduced and the degree of monopoly diminished.

Mr. Harrod was rightly criticized in that there exist other factors which influence the degree of monopoly in the opposite direction. For instance, in the slump, cartels are created to save profits,[2] and this, of course, increases the degree of monopoly, but when trade revives they are dissolved because of improving prospects of independent activity and the emergence of outsiders.

More important still is the fact that in spite of the fall of prices of raw materials and wages some prices of finished goods tend to be relatively "sticky" in the slump; this for various reasons: entrepreneurs avoid price cuts because it may induce their competitors to do likewise; cartels are not afraid that outsiders will appear, etc. It can be stated on the basis of data quoted

[1] *The Trade Cycle*, pp. 86–87.

[2] Joan Robinson, review of R. F. Harrod, *The Trade Cycle*, *Economic Journal*, December 1936.

above that the influence of these factors in raising the degree of monopoly during the slump is stronger than that of the diminishing imperfection of the market.

Indeed, if we look at our data on the relative share of manual labour in the national income we see that in general it does not change much during the business cycle. But the prices of basic raw materials fall in the slump and rise in the boom as compared with wages, and this tends to raise the relative share of manual labour in the slump and reduce it in the boom. If the relative share of manual labour remains more or less constant it can be concluded that the degree of monopoly tends to increase in the depression and decline in the boom.

We now see that, as has already been mentioned, the apparent stability of manual labour's relative share during the cycle is in reality the effect of the opposite changes in the degree of monopoly and in the relation of the prices of basic raw materials to wages.

2. The stability of the relative share of the wage bill W in the national income A in the short period has far-reaching consequences as regards the formation of the prices of finished goods. Let us divide in the equation:

$$\frac{W}{A} = \text{const.}$$

both the numerator and the denominator of the left-hand side by an index of the volume of output of finished goods. Since the money value of the latter is the national income A we obtain:

$$\frac{\text{index of average wage-costs}}{\text{index of the prices of finished home-produced goods}^{1}} = \text{const.} \quad . \quad (5)$$

Now, as stated above, conditions of approximately constant returns prevail in the short period in the economy as a whole. Thus the index of the average cost of manual labour does not depend appreciably on the level of output and employment and with a constant technique and intensity of work does not differ much from the index of wage rates. Consequently the equation (5) shows that with constant technique and intensity of work, prices of finished home-produced commodities change approximately in the same proportion as wage rates. This result clearly is of great importance for the theory of real wages, and will be dealt with in more detail and supported statistically in the essay on "Money and Real Wages." We now propose to apply it to the problem of the prices of investment and consumption goods.

3. Let us consider in an economy the sections which produce consumption and investment goods respectively (including in each the corresponding raw material production). Since our argument throughout the essay is not confined to a closed system the formula (5) applies approximately to each of these two sections. Thus if the technique of production and the intensity of work are unaltered, it may be concluded that the prices of con-

[1] All exported commodities must be here included in "finished" goods. Further "prices" are here, strictly speaking, differences between the actual prices of commodities and the cost of foreign raw materials used in their fabrication.

sumption goods will move proportionately to wage rates in consumption goods industries. A similar development may be supposed to take place in the investment goods industries. It therefore follows that the ratio of the price indices of finished investment and consumption goods $\frac{p_i}{p_c}$ is in the short period approximately equal to the ratio of indices of the corresponding wage rates $\frac{r_i}{r_c}$:

$$\frac{p_i}{p_c} = \frac{r_i}{r_c}$$

And since wage rates move more or less proportionately in the two sections[1] marked cyclical fluctuations in $\frac{p_i}{p_c}$ are unlikely. This result is not impaired if we allow for changes in the technique of production. If the increase in productivity due to technical changes is different in consumption goods industries from that in investment goods industries this will, of course, influence the movement of $\frac{p_i}{p_c}$; but this influence can operate only in the long run, and is not of a *cyclical* nature. In order to investigate the movement of $\frac{p_i}{p_c}$ statistically we have constructed indices of the prices of finished consumption and investment goods in the U.S.A. for the period 1919–35. The index of consumption goods prices is a

[1] Wage rates in investment goods industries might be expected to fluctuate more, due to stronger changes in employment. In fact such is not the case, because trade unions are strongest in the heavy industry.

weighted average of the indices of the cost of living and the prices of motor cars,[1] that of investment goods—a weighted average of the building costs and the prices of movable equipment.[2]

The results are computed in the following table:

TABLE 3

Prices of Consumption and Investment Goods in U.S.A.
1929 = 100

	p_c	p_i	$\frac{p_i}{p_c}$		p_c	p_i	$\frac{p_i}{p_c}$
1919	102	110	108	1928	100	97	97
1920	119	125	105	1929	100	100	100
1921	105	105	100	1930	96	97	101
1922	98	94	96	1931	87	94	108
1923	101	101	100	1932	78	82	105
1924	101	101	100	1933	76	78	103
1925	104	98	94	1934	80	85	106
1926	103	98	95	1935	83	86	104
1927	101	96	95				

We see that variations in $\frac{p_i}{p_c}$ are in general small.

[1] The index of prices of motor cars is obtained from Dr. Kuznets' *National Income and Capital Formation, 1919–35*, by dividing the value of consumers' durable commodities in current prices by their value in 1929 prices (p. 40). The indices of cost of living and prices of motor cars are weighted in the proportion 88 : 12 according to the "composition of consumers' outlay" in 1929 (ibid., p. 59).

[2] The price index of movable equipment is obtained by dividing the value of "producers' durable commodities" at current prices by their value at 1929 prices (ibid., p. 40). The indices of building costs and of prices of movable equipment are weighted in proportion of 2 : 1 according to the amounts spent on these two types of investment (inclusive of maintenance) in 1929 (ibid., pp. 40 and 80).

At any rate, contrary to prevailing views there was no tendency for $\frac{p_i}{p_c}$ to fall in the depression 1930–33.

It is usually supposed that the prices of investment goods fluctuate much more violently than those of consumption goods. This is due to the assumption that increasing marginal-cost curves prevail in the short period; for if such were the case the larger proportionate fluctuations in the output of investment goods as compared with those in the output of consumption goods would lead to correspondingly larger fluctuations in the prices of investment goods. The statistical evidence of approximately proportional changes in the prices of the two types of goods indicates that the assumption of rising marginal-cost curves in the short period is unrealistic, and indirectly supports our assumption about the shape of short-period marginal-cost curves.

The important consequence of the above is that since $\frac{p_i}{p_c}$ has no marked cyclical fluctuations, changes in the ratio of the prices of investment and consumption goods may be neglected in the theory of the trade cycle. We make use of this conclusion in the last essay.

FINAL REMARKS

The results arrived at in this essay have a more general aspect. A world in which the degree of monopoly determines the distribution of the national income is a world far removed from the pattern of free competition.

Monopoly appears to be deeply rooted in the nature of the capitalist system: free competition, as an assumption, may be useful in the first stage of certain investigations, but as a description of the normal state of capitalist economy it is merely a myth.

2

INVESTMENT AND INCOME

GENERAL PRINCIPLES

1. The object of this essay is to clear up some questions arising out of the Keynesian theory of the Multiplier. We shall first deal with the equation between the expenditure on investment I and the value of savings S which has been so much discussed since *The General Theory* appeared. However, before embarking upon further argument we want to examine in detail one point often touched upon in this discussion: whether or not $I = S$ is a tautology. We define (as in the first essay, p. 14) the gross national income as the value added by all enterprises of an economy. Thus it is equal to total sales of all enterprises except those producing raw materials; i.e. to sales of goods to ultimate consumers + sales of newly produced fixed capital equipment + any increase in stocks and working capital. Sales of fixed capital equipment + increase in working capital and stocks may be called gross investment. Thus we have *by definition*:

$$\text{National income} = \text{Sales of investment goods}^{1} + \text{Sales of consumption goods}$$

[1] Inclusive increase in working capital and stocks. This type of investment does not often involve a sale, the increase of inventories of a firm being created by its own production. Such case, however, may be considered as the firm's sale to itself.

where both national income and investment are gross concepts (from which maintenance and depreciation must be subtracted in order to obtain net national income and net investment respectively). Further, we shall call saving the difference between the national income as defined above and the expenditure on consumption. Thus we have, again *by definition*:

$$\text{Sales of investment goods} + \text{Sales of consumption goods} = \text{Saving} + \text{Expenditure by consumers}$$

saving again being a gross concept. We have now the further equation:

$$\text{Sales of consumption goods} = \text{Expenditure by consumers}$$

which, however, is *not* a tautology since it represents the exchange process on the market of consumption goods (though it is an identity in the sense that it is fulfilled in all circumstances). Thus the equation derived from this exchange equation and the proceeding tautology:

$$\text{Sales of investment goods} = \text{Saving}$$

is also not a tautology. Now we take into account the exchange equation for the market of investment goods:

$$\text{Sales of investment goods} = \text{Expenditure on investment}$$

and we get finally:

$$\text{Expenditure on investment} = \text{Saving}$$

or:

$$I = S$$

It is useful to show how an increase in expenditure on investment by ΔI causes—by means of the exchange process on the market of investment and consumption goods—saving S to increase by an amount ΔS equal to ΔI.

If in a certain period the expenditure on investment is I and in the next $I + \Delta I$, sales of investment goods must increase by ΔI. If the output of them was not changed, the total amount ΔI is an addition to income of capitalists (entrepreneurs and rentiers), but if output and employment also increase a part of ΔI is received by workers. Out of the addition to income ΔI flowing to the investment goods industries a part ΔS_1 is saved while another part $\Delta I - \Delta S_1$ is consumed. This last amount makes for an additional expenditure on consumption goods.

Consider now the consumption goods industries: a part of the total sales of consumption goods is bought by the capitalists and workers in consumption goods industries, the rest is purchased by the capitalists and workers in investment goods industries. And it is the value of this latter which is equal to the savings "in consumption goods industries" S , for it is equal to the difference between the total sales of consumption goods and the expenditure on consumption by the capitalists and workers drawing income from their production. Thus an additional expenditure on consumption by the capitalists and workers in the investment goods industries creates an equal additional saving ΔS_2. We have:

$$\Delta I - \Delta S_1 = \Delta S_2$$

or:

$$\Delta I = \Delta S_1 + \Delta S_2 = \Delta S$$

and we see how an additional expenditure on investment ΔI creates an equal addition to saving ΔS.

2. It may be interesting to notice that the above equations are contained in the famous Marxian scheme of "extended reproduction."[1] Marx even considers the questions of how to provide "means" for increased expenditure on investment.[2] It must be added, however, that the problems discussed here are treated by Marx from a rather special point of view. He is interested in finding out, with the help of exchange equations, the pace of investment in investment and consumption goods industries respectively, which is necessary in order to secure a steady expansion of output. (The rates of profit in both divisions of industry are assumed to be equal throughout and on this basis the process of expansion is constructed so as to make investment in each, at the end of every "production-exchange cycle," equal to its saving so that there is no "shift of capital" from consumption to investment goods industries or conversely.) He does not pay attention to the problem of what happens if investment is inadequate to secure the moving equilibrium, and therefore does not approach the idea of the key position of investment in the determination of the level of total output and employment.

Exactly the reverse attitude is represented by one of his eminent pupils, Rosa Luxemburg. In her *Akkumulation des Kapitals* she stressed the point that, if capitalists are saving, their profits can be "realized" only if a

[1] *Capital*, Vol. II, *The process of circulation of Capital*, London, Swan Sonnenschein & Co., pp. 571–611. [2] Ibid., p. 593.

corresponding amount is spent by them on investment. She, however, considered impossible the persistence of net investment (at least in the long run) in a closed capitalist economy; thus, according to her, it is only the existence of exports to the non-capitalist countries which allows for the expansion of a capitalist system. The theory cannot be accepted as a whole, but the necessity of covering the "gap of saving" by home investment or exports was outlined by her perhaps more clearly than anywhere else before the publication of Mr. Keynes's *General Theory*.

3. We tacitly assumed in the first paragraph that we were dealing with a closed economy. In an open economy the national income is equal to home sales of goods to consumers + home sales of (newly produced) fixed capital equipment + increase in working capital and stocks + foreign balance of goods and services. Following an argument analogous to that of the first paragraph we obtain the equation:

$$\left.\begin{array}{l}\text{Expenditure on investment}\\ \text{Balance of foreign countries'}\\ \qquad\text{expenditure}\end{array}\right\} = \text{Saving}$$

An increment in the balance of foreign countries' expenditure home investment remaining constant, creates in the same way as shown in the first paragraph an equal increament of savings. (This, I think, is the correct interpretation of the theory of Rosa Luxemburg.)

4. We simplified tacitly in another respect also our argument in paragraph one, namely, we abstracted the

complications arising out of Government income and expenditure. The value added by private enterprise does not coincide with the total income of capitalists and labour, for a part is transferred by taxation to the Government.[1] We do *not* consider, as is often done, this part as the equivalent of consumption of Governmental services. (We mean here by consumption only the voluntary spending for goods and services.) The Government in turn spends its revenue partly on officials' salaries, doles for unemployed, etc., and interest on the public debt; while the rest of the revenue, being devoted to Governmental investment[2] and to the increase in Governmental claims, constitutes Governmental saving.

Thus the consumption of people drawing their income from the Government is included in consumption; a part of saving is done by the Government; and a part of the output of investment goods is sold to the Government. The national income can therefore be represented in the following two ways:

Private investment[3]	Private saving
Governmental investment	Governmental saving
Balance of foreign countries expenditure	Consumption
Consumption	

Let us subtract from both sides Governmental saving. As Governmental investment less Governmental saving

[1] By Government are meant here all public authorities.
[2] Armaments, public buildings, etc.
[3] Inclusive residential building.

constitutes the budget deficit or the "balance of Government's expenditure" we obtain:

Private expenditure on investment	Private saving
Balance of Governments' expenditure	Consumption
Balance of foreign countries' expenditure	
Consumption	

The sum of private saving plus (voluntary) consumption may be called private national income Y. It is equal to the value added by all enterprises less Governmental saving and also to the sum of all private incomes after the deduction of taxes.[1] It is this definition of "national income" which we shall mean in the following argument. The sum: private home investment + balance of foreign countries expenditure + balance of Governmental expenditure will be denoted by I, and private saving by S. Thus the equation:

$$I = S$$

refers now to investment in the above sense and to private saving.

It may be useful to show how the increase in the balance of Governmental expenditure (the other two components of I remaining constant) creates an equal increase in private saving. Let us suppose, e.g., that

[1] Both direct and indirect. Thus the value of consumption is here reckoned at prices from which excise, etc., have been deducted.

the Government increases officials' salaries by ΔI by borrowing to that extent. The officials save out of their additional revenue ΔS_1 and spend $\Delta I - \Delta S_1$. Thus the sales of consumption goods industries to people other than capitalists and workers attached to these industries increases by the amount of officials' additional expenditure $\Delta I - \Delta S_1$. But the sales of consumption goods industries to "outsiders" is equal to the saving of capitalists and workers attached to these industries. Consequently savings "in consumption goods industries" rise by $\Delta I - \Delta S_1$. Since the savings of officials increase by ΔS_1 total private saving rises by $\Delta I - \Delta S_1 + \Delta S_1 = \Delta I$, i.e. by the increment in the balance of Government's expenditure.

It is interesting to notice that here the rise of "investment" by ΔI (creating an equal increase in private saving) causes *directly* a rise of consumption by $\Delta I - \Delta S_1$. If the Government spends the amount borrowed ΔI for additional dole payment, ΔS_1 may be supposed equal to zero because dole receivers do not save. Then the rise of "investment" by ΔI *directly* increases consumption also by ΔI.

5. Changes in the three components of I: private investment, the balance of Governmental expenditure and the balance of foreign countries' expenditure are in general interconnected. The most typical interconnection is the influence of a "primary" change in private investment on the other two components. An increment in home private investment, by raising employment and income, reduces dole payments and increases the tax

revenue so that the deficit tends to fall. An increase in output and consumption also requires more foreign raw materials, foodstuffs, etc., which tends to diminish the balance of trade. Thus the stimulating influence of an increase in private home investment on employment and income is hampered by a decrease in the other two components of I.

SPECIAL ASSUMPTIONS

1. In our further argument we shall use some results reached in the first essay. We saw there that the relative share of manual labour in the national income shows great stability in a moderately long period. In the first essay we defined national income as the value added by all enterprises of an economy; now, however, we mean by it "private national income" which is less than the value added by all enterprises by the amount of Governmental saving. But since the latter bears a small proportion to the national income, the ratio of the wage bill to the "private national income" Y is not appreciably changed.

The wage bill is the income of employed manual workers before the deduction of taxes. Their spendable income is thus less than the wage bill, but if changes in the system of taxation do not occur we can assume it approximately proportionate to the wage bill. From that we can conclude that the ratio of manual workers' spendable income to Y, which we denote by α, must also show great stability. The rest of the national income represents the income of all non-wage earners after the deduction of taxes. We denote it by y; it includes the incomes of capitalists, salary earners, and also dole receivers. We have then:

$$y = (1 - \alpha)\, Y^{1} \quad . \quad . \quad . \quad . \quad . \quad (6)$$

The savings of manual workers are so small that we can neglect them[2] and thus identify total private saving S with non-wage earners' savings. Hence we can now write the investment-saving equation in the form:

$$I = S = s$$

But s is, of course, equal to the difference between income y and consumption c of non-wage earners.

$$I = y - c \quad . \quad . \quad . \quad . \quad . \quad . \quad (7)$$

It is clear that the equations (6) and (7) establish a functional relation between investment I and national income Y if such a relation exists between non-wage earners' income y and the consumption out of it c. Here, however, we touch upon the problem how to measure the amounts dealt with. For we clearly cannot expect a definite functional relation between income and the consumption out of it unless both are expressed in "real" terms.

2. We shall express investment, income, and consump-

[1] Since α is equal to about 0·38 in Great Britain and about 0·32 in U.S.A. (with shop assistants classified as manual labour) the stability of $1 - \alpha$ is much greater than that of α.

[2] α is in general smaller than $1 - \alpha$, while the proportion of savings in workers' income is incomparably lower than that in y.

tion in "stable values" by deflating them with the index of prices of finished (consumption and investment) goods. This index has for this purpose the following advantage. It was established in the preceding essay (pp. 38–39) that the index of prices of finished consumption goods (cost of living) and the index prices of finished investment goods (building costs and prices of movable equipment) tend to deviate only slightly from each other. Thus if we deflate income and consumption with the joint index of prices of finished goods (composed of these two indices) we get figures approximately equal to "real" income and consumption, i.e. to income and consumption deflated with the index of finished consumption goods. And similarly investment (which is largely in *fixed* capital) is deflated with an index not much different from that of prices of finished investment goods.

We do not use here the Keynesian wage-units because even in not very long periods there is a considerable change in the productivity of labour due to technical progress. Thus income measured in wage-units often fails to be an adequate indicator of the "real" income.

INVESTMENT AND INCOME IN A SIMPLIFIED MODEL

1. We noticed above that the equations:

$$y = (1 - a)Y \quad . \quad . \quad . \quad . \quad . \quad (6)$$

and

$$I = y - c \quad . \quad . \quad . \quad . \quad . \quad . \quad (7)$$

enable us to establish a functional relation between national income Y and investment I provided we can establish such a relation between the income of non-wage earners y and their consumption c. Before inquiring into the connection between y and c in the real world we shall apply the above equations to the analysis of investment and income in a simplified model.

We assume that in this hypothetical economy the joint consumption of capitalists, salary earners and dole receivers c expressed in "stable values" is constant. We denote this constant by c_0 and thus we obtain from equations (1) and (2):

$$Y = \frac{1}{1-a} I + \frac{c_0}{1-a}$$

It is easy to see that the ratio of an increment of income ΔY to the corresponding increments of investment ΔI is equal to $\frac{1}{1-a}$:

$$\frac{\Delta Y}{\Delta I} = \frac{1}{1-a}$$

Thus $\frac{1}{1-a}$ is the multiplier which has in our system a constant value. It does not follow, of course, that the ratio of income to investment $\frac{Y}{I}$ is also constant. On the contrary, it follows from the above equation that $\frac{Y}{I}$ falls with the increase of investment. This means that investment must fluctuate more than national income and *a fortiori* more than consumption (for national income is the sum of consumption and investment).

The formula of the multiplier shows that if some

increase in the rate of investment has occurred income must have increased by an amount which is $\frac{1}{1-a}$ times as great. Therefore, the multiplier cannot tell us what would happen if, e.g., public works financed by State borrowing were undertaken since other kinds of investment might increase or fall off in consequence. If, however, we can demonstrate that in the period considered this influence is negligible, then the multiplier will show approximately what will be the increase in income.

Our discussion of the investment-saving equation in the first section demonstrates that there is no "magic" in the working of the multiplier. Suppose we know that in a certain year the total expenditure on investment was greater by ΔI than in the preceding year, then savings must have increased by the same amount. But since the manual workers do not save and since in our model the consumption of other classes is constant, this means that the incomes of the latter increased by the amount ΔI. As, however, the ratio of the distribution of income between manual workers and all other classes is steadily $\frac{a}{1-a}$ output must have expanded so that the rise of non-wage earners' incomes by ΔI was accompanied by a rise of $\frac{1}{1-a} \cdot \Delta I$ in the wage bill, the total increase in income being:

$$\Delta I + \Delta I \cdot \frac{a}{1-a} = \frac{\Delta I}{1-a}$$

2. There is a point in the "working of the multiplier" which, I think, requires special explanation. If an increase in the expenditure on investment, e.g. in fixed capital, takes place, an additional demand for consumption goods arises. But how can the production of them, which even with given capital equipment requires a certain time, immediately rise? Such a rise is not at all impossible, because existing stocks of raw materials and semi-manufactures may be immediately converted into working capital and enable the factories to supply the market without delay with finished consumption goods. If, however, for this or any other reason such a process of adjustment does not occur with sufficient speed, stocks of finished consumption goods are depleted and in the formula of the multiplier ΔI is equal to the difference between the additional investment in fixed capital and any consequential dis-investment in stocks in the period considered.

What happens, however, if no reserves of raw materials, semi-manufactures, and finished consumption goods are in existence, and thus the supply of consumption goods is fully inelastic at the time? The multiplier is then equal to *1*, since the volume of consumption does not increase and our formula appears wrong. This is due to the fact that our assumption of the constancy of the relative share of manual labour a in the national income is incompatible with an inelastic supply of consumption goods. For in this case the increase of employment in investment good industries must cause a shift in the national income to the disadvantage of the workers.

Since according to statistical evidence a tends to be stable we can exclude from our consideration the case of an inelastic supply of consumption goods.

INCOME AND CONSUMPTION IN THE REAL WORLD

1. We pass now from our simplified model to real conditions. The consumption of non-wage earners is no longer supposed to be stable. It is clear that there must be *some* connection between their income y and the consumption c out of it. (Both are supposed to be expressed in "stable values.") Various objections, however, may be raised against this connection being close.

The first is that consumption out of a given income or "the propensity to consume" is greatly affected by the level of the rate of interest. In classical economics the stimulating influence of a rise in the rate of interest upon the thrift was strongly emphasized. It has, however, long been indicated that it is not at all certain whether consumption is really encouraged or discouraged by a higher rate of interest. But all this discussion appears to be of a rather academic character, at least as concerns development in the moderately long period with which we are here concerned. For in such periods the long-term rate shows but small changes (see pp. **112–113**), and clearly this is the rate which is relevant here. Thus we can safely neglect the influence of the rate of interest in the analysis of the connection between y and c.

2. Another very important objection is that capitalists' expenditure is only loosely connected with their income because their "propensity to consume" depends to great

extent on the actual level of capital values; in particular on that of stock exchange prices. For if he feels wealthier, the capitalist may assume less thrifty habits, even though his current real income has not altered.

Or one can imagine him being influenced not by the *level* of actual capital valuations but by the *change* in these valuations within the period considered. For he may be supposed to consider as income not only his current revenue but also the windfall gain or loss due to changes in the valuation of his assets.

It is idle to discuss theoretically the problem of whether these factors are more or less important in the determination of capitalist consumption. And since the period of American stock exchange boom 1926–29 is often considered typical in this respect, it will be useful to look at the revelant figures in these years.

In the table on p. 58 are given the gross and net income of capitalists,[1] the approximate value of capitalists' consumption,[2] the index of stock exchange prices, and

[1] Based on Dr. Kuznets' *National Income and Capital Formation, 1919–1935*, p. 24. Income tax not deducted.

[2] This is calculated in the following way. We deduct from the income of capitalists the total investment (also Kuznets' estimate) and thus obtain the capitalists' consumption less the saving of workers (chiefly of salary earners because that of manual workers is small). Further, from *America's Capacity to Consume* we estimate the average rate of saving of all workers (black coat and manual) in 1929 as 6 per cent. Since the size and distribution of workers' income did not change very much in the period 1920–29, we applied the same rate to all years and thus obtained approximate figures for workers' saving, which we added to the figures of capitalists' consumption less the saving of workers.

the change of this index from the beginning to the end of each year. It must be added that in the period 1926–29 commodity prices were stable and thus there is no necessity to deflate the money values.

	($ *milliards*)			
	1926	1927	1928	1929
Gross capitalists' income (before deduction for depreciation and maintenance)	41·9	39·3	42·1	42·9
Net capitalists' income (after deduction for depreciation and maintenance)	26·5	24·1	25·7	25·9
Approximate capitalists' consumption	21·7	19·0	22·4	20·7
Prices of shares (Standard Statistics, 1926 = 100, yearly averages) ..	100·0	118·3	149·9	190·0
Change in the prices of shares (the change of the same index from the beginning to the end of a given year)	+ 3·8	+ 31·6	+ 40·1	− 33·7

Both capitalists' income and capitalists' consumption show small changes in the same direction. Share prices are violently rising throughout the period and the change of share prices from the beginning to the end of the year (measuring the windfall loss or gain) varies greatly in different years. (In 1928 *both* figures are much greater than in the preceding years.) The only possible interpretation of these data is that the influence of the stock exchange on capitalists' consumption in U.S.A. in 1926–29 was not very great. But if the stock exchange did not greatly influence the capitalists' propensity to consume even under such favourable circumstances its influence cannot generally be very important.

3. Another argument is directed against the existence not so much of a functional relation between the consumption and income of capitalists but rather of one between their current consumption and their current income. It is not here denied that an appreciable time-lag exists between y and the corresponding c (as opposed to income and consumption of manual workers). This modifies but does not invalidate the "theory of the multiplier." We are introducing this modification at the final stage of our argument (see pp. 66–68).

4. A further argument against a close connection between c and y refers to the variations in the distribution of income. The earners of y fall into various groups with "different propensities to consume" and, consequently, it is not only the change in the amount of y but also the shifts in its distribution which determine the fluctuations of c.

We can distinguish the following groups among non-wage earners: (1) dole receivers (unemployed, etc.); (2) salaried employees; (3) small entrepreneurs; (4) rentiers; (5) dividend receivers; (6) joint stock companies (the gross income of the last consists of depreciation and net corporative savings).

Considerable shifts in the distribution of income among these groups occur in the trade cycle and obviously affect their joint consumption c, but it can be shown that these shifts are strongly correlated with changes in the volume of y (expressed in stable values) and thus c is a fairly close function of y.

It is easy to see that the distribution of non-wage earners' income y among the various groups is *grosso modo* determined by: (1) the volume of y itself; (2) the index of prices of finished goods, p, with which we deflated the incomes; (3) the dole rate; (4) the average salary rate. Indeed y and p determine the money value of non-wage earners' incomes yp. Further, y bears a constant proportion to national income Y and the latter varies inversely with the amount of unemployment. Thus given y and the dole rate, the aggregate dole payment is determined. In a similar way y and the average salary rate determine the salary bill. Subtracting dole payments and the salary bill from yp, we obtain the money value of capitalists' incomes. Now the aggregate interest on loan debt is approximately stable (in money terms) over the moderately long period and can be considered as given. Subtracting it from total capitalist income, we obtain dividends and entrepreneurial incomes. It may now be easily shown that the changes in the distribution of non-wage earners' income y depend to great extent on those in its volume. For a fall, say, in y (which is proportionate to the national income Y) means, of course, a decline in output and employment, and this depresses in a more or less definite way the salary rate and the prices of finished goods (which, according to results arrived at in the preceding essay, p. 37, move more or less proportionately to the wage cost). Thus the chief factors determining the distribution of non-wage earners' income can be reduced to function of its volume y.[1]

The effect of the fall in y will be to increase the relative share of dole receivers, salary earners, and rentiers. This is clear as regards dole receivers and rentiers. As concerns salary earners, the proportionate fall in the salary bill in the slump is always smaller than that in the wage bill; while, as the relative share of manual labour in the national income is constant, the total income of non-wage earners must change proportionately to the wage bill. Thus the proportion that the salary bill bears to the total non-wage earners' income must rise when y falls.

To the rise in the relative share of dole receivers, salary earners, and rentiers in y as y diminishes, corresponds the sharp fall in the relative share in y going to corporations (in the form of depreciation and net corporative savings). The change in the income of small entrepreneurs and in dividends follows a middle course and is likely neither to rise nor to fall very much relatively to the total income of non-wage earners.

It therefore follows that the shift in the distribution of non-wage earners' income y when it is declining tends to hamper the fall of consumption c out of it, i.e. c falls less than it would if the distribution of y did not alter. If y rises c increases less than it would if there were no shifts in the distribution of y.

[1] Except the dole rate, which thus must be treated as datum.

INVESTMENT AND INCOME IN THE REAL WORLD

1. As a result of the above investigation it can be said that on certain assumptions—which are usually fulfilled in the moderately long period—and neglecting provisionally the time lag between income and consumption, a more or less close connection between c and y is likely to exist. Thus we can write:

$$c = \eta(y) \qquad \text{. . . . . (8)}$$

As already mentioned above (p. 51), this equation enables us to establish the functional relation between investment I and national income Y. For besides the equation (8) we have the equation

$$I = y - c \qquad \text{. . . . . (7)}$$

which expresses the fact that investment, since it is equal to total saving, is also equal to that of non-wage earners alone, because the saving of wage earners is negligible. Further, the relative share of manual labour in the national income is a constant α and thus we have for non-wage earners income y:

$$y = (1 - \alpha)Y \qquad \text{. . . . . (6)}$$

From the equations (7) and (8) it follows that I is a function of y, which in conjunction with equation (6) shows that there must be a functional relationship between investment I and the national income Y.

Consequently we can write

$$Y = f(I) \qquad \text{. . . . . (9)}$$

where f is, of course, an increasing function, and from this equation we obtain the multiplier:

$$\frac{\Delta Y}{\Delta I} = f'(I)$$

It is interesting to see how the multiplier works in the real world. If we have an increase in investment from level I to a given level $I + \Delta I$, there is an increase in employment, output, and national income. If, as in our simplified model, the consumption of non-wage earners c remained stationary, this increase would be pushed to the point at which non-wage earners' income increases by ΔI; for at that point non-wage earners save ΔI more, and by assumption they would not tend to expand their consumption. But in reality when their income increases they do consume more. And thus the rise of employment output and income stops only when that level of non-wage earners' income is reached at which their increased saving and consumption are such as to correspond to their propensity to consume. Consequently the multiplier is in the real world greater than in our simplified model. And since in the latter it was equal $\frac{1}{1-a}$ (where a is the relative share of manual labour in the national income) we have:

$$\frac{\Delta Y}{\Delta I} = f'(I) > \frac{1}{1-a}$$

How much $f'(I)$ exceeds $\frac{1}{1-a}$ depends on the thrift habits of the various groups of non-wage earners and on the redistribution of income between these groups associated with the rise of their total income y.

2. The consumption of non-wage earners, c, changes always in a lesser proportion than their income y, and for two reasons. First, each individual's consumption is less elastic than his saving; and, second, the redistribution of y associated with the change in its amount, is—as shown above—such as to reduce the resultant change in c (since a rise of y is accompanied by an increase in the relative share of it going to corporations and conversely).

Since the consumption of non-wage earners changes in a lesser proportion than their income the reverse must be true of their saving, i.e. the latter must change always in a greater proportion than y. From this results an important feature of the function connecting national income Y with investment I. Since I is equal to the saving of non-wage earners it must change always in a greater proportion than their income y. But the latter bears a constant proportion to the national income Y. Thus investment rises or falls always in a greater proportion than the national income. The shape of the function f is such that $\frac{I}{f(I)}$ increases when I rises. In other words, investment fluctuates more violently than national income and *a fortiori* more violently than consumption.

3. The last proposition has been known in economics for a long time, but it was deduced from the so-called acceleration principle. The argument ran thus: Let us assume that at a certain time the volume of capital

equipment is 20, the output of consumption goods 10, and gross investment 1·5, of which depreciation is 1 and new investment 0·5. If now consumption increases in a period by 10 per cent to 11, equipment must increase in the same proportion to 22. Thus net investment in this period must be 2. (There will also be some increase in depreciation because of the increase in the amount of capital equipment, but it will be negligible.) Thus while consumption increases by only 10 per cent, gross investment rises from 1 + 0·5 to 1 + 2, i.e. by 100 per cent.

The argument is apparently based on the unrealistic assumption that the degree of use of equipment is constant; while it is clear from trade cycle statistics that it is precisely the fluctuation in the use of equipment which accounts chiefly for changes in output, and the proportionate increase or decrease of equipment is of minor importance. Consequently the connection between investment and consumption given by the acceleration principle is also unrealistic: for according to this principle investment is an increasing function of the rate of *change* in consumption. Thus on the top of the boom when consumption is stationary investment should fall to the level of depreciation, while the statistics show that its maximum is reached almost simultaneously with that of consumption. (See, e.g., statistical data in the next section.)

This is, however, in accordance with the connection between investment and consumption which was established above on a quite different basis. Starting from the equation of saving and investment and making some assumptions about the distribution of the national income among various classes and about their propensity to consume, we demonstrated that national income and, therefore, consumption is an increasing function of investment, which, however, changes always in a greater proportion than consumption.[1]

4. We have now to make the modification which we promised in connection with the existence of the time-lag between non-wage earners' income y and consumption

[1] A new interpretation of the acceleration principle was given by R. F. Harrod in *The Trade Cycle*. The material modification introduced by him is that it is not the actual investment but investment decisions or orders which are a function of the rate of change in consumption. In this form the acceleration principle *is* compatible with the theory of the multiplier. For there is a time-lag between investment orders and actual investment, and thus they are in general not equal; consequently it is possible that the rate of investment decisions is an increasing function of the *change in consumption*, while *consumption itself* is a function of the rate of actual investment.

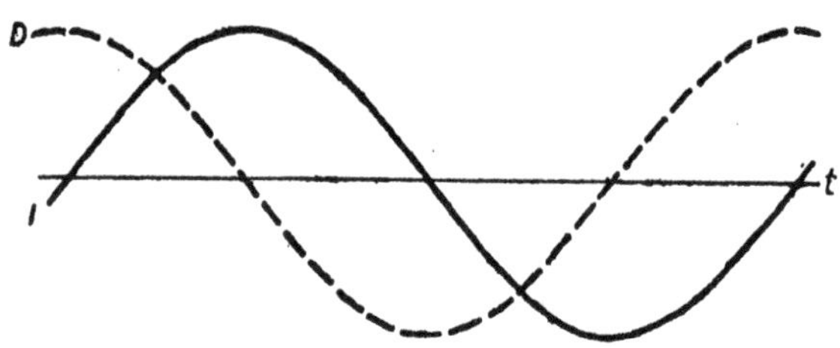

But this theory is also unrealistic. It implies that the rate of investment decisions D is an increasing function of the change in the rate of actual investment I, and therefore that the respective time curves are situated as shown on the chart. It is easy to see that the period is then four times the time-lag between D and I. Since the average time-lag between investment decisions and investment output is unlikely to be greater than half a year (see p. 127), the period of trade cycle would be less than 2 years; while its actual length is 7–12 years.

out of it *c*. This time-lag results in the present national income being influenced not only by the present but also by past investment. Consequently the system behaves as if a certain delay were involved in the functional connection between investment and income. Thus if we denote investment and income at time t by I_t and Y_t respectively our equation (9) must be written:

$$Y_t = f(I_{t-\lambda}) \quad . \quad . \quad . \quad . \quad . \quad (10)$$

where λ is the time-lag between investment and income.[1]

The multiplier may be defined as:

$$\frac{\Delta Y_t}{\Delta I_{t-\lambda}} = f'(I_{t-\lambda})$$

[1] Let us denote the time-lag between y and c by ω. Then we have:

$$c_t = \eta(y_{t-\omega})$$

and the equation between investment and non-wage earners' saving gives:

$$I_t = y_t - \eta(y_{t-\omega})$$

On the other hand, it is clear from p. 62 that the formula (10) can be established if the time-lag fulfils the equation:

$$I_t = y_{t+\lambda} - \eta(y_{t+\lambda})$$

Thus λ must fulfil the equation:

$$y_t - \eta(y_{t-\omega}) = y_{t+\lambda} - \eta(y_{t+\lambda})$$

or:

$$y_{t+\lambda} - y_t = \eta(y_{t+\lambda}) - \eta(y_{t-\omega})$$

We divide this equation by $y_{t+\lambda} - y_{t-\omega}$:

$$\frac{y_{t+\lambda} - y_t}{y_{t+\lambda} - y_{t-\omega}} = \frac{\eta(y_{t+\lambda}) - \eta(y_{t-\omega})}{y_{t+\lambda} - y_{t-\omega}}$$

If the time-lags are small and the time-curve y_t continuous, we obtain as a good approximation:

$$\frac{\lambda}{\lambda + \omega} = \eta'(y_t)$$

which defines λ in terms of ω and η'. If ω and η' are slowly changing variables, as they are likely to be, the same is true of λ.

The time-lag λ being in general not constant, and the function not quite stable, what is the real meaning of equation (10)? It may be formulated in the following way: there exists such a function f and such a constant λ that the deviations of Y_t from $f(I_{t-\lambda})$ are relatively small.

A STATISTICAL ILLUSTRATION

1. We are using, as a statistical illustration of the above, data on national income and investment in the U.S.A. computed in Dr. Kuznets' *National Income and Capital Formation, 1919–35.*

In order to obtain the "gross private national income" Y we subtract from gross income (including repairs of equipment) of all private industries the Government's[1] gross saving (pp. 14, 80, 18).

The latter subtracted from gross capital formation (inclusive of repairs, pp. 40, 80) gives investment I in our sense of the term. The results are represented in the following table:

TABLE 4

Gross National Income and Investment in the U.S.A.

($ milliards)

	Y	I		Y	I
1919	79·3	31·3	1928	86·0	22·9
1920	82·4	29·1	1929	89·7	25·5
1921	65·3	17·1	1930	79·6	19·4
1922	64·6	17·7	1931	63·0	13·6
1923	74·8	22·4	1932	44·6	7·0
1924	74·7	18·9	1933	42·1	7·4
1925	78·7	22·7	1934	51·8	10·6
1926	84·3	23·2	1935	58·7	14·9
1927	81·8	22·3			

[1] We mean by Government as above all public authorities.

In order to obtain "stable values" we must deflate these items with the index of prices of finished goods given in the next table. This was constructed from the indices of prices of finished consumption and investment goods in the U.S.A. computed on p. 39.[1]

TABLE 5

Index of Prices of Finished Goods in the U.S.A

1929 = 100

1919	104	1925	102	1931	89
1920	120	1926	102	1932	78
1921	105	1927	100	1933	76
1922	97	1928	99	1934	81
1923	101	1929	100	1935	84
1924	101	1930	96		

Deflating with this index the money values of national income and investments contained in Table 2, we obtain:

TABLE 6

Gross National Income and Investment in the U.S.A.
(In $ milliards at 1929 prices)

	Y	*I*		*Y*	*I*
1919	76·1	30·0	1928	86·9	23·1
1920	68·7	24·2	1929	89·7	25·5
1921	62·3	16·3	1930	82·8	20·2
1922	66·6	18·2	1931	70·8	15·3
1923	74·0	22·2	1932	56·5	8·9
1924	74·0	18·7	1933	54·4	9·7
1925	77·1	22·3	1934	64·0	13·1
1926	82·6	22·5	1935	70·0	17·8
1927	81·8	22·3			

[1] We have weighted them in the proportion 3 : 1 according to the composition of the gross national product inclusive of repairs in 1929. *National Income and Capital Formation*, pp. 45, 80.

2. Plotting the figures on a diagram (see Fig. 3), we see at a glance that while the points corresponding to the period 1924–35 are scattered round the straight line AB, those corresponding to 1919–23 lie far above it. The points 1919 and 1920 are the highest, and below them are the points 1921, 1922, and 1923 round the straight line A_1B_1 parallel to AB.

This can be interpreted as a shift of the investment-income curve. There was evidently a sharp increase in the propensity to consume in the period 1919–24. A shifting of the investment-income curve in the long run is of course a quite normal phenomenon. Here, however, we have a change of a rather discontinuous character. We do not here attempt to account for this shift, which presents a problem requiring special investigation, but will only examine in more detail the period 1924–35, during which we notice a more or less stable connection between investment and income.

The way in which the points 1924–35 are scattered round AB shows a certain regularity: looking at them in the chronological order (treating both 1926–27 and 1928–29 as biennia, which are denoted on the chart by white circles), they form a polygon rotating in a clockwise direction. This shows that there is a time-lag between investment and income. Indeed, the straight line AB represents in such circumstances the approximate connection between investment in a year considered and income at a later date. For instance, to investment in 1931 corresponds the abscissa of the point M lying between 1931 and 1932. On the

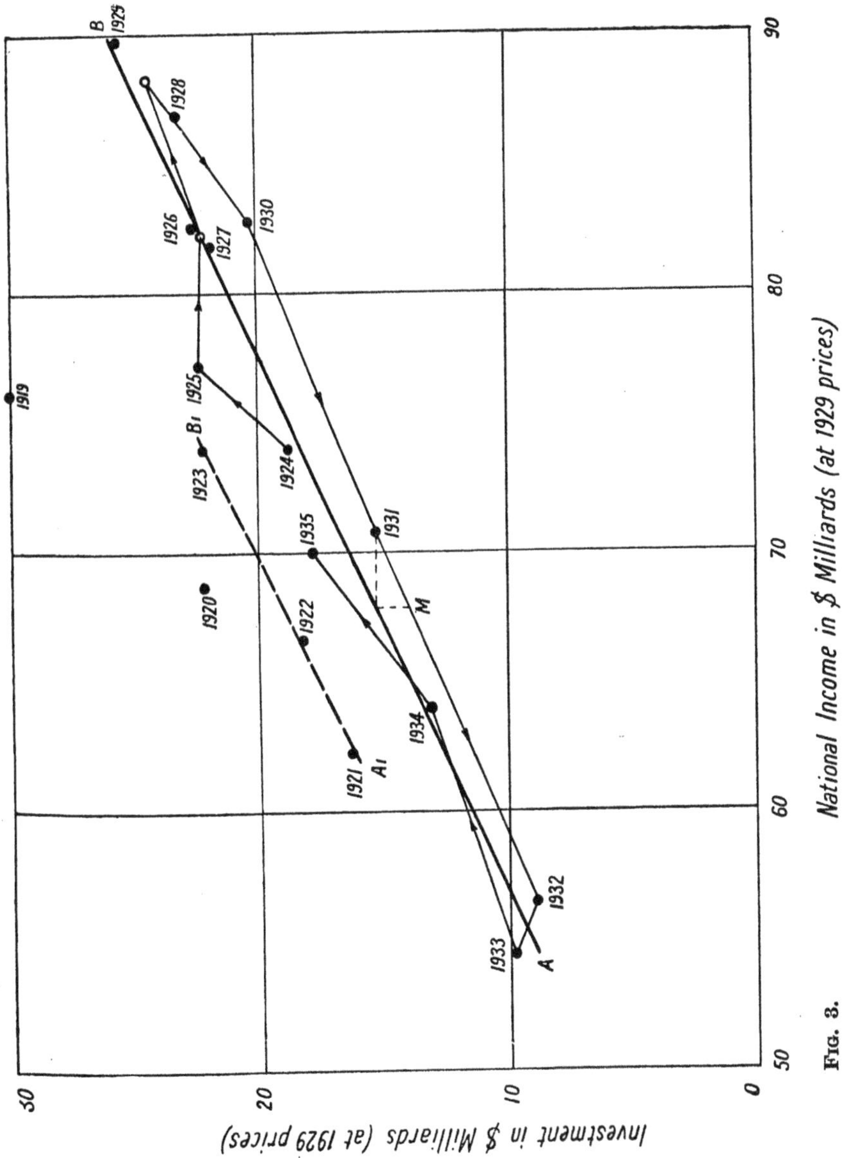

National Income in $ Milliards (at 1929 prices)
Investment in $ Milliards (at 1929 prices)
50
60
70
80
90
0
10
20
30
1919
1920
1921
1922
1923
1924
1925
1926
1927
1928
1929
1930
1931
1932
1933
1934
1935
A
B
A1
B1
M

FIG. 3.

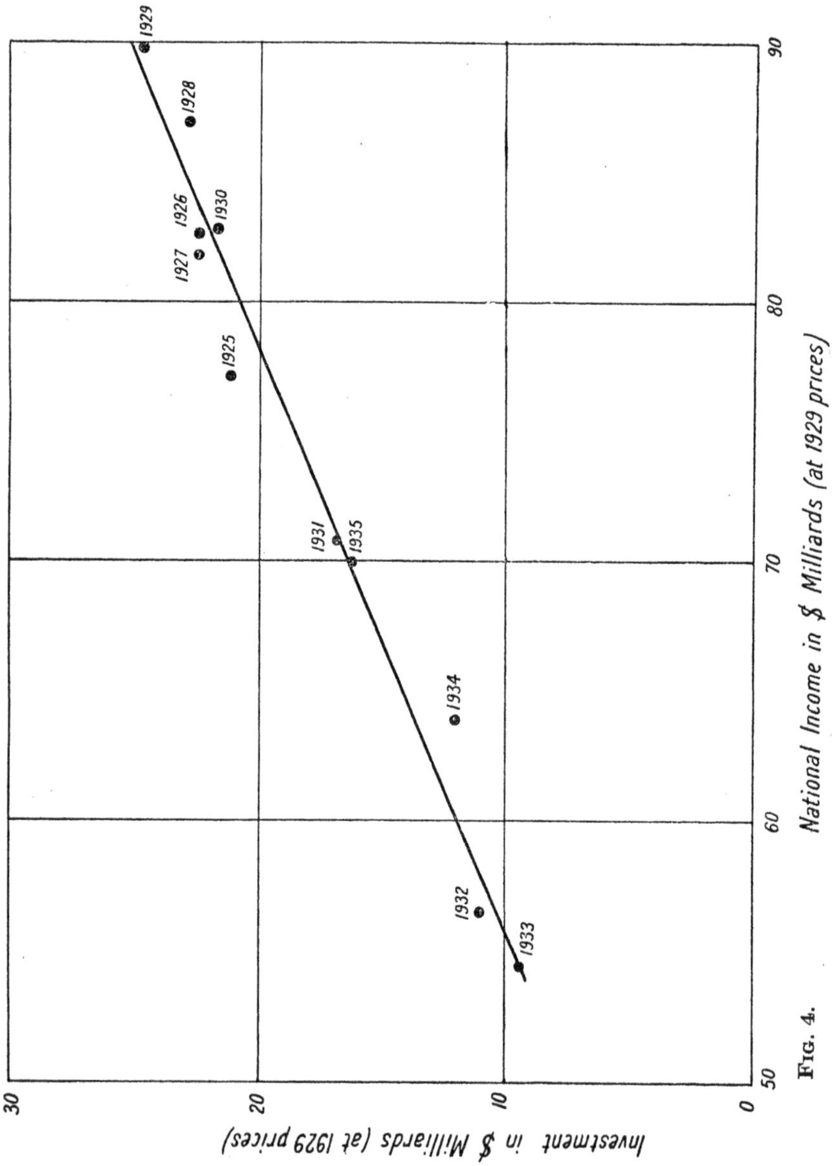
National Income in $ Milliards (at 1929 prices)
Investment in $ Milliards (at 1929 prices)
50
60
70
80
90
0
10
20
30
1925
1926
1927
1928
1929
1930
1931
1932
1933
1934
1935

FIG. 4.

basis of our polygon it is possible to determine the average time-lag. It appears that it is here equal to about four months.

Thus we see that a correlation between present income and investment 0·33 years ago must obtain. (For instance, the income in 1931 corresponds to investment four months earlier which we determine by adding $\frac{2}{3}$ of investment in 1931 to $\frac{1}{3}$ of investment in 1930.) The results are again plotted on a diagram (Fig. 4). The ordinates of the points plotted now represent not I_t but $I_{t-0\cdot33}$. The deviations from the line of best fit are now relatively small. The equation of this line is:

$$Y_t = 2\cdot25\, I_{t-0\cdot33} + 33\cdot2 \qquad (11)$$

It represents the function f for U.S.A. in the period 1924–35. It proves, as is easy to see, the rule (p. 64) that income changes in a lesser proportion than investment. (It is obvious that the ratio $\frac{Y_t}{I_{t-0\cdot33}}$ falls when investment increases.) The multiplier $\frac{\Delta Y_t}{\Delta I_{t-0\cdot33}}$ is equal to 2·25. As shown on p. 63 the multiplier must be greater than $\frac{1}{1-\alpha}$ where α is the relative share of manual labour in the national income. According to my rough estimate α for U.S.A. is about 0·32, and thus $\frac{1}{1-\alpha}$ is about 1·5. Thus this rule also is proved.

The line of best fit is here a straight one. But probably this is not the case outside the range of income and investment here considered.

Fig. 5 compares the actual national income and that calculated from formula (11).

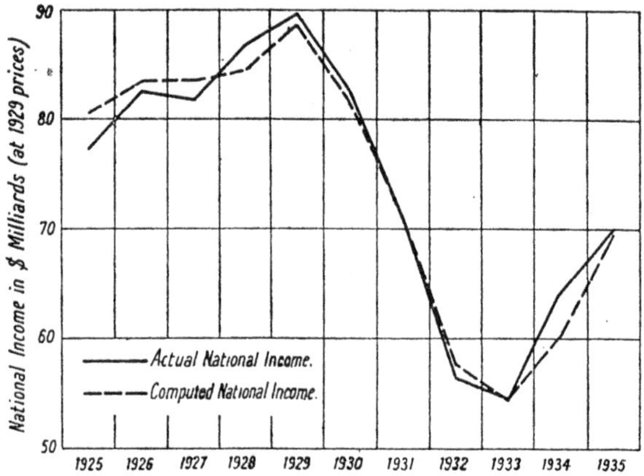

FIG. 5.

3

MONEY AND REAL WAGES

INTRODUCTION

We intend in this essay to discuss at some length the Keynesian theory of wages. We are limiting ourselves to the consideration of a closed economy, for this is the only case to which the Keynesian argument fully applies. To take an extreme example, let us imagine an economy which exports all its produce and imports all consumption goods. It is obvious that in such an economy a reduction in money wages is equivalent to one in real wages, and increases output and employment (but not necessarily the real wage bill).

A SIMPLIFIED MODEL

1. In order not to confuse the various questions involved we shall first consider the problem of wages in a highly simplified model. We assume for the moment: (1) that free competition prevails; (2) that the salary earners and manual workers do not save; (3) that the various types of wages and salaries change always in the same proportion; (4) that entrepreneurs and rentiers have an equal propensity to consume; (5) that the rate of interest is kept constant. All these simplifying assumptions will be gradually removed afterwards.

2. Since in our model free competition prevails, the

short-period equilibrium of a firm is reached at the point of intersection of the horizontal "individual" demand curve and the upward sloping part of the short-period marginal-cost curve. Thus with an increase in employment the ratio of prices to wages must increase, or, what amounts to the same, the real wages must fall (if there is no rise in the productivity of labour due to changes in technique or intensity of work). This is the "classical" doctrine of real wages, and is admitted also by Keynes. As we shall see below, this rule does not apply to real conditions of imperfect competition as described in the essay on "The Distribution of the National Income," but it holds good in the model now considered.

3. We will now deal with the problem of changes in money wages in our system. But before going into the matter some general remarks are necessary.

The national income may be represented in two ways as follows:

Capitalists' income	Investment
Wages and salaries	Consumption

Since in our model the consumption of salary earners and manual workers is equal to their income, we obtain by subtracting wages and salaries from both sides:

$$\text{Capitalists' income} = \text{Investment} + \text{Capitalists' consumption}$$

This equation is very important for the further argument. It follows from it that capitalists' income expressed in "stable values" is fully determined by the volume of investment and capitalists' consumption.

It will perhaps be useful to look at this simple but paradoxical theorem in a different way.[1] Let us schematically represent our economy as consisting of three industries, producing wage-goods, investment goods, and goods consumed by capitalists (or luxury goods) respectively. Wage-goods are in part consumed by the workers producing them, while the surplus sold to workers of the other two industries constitutes capitalists' income derived from the wage-goods industry. Thus employment in the investment and luxury goods industries determines capitalists' income in the wage-goods industry expressed in "stable values." But capitalists' incomes drawn from investment and luxury goods production (expressed in "stable values") are of course also determined by employment in these two industries. Thus the output of investment and luxury goods determines total capitalists' income expressed in "stable values." And because capitalists' income from the wage-goods industry is equal to workers' income in the other two industries the value of capitalists' total income is equal to the value of the output of investment and luxury goods.

4. Let us now consider what happens when all wages and salaries are reduced in the same proportion. If the

[1] The above equation is of course equivalent (under the assumption that the salary earners and manual workers do not save) to the equality of saving and investment which can be obtained from it by subtracting the capitalists' consumption from both sides.

capitalists, having succeeded in cutting wages, immediately raise the volume of their consumption and investment in the expectation of higher profits, employment must increase. Indeed, capitalists' income expressed in "stable values" must rise by the same amount that the volume of their consumption and investment has risen, and this can be attained only by an increase in employment. And the latter is connected in our model with the fall of real wages, which therefore decline as a result of a decline in money wages.

Or to represent this process in a different way: employment in the luxury goods and investment goods industries increases because of the rise in effective demand on the part of capitalists and employment in the wage-goods industry rises because of the demand on the part of workers set to work in the other two industries. This rise in employment, as shown in the preceding paragraph, is just sufficient to raise profits by the same amount that capitalists' consumption and investment have risen.

Such a state of affairs is, however, extremely unlikely. First, entrepreneurs will in general not hurry with new investment orders simply on the strength of a successful wage reduction, but will rather wait until the expectations of higher profitability have been realized. Even should they give new orders at once, the technical time-lag between investment orders and the actual production of investment goods would prevent the latter from increasing immediately.

The position as regards capitalists' consumption is similar, in that it is actual rather than expected income which influences the capitalists' standard of living, and, as was shown in the preceding essay, even this influence operates with considerable delay.

If the above is a true description of the course of events, then a wage cut cannot raise capitalists' incomes expressed in stable values either immediately or later. Immediately after a wage reduction the volume of investment and capitalists' consumption remains unaltered, and thus so does the capitalists' income expressed in stable values. Employment does not alter, while all prices fall in the same proportion that wages have been reduced. Thus nothing is changed by wage reduction except the "general level" of prices, and thus there is no reason for capitalists to increase the volume of their consumption and investment later if they did not so at the beginning.[1]

Or, to put it in a different way: The volume of capitalists' consumption and investment is initially unchanged. Thus there is no increase in output and employment in the luxury and investment goods industries. It follows that the demand for wage-goods falls proportionately to wages, so that since prime costs are reduced also in the same proportion there is no change in the output of the wage-goods industry. Consequently output and employment in all three industries are unchanged and prices fall uniformly in the proportion of the wage reduction.

[1] I have already treated the problem of wages in this way in my article "Essai d'une Théorie du Mouvement Cycliques des Affaires," *Revue d'Economie Politique*, March–April 1935, pp. 301–2.

But then capitalists have no incentive to raise their consumption or investment, for their income expectations are not realized.

Since capitalists' consumption and investment do not increase immediately, their income is initially unchanged; since their income is initially unchanged, their consumption and investment and consequently their income also fails to increase later on.

IMPERFECT COMPETITION INTRODUCED

1. We are going now gradually to remove our assumptions. We drop first that of free competition and examine the relation between real wages and employment in a system such as described in the first essay, in which imperfect competition prevails and average wage-cost curves in the majority of enterprises are more or less horizontal. We have shown there (pp. 36–39): (1) That in such a system the ratio

$$\frac{\text{index of average wage cost}}{\text{index of prices of finished goods}}$$

is approximately constant; (2) that the index of average wage cost does not depend appreciably on the level of output and employment, and thus, with a constant technique and intensity of labour, the index of average wage-cost does not differ greatly from the index of wage rates; (3) that the index of prices of finished goods does not greatly deviate from that of the cost of living.

It follows from these three points that the index of real wages tends to be more or less stable provided the technique of production and intensity of labour do not alter. Consequently in actual fact the index of real wages must show a steady tendency to rise, since there is a strong secular trend in the productivity of labour due to improvements in technique and the increase in intensity of work. But if we eliminate the trend from the index of real wages, we can expect a series of great stability, though *some* fluctuations must be present, as both the technique of production and the intensity of labour may show some rather irregular changes apart from the secular trend, and in addition the ratio

$$\frac{\text{index of average wage cost}}{\text{index of prices of finished goods}}$$

is only approximately constant. (The small fluctuations in it depend partly, as we shall see, on changes in money wages.) To sum up, we should expect that in a closed system real wages, after the elimination of secular trend, would show relatively small changes which would not be likely to have any strong (positive or negative) correlation) with the level of employment.

We shall use as a statistical illustration the data on real wages in the U.S.A.—which may be considered an approximately closed system—for the period 1919–35. We have computed for this purpose a combined index of hourly wages in the manufacturing, building, railroads, and agriculture, and divided it by an index of the cost of living.[1]

[1] We used the data on hourly (for agriculture monthly) wages, published in *Survey of Current Business*. The indices of wages of the four industries mentioned were weighted in proportion of their wage bills in 1929 as given in Dr. Kuznets's *National Income and Capital Formation, 1919–1935* (pp. 62, 63).

81 F

TABLE 7

Real Wages in the U.S.A.

1929 = 100

1919	81	1925	92	1931	108
1920	86	1926	92	1932	106
1921	87	1927	96	1933	109
1922	87	1928	98	1934	118
1923	91	1929	100	1935	117
1924	93	1930	103		

We see at a glance a strong trend, doubtless due to technical progress, etc., which amounts on an average to 2·25 per cent per year. The series obtained after eliminating the trend is given in Table 8, together with the index of output in the U.S.A. (gross national product at 1929 prices).[1]

TABLE 8

Real Wages after Elimination of Trend and Output in the U.S.A.

1929 = 100

	Real Wages	*Output*		*Real Wages*	*Output*
1919	100	71	1928	100	97
1920	103	73	1929	100	100
1921	102	69	1930	101	91
1922	100	74	1931	104	78
1923	103	82	1932	100	61
1924	103	83	1933	100	63
1925	100	86	1934	106	73
1926	98	92	1935	103	78
1927	100	92			

[1] Inclusive of repairs, Dr. Kuznets's *National Income and Gross Capital Formation*, pp. 8, 80.

The fluctuations in real wages are small, and it is easy to see that no clear negative or positive correlation with those of output exists. Real wages at the bottom of the slump (1932, 1933), e.g. are equal to those at the top of the boom (1928, 1929).

2. Let us next examine the process of wage reduction. So long as we assume that the degree of monopoly (i.e. the ratio of prices to marginal costs) remains unaltered, the effect of an all-round wage reduction is just the same as with perfect competition. For if it is assumed that the volume of capitalists' consumption and investment does not change immediately, there is initially no change in employment; while prices, since they change proportionately to prime costs, are in this case reduced proportionately to wages. But since the only change in the system is that in the "general price level," there will be no inducement for capitalists to increase their consumption and investment at a later date.

It is doubtful, however, whether the degree of monopoly really remains unaffected by the process of wage reduction. Some prices are likely to be "sticky," i.e. not to fall at all, or to fall less than marginal costs.[1] This has an important influence upon the result of a wage cut. The output of investment and luxury goods does not change immediately after a wage reduction (according to our fundamental assumption), and thus employment in the industries making these goods is unaltered. The money demand of workers is consequently

[1] See pp. 35–36.

reduced (as in the cases considered above) proportionately to wages, but the prices of wage-goods do not decline on the average to the same extent. As a result the "real" demand for wage-goods falls off, and so does the output and employment in the wage-goods industry. Thus, paradoxically, both employment and real wages are here reduced by the wage cut. And when this has occurred, there will still be no incentive for capitalists to increase their consumption and investment.

Indeed, as the volume of capitalists' consumption and investment is initially unaltered, capitalists' money income (being equal to the value of these two items) is reduced in the same proportion as the prices of luxury and investment goods. If the respective prices of these two types of goods are reduced roughly in the same proportion, the ratio of profits to the price of investment goods is unchanged, and so is also the profitability of new investment. Thus neither investment nor capitalists' consumption is encouraged at a later stage provided it did not rise at the beginning.

To sum up, any increase in the degree of monopoly due to a wage cut reduces employment, the real wage rate and (for both these reasons) the real wage bill, but it does not increase the capitalists' income expressed in stable values.

3. If the wage cut increases the degree of monopoly and thus reduces the relative share of manual labour in the national income, it may be asked how it is possible for this relative share to remain approximately stable throughout the business cycle. We have already stated

in the essay on "The Distribution of the National Income" that in a depression the degree of monopoly increases (because of wage reductions and for other reasons), but this adverse influence upon the share of manual labour is counterbalanced by the fall in raw material prices relative to wages (see pp. 36 sqq.). In the boom the reverse occurs.

As a result, the influence of a change in money wages upon real wages via the degree of monopoly is obscured and only sharp fluctuations in the former are reflected in the latter. This is illustrated by Table 9, in which have been computed the indices of money wages in the U.S.A. (the combined index of wage rates in agriculture, manufacturing, building, and railways used above) and real wages (the corresponding series after elimination of secular trend calculated above).

TABLE 9

Real Wages after Elimination of Trend and Money Wages in the U.S.A.

1929 = 100

	Money Wages	*Real Wages*		*Money Wages*	*Real Wages*
1919	83	100	1928	98	100
1920	102	103	1929	100	100
1921	89	102	1930	100	101
1922	84	100	1931	94	104
1923	91	103	1932	82	100
1924	95	103	1933	81	100
1925	96	100	1934	94	106
1926	96	98	1935	97	103
1927	98	100			

As we see, the fluctuations in money wages are much more violent than those in real wages. The "jumps" in the former (1919–20, 1920–21, 1931–32, 1933–34) are reflected on a much smaller scale by the latter.

FURTHER ASSUMPTIONS REMOVED

1. We have supposed so far that salary earners and manual workers do not save, and that the various types of salary and wage rates change always in the same proportion. We shall now make more reasonable assumptions.

We divide the salary earners into two categories, which we shall typify as "clerks" and "managers." We assume that the salary rates of the first group move porportionately to wage rates, and that both manual workers and "clerks" do not save (for their saving is in fact unimportant). However, we do allow for "managers" saving, and suppose their salaries to change in the same direction as capitalists' incomes, but in a lesser proportion.

The "balance sheet" of the national income can now be written as follows:

Capitalists' income	Investment
"Managers' " salaries	Consumption
Wages and "clerks' " salaries	

Since manual workers and "clerks" do not save, we obtain by subtracting their joint incomes from both sides

Capitalists' and "managers' " income = Investment
+ Capitalists' and "managers' " consumption

If the money income of "managers" always moved proportionately to that of capitalists, our previous argument on wage reduction would fully apply to the case now considered with this one change, that capitalists' and managers' income or consumption must be substituted for capitalists' income or consumption respectively.

But the fact that the income of "managers" varies to a lesser extent than that of capitalists' modifies to a certain degree the results of a wage cut. Indeed, the relative shift of income from capitalists' to "managers" increases their joint consumption, for the latter have a greater propensity to consume than the former (capitalists' incomes include the corporative saving). Thus employment is stimulated. On the other hand, this shift unfavourably affects the profitability of investment, and thus exerts a certain pressure on investment and consequently upon employment. On balance it is uncertain how employment will be affected, but the effect of the shift of income from capitalists to managers caused by wage reduction is not likely to be great.

2. A similar problem arises when we discard our assumption that the entrepreneurs and rentiers have an equal propensity to consume. In reality that of rentiers is usually higher because entrepreneurial incomes include the corporative saving. Thus when the total money income of capitalists declines as the result of a wage cut and the relative share of rentiers in it increases, the volume of capitalists' consumption tends to increase. And this consequently affects favourably total capitalists'

income (expressed in stable values) and employment. As a result also investment becomes more profitable, for (with a given rate of interest) the increased burden of payments to rentiers does not concern new investments, but only past ones. This in turn strengthens the tendency for employment and capitalists' income to rise. However, the change in capitalists' propensity to consume because of the shifts in the distribution of income between entrepreneurs and rentiers described above is not likely to be very important, and so its final effect must not be overestimated.[1]

3. We can now sum up the modifications introduced by passing from our simplified model towards real conditions.

(1) Real wages have no close (positive or negative) correlation with employment because in reality imperfect competition and more or less horizontal curves of average wage-cost prevail in the majority of enterprises.

(2) A wage cut tends to raise the degree of monopoly, and consequently to reduce real wages and to affect employment unfavourably.

(3) A wage cut causes a relative shift of income from capitalists to "managers." As a result, consumption tends to increase and investment to fall off. How it affects employment is uncertain, but the change in either direction is likely to be small.

(4) A wage cut causes also a relative shift of income

[1] The more so that as a result of the redistribution of capitalists' income the saving of enterprises is smaller in relation to total saving, and this tends to discourage investment. See below, p. 132.

from entrepreneurs to rentiers. This tends to increase capitalists' propensity to consume, and consequently employment and "real" capitalists' incomes.

On the balance we can say that:

(1) A wage reduction may change employment in either direction, but this change is likely to be small.

(2) It tends to redistribute income to the disadvantage of the workers. (The fall in real wages is, however, much smaller than that in money wages.)

Of course in the case of a rise in money wages the statements must be reversed.

4. One last assumption was still left unremoved; that of the rate of interest being kept constant. As we have seen, a wage cut does not cause any important change in employment and output, while prices decline. As a result, the value of output must diminish and the demand for cash for transactions fall off. Thus the rate of interest tends to decline, and this encourages investment so that we have yet another possible way for a wage cut to raise employment.

This argument, though theoretically quite correct, is, however, without practical importance. The increase in the demand for cash in general affects only slightly the long-term rate of interest, which is the most important rate in the determination of the level of investment.[1] Thus it seems to be quite justifiable to neglect this channel through which a wage reduction could influence the level of employment.

5. We gave above a statistical illustration of there

[1] See below, pp. 112–113.

89

being no close connection between real wages and employment and of the influence of change in money wages upon real wages. The effect of a change in money-wages on employment is much more difficult to trace statistically because the latter is usually subject to many other influences. In the slump, e.g., both wages and employment decline, which does not prove, however, that wage reductions depress employment.

A crucial test in which most of the irrelevant factors were absent was provided by the Blum Experiment. The detailed account of this investigation was published elsewhere,[1] and we will here refer only shortly to the chief conclusions.

In the article concerned we came to the conclusion that the results of the Blum Experiment (lasting from the spring of 1936 till the spring of 1937) were approximately equivalent to the consequences of an increase of wages in a closed economy by 60 per cent. It was further stated that this great change hardly affected output, and that real wages per hour rose by 26 per cent. (The long-term rate of interest was approximately stable.) This is in full accordance with the theory developed above. It must be noticed that some factors (e.g. Governmental control of rents, railway tariffs, prices of bread, etc.) strengthened the natural tendency of some prices to remain "sticky," and thus the rise in real wages was greater than if "natural" conditions had prevailed. (In other words, the fall in the degree of monopoly was unusually great.)

[1] *Economic Journal*, March 1938.

FINAL REMARKS

1. There are certain "workers' friends" who try to persuade the working class to abandon the fight for wages, of course in its own interest. The usual argument used for this purpose is that the increase of wages causes unemployment, and is thus detrimental to the working class as a whole.

The Keynesian theory undermines the foundation of this argument. Our investigation above has shown that a wage increase may change employment in either direction, but that this change is unlikely to be important. A wage increase, however, affects to a certain extent the distribution of income: it tends to reduce the degree of monopoly and thus to raise real wages. On the other hand, "real" capitalists' incomes tend to fall off because of the relative shift of income from rentiers to corporations which lowers the capitalists' propensity to consume.

If viewed from this standpoint, strikes must have the full sympathy of "workers' friends." For a rise in wages tends to reduce the degree of monopoly, and thus to bring our imperfect system nearer to the ideal of free competition. On the other hand, it tends to increase the thriftiness of capitalists by causing a relative shift of income from rentiers to corporations. And "workers' friends" are usually admirers both of free competition and of thrift as a virtue of the capitalist class.

2. Another question may arise in connection with the Keynesian theory of wages. Is not the struggle of workers for higher wages idle if they lose whatever gain they

may make in the form of a higher cost of living? We have shown that wage reduction causes a change in the distribution of the national income to the disadvantage of workers, and that in the event of an increase in wages the reverse occurs. This is not to deny, however, that changes in real wages are much smaller than those in money wages; but nevertheless they may be quite material; especially as we are dealing with averages which reflect only slightly great fluctuations in real wages in particular industries.

We noticed above the great stability of the relative share of manual labour in the national income. This is not in contradiction with the influence of money wages upon the distribution of the national income. On the contrary, the resistance to wage cut prevents the degree of monopoly from rising in the slump to the extent it would if "free competition" prevailed on the labour market. Though in fact the relative share of manual labour is more or less stable, this would not obtain if wages were very "elastic."

It is quite true that the fight for wages is not likely to bring about fundamental changes in the distribution of the national income. Income and capital taxation are much more potent weapons to achieve this aim, for these taxes (as opposed to commodity taxes) do not affect prime costs, and thus do not tend to raise prices. But in order to redistribute income in this way, the Government must have both the will and the power to carry it out, and this is unlikely in a capitalist system.

Part Two

4

THE PRINCIPLE OF INCREASING RISK[1]

THE PROBLEM

1. The subject of this essay is the determination of the amount of investment undertaken at a given time by a single entrepreneur. He intends, for instance, to build a factory for the production of a certain product. He is faced with given market conditions: he knows the price of the product in question, the level of wages and the prices of raw materials, the cost of construction and the rate of interest. Besides, he has some rather vague ideas as to the probable future change in prices and costs. This knowledge is the basis for the planning of investment, i.e. for the choice of the amount of capital k (measured in terms of money) to be invested and the method of production to be applied.

With a *given* amount of capital k and a given method of production the entrepreneur is able to estimate the series of future returns (differences between revenues and effective costs) $q_1, q_2 \ldots q_n$ during the prospective life of the factory. We shall call the rate ϵ at which the series of returns must be discounted in order to obtain the amount invested k, the prospective rate of profit,[2]

[1] This essay is an altered version of the article published in *Economica*, November 1937.

[2] This definition corresponds to Professor Fisher's "rate of return over cost," Mr. Boulding's "internal rate of return," and Mr. Keynes's "marginal efficiency of capital."

while by prospective profit π we mean the product $k \,.\, \epsilon$. Now we can assume that with a given amount to invest k the entrepreneur will choose such a method of production as will maximize the prospective rate of profit, or, what amounts to the same (k being given), the prospective profit $\pi = k\epsilon$. Thus to every value of k there corresponds a definite maximum prospective profit π_m.

The method of production having been chosen for each value of k, the entrepreneur has still to decide on the optimum k, i.e. the size of investment. He must charge the capital invested at the market rate of interest ρ and also make some allowance for risk, the rate of which we denote by σ. Thus the entrepreneur's prospective gain g is:

$$g = \pi_m - (\rho + \sigma)k$$

The entrepreneur will obtain the maximum gain at the value of k which satisfies the equation

$$\frac{d\pi_m}{dk} = \rho + \sigma$$

and this value of k is the optimum amount of investment. Now $\frac{d\pi_m}{dk}$ is simply the prospective rate of profit of a small capital addition dk to the amount invested k, supposing that both k and $k + dk$ are invested with the appropriate optimum method of production. We shall call $\frac{d\pi_m}{dk}$ marginal prospective rate of profit, or for the sake of brevity marginal rate of profit. We can consequently say that the size of investment k_0 is determined by that level at which the marginal rate of profit is equal to the sum of the rate of interest ρ and rate of risk σ. (See Fig. 6.)

2. It can easily be seen from the chart that the

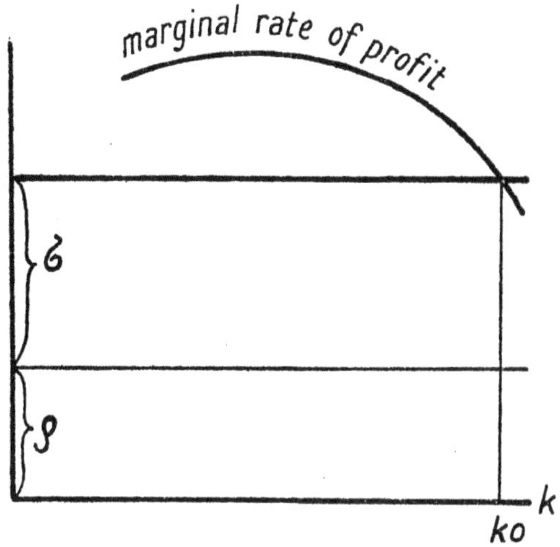

FIG. 6.

optimum amount k_0 to be invested is finite only if the marginal rate of profit falls when k exceeds a certain value. It is commonly believed that such a fall does in fact occur, and for two reasons: (1) large-scale diseconomies; (2) imperfect competition. The first reason seems to be unrealistic. Clearly it has no technological basis. True, every machine has an optimum size, but why not have ten (or more) machines of this type?

There remains the argument of difficulties of management arising out of large-scale enterprise. But this also is doubtful (why not start ten factories instead of one with ten independent directors?), and anyway could apply only to industrial giants far above the average size of existing enterprises.

The second reason for the limited size of investment is quite realistic, but does not cover the ground fully. The effect of imperfect competition in limiting the amount of investment k may often be overcome by spreading the latter over various fields: imperfect competition then operates to limit the portion of k invested in any particular field, but not to limit the total amount of k. On the other hand, imperfect competition cannot account for the fact that in a given industry at the same time large and small enterprises are started. Thus there must be yet another factor restricting the size of an investment.

INCREASING RISK

1. We have assumed so far—as is usually done—that the rate of risk is independent of the amount invested k. It is this assumption which has to be dropped, I think, in order to obtain a realistic solution of the problem of limited investment. It is reasonable to assume that marginal risk increases with the amount invested. For the greater the investment the greater is the reduction of the entrepreneur's income from his own capital when the average rate of profit falls short of the rate of interest. Suppose the rate of interest is 5 per cent, the entre-

preneur's own capital £1,000,000, and the credit taken also £1,000,000. If the average rate of return is only 3 per cent, the total income of the entrepreneur is £10,000 as compared with £30,000 if he had borrowed nothing; while with £2,000,000 credit he suffers a net loss of £10,000, which, if it continues long enough, will drive him into bankruptcy.

If, however, the entrepreneur is not cautious enough in his investment activity, it is the creditor who imposes on his calculation the burden of increasing risk, charging the successive portions of credits above a certain amount with a rising rate of interest.[1]

The amount invested k_0 *is now given by the condition of the marginal rate of profit being equal to the sum of the marginal rate of risk* σ *and the rate of interest* ρ. *The* $\rho + \sigma$ *curve is not a horizontal curve* as in Fig. 6, *but an upward sloping one.* The point of its intersection with the marginal rate of profit curve determines the amount of the investment in the absence of large-scale diseconomies and imperfect competition (Fig. 7).

Now the various sizes of enterprises started in the same industry at a given time can be easily explained. The smaller the private capital of an entrepreneur investing an amount k the greater the risk of impairing his income. Thus the smaller the private capital the higher is the $\rho + \sigma$ curve, and—as is easy to see from the chart—

[1] See M. Breit, "Ein Beitrag zur Theorie der Geld-und Kapitalmarktes," *Zeitschrift fuer Nationaloekonomie*, Band VI, Heft 5, p. 641. The principle of increasing risk is a generalization of Mr. Breit's ideas.

the smaller the amount invested k_0. The enterprises started in a given industry at a given moment are not of equal size because the private capital of the various entrepreneurs is not the same. "Business democracy" is a fallacy: the amount of the entrepreneur's private capital is a "factor of investment."

2. Legitimate doubt may arise as to whether the

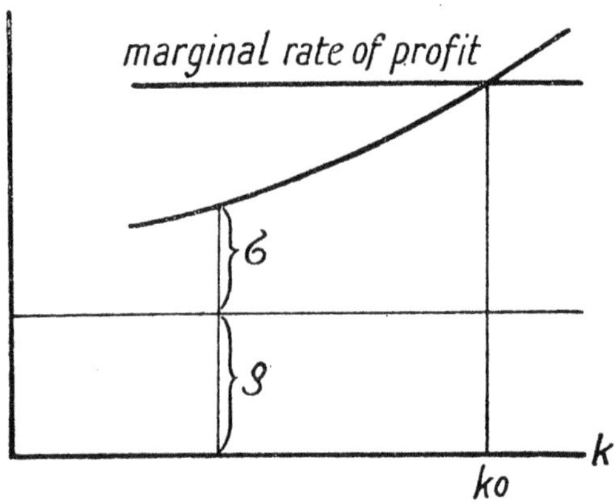

FIG. 7.

results arrived at above are applicable to the case of joint-stock companies. If a company issues bonds or debentures the situation is not materially altered. The greater the issue the more are dividends impaired in the event of unsuccessful business. The position is also similar in the case of an issue of preference shares (the fixed interest on which is paid from profit before dividends on ordinary shares are distributed). But what about an issue of ordinary shares? *Prima facie* it would seem that no limits are set to such an issue, but in fact this is not the case. It is clear that the shareholders of an existing company or the promoters of a new one have no reason whatsoever to grant to new shareholders the full rate of profit from the investment undertaken: on the contrary, they will keep back a part for themselves either by accepting bonus shares, or by issuing the new shares above par and adding the agio gains to reserves. But a limit is set to these efforts to "cheapen" the capital received from new shareholders by the fact that the narrower is the margin between the prospective dividend on new shares and the rate of interest the smaller will be the market for the new shares. Thus there exists an "optimum size" of issue which is relatively small. (Even if the company tries to increase it by "exaggerating" the prospects of the enterprise the limit is set by the cost of advertisement and kindred "services.") This explains the fact that issues of ordinary shares do not play at all a very important part as compared with issues of bonds and preference shares.

The fundamental factors determining the optimum size of an issue of ordinary shares are essentially the same as in the case of floating a loan: the prospective rate of profit and the rate of interest. But their influence is here exerted in a much more complicated way, and may be distorted by speculative demand for shares which is often only loosely connected with the actual profitability of the enterprise. However, it seems justifiable to assume as a first approximation that conditions of investment activity are such as would obtain if all finance was by way of loans; this the more so, because, as mentioned above, ordinary shares do not play a very important part in the finance of investment.

THE RATE OF INTEREST AND THE METHOD OF PRODUCTION

1. In the case represented in Fig. 7 we have constant returns and imperfect competition is abstracted. Though in the general case Fig. 6 there corresponds to each point on the marginal rate of profit curve a different method of production, it is clear that with constant returns and perfect competition technique does not change with the amount invested: the maximum rate of profit is obtained by the application of the same method of production, whatever the scale of enterprise.

Let us now consider what happens if the rate of interest is lowered. The $\rho + \sigma$ curve shifts down, and its point of intersection with the marginal efficiency curve moves to the right (Fig. 8). The method of production chosen by the entrepreneur in his plan does not change as the size of investment increases. *Consequently so long as constant returns prevail, and we abstract the influence of imperfect competition, the change in the rate of interest does not affect the method of production chosen by the entrepreneur, but only the size of the investment planned.*

2. This statement seems to be in contradiction with the classical theory of marginal productivity of capital and labour, but the contradiction is only apparent. The

point of departure of the classical doctrine is a drastically simplified model of production in which the quantity of product is a definite function of the amount of "real" capital and labour used. A necessary condition of long-run equilibrium is equality between the marginal productivity of each factor and its price divided by the price of product. In the case of constant returns (homo-

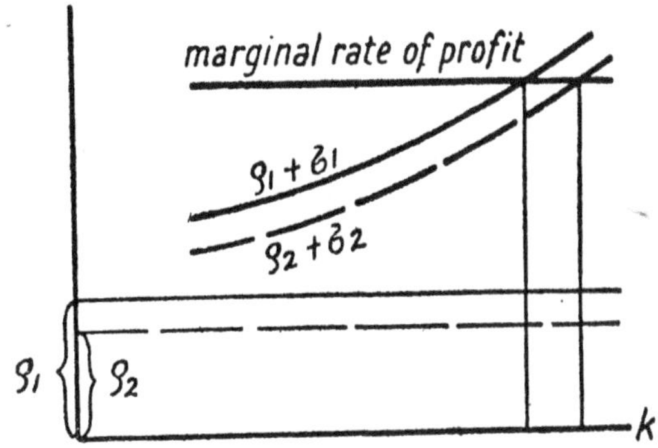

FIG. 8.

geneous production function) this is also a *sufficient* condition for long-run equilibrium, for with constant returns the marginal productivity equations exclude the existence of entrepreneurial gain. If the rate of interest falls, a shift towards a new long-run equilibrium must take place in which the marginal productivity of capital is lower, that of labour higher, and more capital is used in proportion to labour. But the theory says nothing about the immediate influence of a fall in the rate of interest on the plans of the entrepreneur. Such a fall in the case of constant returns (if our principle of increasing risk is not taken into account) must create a tendency to plan investment of infinite size and with an indefinite method of production.[1]

However, after the output of the product has suddenly increased, its price falls, and this makes possible the restoration of another long-run equilibrium in which the marginal productivity equations are satisfied.[2]

Thus our problem was quite different from that of classical theory. We examined the planning of the entrepreneur in a given situation which in general was *not* the position of long-run equilibrium. We tried to find the factor limiting the size of the investment planned, and this factor, as we see, is non-existent in the classical theory in the case of firms subject to constant returns and not in the position of long-run equilibrium. And our statement that the fall in the rate of interest does not affect the method of production, but only the scale of investment plans, referred only to the *plans* and not to the situation arising out of their realization.

The classical thesis that a low rate of interest causes the use of more capitalistic method of production was

[1] It is sometimes considered obvious that the method of production is chosen so as to minimize average costs. This assumption, however, attributes to the entrepreneur the tendency to maximize the profit per unit of output, while he of course tends to attain the maximum total profit. Both tendencies are equivalent only if a given output is planned.

[2] This treatment is, however, very formal, for in reality an upward self-stimulating process begins which causes (if the rate of interest is not raised) either hyperinflation or fluctuations about the new position of long-run equilibrium.

often applied not only to the long-run equilibrium position, but also to entrepreneurs' planning in "dis-equilibrium." This interpretation is of course wrong, and, as we have shown above, if we abstract imperfect competition and introduce the principle of increasing risk, the fall in the rate of interest has no immediate effect on the method of production decided upon by entrepreneurs in making their plans.[1]

"COMMITMENTS" AS A FUNCTION OF MARGINAL NET PROFITABILITY

So far we have dealt with the investment of a firm starting afresh, with a given capital of its own. This is of course a special case. In general investments undertaken by firms are not their "maiden" ones. The burden of risk borne by a firm does not depend solely on investment currently planned. This burden is the result of all its "commitments," by which term we mean here all its investments past and present minus its own (present) capital. Thus its "commitments" are equal to the cost of the past investment constituting its capital equipment plus investment orders in execution, or recently given, minus private capital consisting of the firm's own capital

[1] It may be shown, however, that if imperfect competition is operative, the decline in the rate of interest exerts some influence towards more capitalistic methods of production in investment plans. This different effect of increasing risk and imperfect competition upon the method of production depends on the fact that the marginal risk increases with the amount of *capital* invested, while the marginal revenue falls with the increase in *output*.

at the start, and the amounts accumulated since (inclusive of amortization). If, e.g., the cost of the capital equipment of a firm is £1,000,000, the investment orders in execution £100,000, the investment orders given to-day £50,000, while the original capital of the firm and the amount accumulated since (inclusive of the amortization fund), £800,000; the "commitments" of this firm are

$$£1,000,000 + £100,000 + £50,000 - £800,000 = £350,000$$

Now it is easy to see that in general it is to the total amount of "commitments" that the curve of increasing risk relates. The investment plans undertaken to-day must be such as to "push" commitments to the point at which marginal risk is equal to the difference between the marginal rate of profit and the rate of interest. Or if we call this difference the marginal net profitability, we can say that the "commitments" of a firm are an increasing function of the marginal net profitability.[1]

It is important to notice that if a firm's investment in a certain period is equal to its saving, its commitments are unaltered, and the marginal risk incurred is not increased.

The connection due to increasing risk, between commitments and net profitability, plays an important part in the theory of business cycle developed in the last essay.

[1] If we consider a long period in which the proportionate rise of the private capital of the firm may be substantial, it is really the ratio of "commitments" to private capital which is the function of the marginal net profitability.

5

THE LONG-TERM RATE OF INTEREST

THE FINANCE OF INVESTMENT

We propose in this essay to analyse briefly the monetary phenomena accompanying investment in fixed capital equipment. In particular we intend to examine the influence of the latter upon the long-term rate of interest, and also to explain the remarkable stability of this rate.

We assume throughout the essay a closed economic system.

Liabilities of the Banks are regarded as being composed of Deposits on which interest is paid and Current Accounts on which none is paid, while assets consist of Notes, Bills, Bonds, and Advances. The ratio of Notes to Liabilities is kept more or less constant. The Central Bank is supposed to behave as in Great Britain, i.e. to supply the economy with cash by buying bills and bonds on the market.

2. We shall first consider the financing of investment in fixed capital under simplifying assumptions which will eventually be removed. We assume for the time being: (1) that on each day of the construction period of a given object of investment bank advances are taken to the extent of the expenditure made during the day; (2) that on the next day a loan of the same amount

is floated and the advance of the preceding day repaid; (3) that savings accumulated in any one day are used in the next to buy bonds.

What will happen under these conditions if additional investment is undertaken can easily be seen. Since saving is equal to investment, to-day's additional accumulation of savings on current accounts equals advances taken for additional investment. To-morrow the flotation of loans to the amount of to-day's investment will be met out of to-day's savings. In this way an increase in the rate of investment will directly result in only a negligible addition to the advances and current accounts of the banks.

The increase in the rate of investment, however, brings about a rise of output in both investment and consumption goods industries, and this creates a greater demand for money for transactions. Current accounts and advances tend to increase, and the banks are obliged to sell bills and bonds in order to be able to expand their credits.

We will consider the results of these sales in detail later on, but first we shall remove our simplifying assumptions and thus show other factors tending to intensify the pressure on the bill and bond market.

3. We suppose now that, instead of financing construction day by day with advances for one day only, the cost of a given object of investment is advanced *en bloc* at the time when its construction is begun. A deposit account (of the same amount as the total cost of the investment object) is opened, out of which the

expenditure on construction is financed. We shall call this account the "investment finance fund."[1] It diminishes gradually as construction proceeds, and is fully spent when the object of investment is finished. (Thus the average period of turnover of the "investment finance fund" is half the construction period.)

The sums spent on construction create equal amounts of saving, which, let us suppose, are accumulated for the time being also on the deposit account, and which are consequently equal in value at the end of construction to the total credit advanced. The loan then floated in order to fund this credit is exactly taken up by the accumulated savings. We shall call the savings which accumulate on deposit account the "intermediate savings fund." Its average period of turnover is also half the construction period.

Now it is easy to see that if the money value of the rate of investment in fixed capital I_m prevails at a certain level and the average construction period is θ, the bank advances for construction must be equal to $I_m \, . \, \theta$. And on deposit accounts there is an "investment finance fund and an "intermediate savings fund," each of the value $I_m \, . \, \frac{\theta}{2}$. If I_m increases, all these items rise proportionately.

It must be added that the above representation is based on the assumption that the time-lag in directing savings towards the purchase of securities is just half the construction period. If it is not, certain complications

[1] It is this fund which has been called by Keynes "finance."

arise which, however, do not materially affect our result, and thus we abstract them from our argument.

4. We see now that if investment in fixed capital increases, bank advances tend to rise, not only because of the increase in the demand for money for transactions, but also because the "investments finance fund" and "intermediate saving fund" are expanding. In this way additional pressure is exerted on the banks to sell bills and bonds. Before we start to consider the influence of this pressure upon the rate of interest, we must remove another simplification involved in the above argument.

We have supposed so far throughout the argument that new savings are (with a certain delay) fully used for the purchase of securities. It is quite possible, however, that they may be devoted partly for the repayment of advances (or what amounts to the same thing in periods of increasing activity when the demand for money for transactions rises they are left on current account while advances increase *pro tanto* less). This, however, does not materially affect the course of our argument. A part of the loans floated is then not taken up by savers, but the banks are *pro tanto* relieved from advances and enabled to take up loans instead. Here, however, a complication arises, since in general banks use the amounts released by repayment of advances partly for the purchase of bills and not of bonds. As a result, the pressure on the bill market is relieved, and that on the bond market *pro tanto* strengthened.

THE INFLUENCE UPON THE RATES OF INTEREST

1. We stated above that an increase in investment causes the banks to sell bills and bonds in order to be able to expand advances. If we ignore for a moment that a part of this supply may be purchased by the Central Bank, the only possible eventual buyers are the owners of deposits and current accounts. Let us first consider how this works as regards bills.

The sales of bills increase of course the discount rate, and this makes bills more attractive to the potential buyers. But it is easy to show that the demand for them is rather inelastic. Indeed, the most likely buyers are the owners of deposits, for the latter bear more or less the character of reserves. The rate paid on the deposits, however, moves usually parallel to the discount rate, and thus there is no change in comparative advantage. Therefore the bills must eventually be bought by the owners of current accounts. The higher rate of discount induces people to manage their transactions with smaller amounts of money, and thus enables some bills to be bought (or permits repayment of advances, the rate on which moves parallel to the rate of discount; and so reduces the sales of bills by banks). It is clear, however, that in order to produce this effect the change in the rate of discount must be appreciable.

Of course the Central Bank in buying bills reduces very much the pressure of sales. For banks may obtain in this way additional amounts of notes, and this enables them to expand credit by, say, £10 for each £1 note obtained. But the effect of the Central Bank's buying is partly counterbalanced by the fact that with increasing activity the demand for notes "in circulation" rises. At any rate there is an inherent tendency in the system for strong fluctuations in the discount rate, which in fact often makes itself felt.

2. What, however, about the sale of bonds? It is known that their yields fluctuate much less than the discount rate. Why do sales of bonds taking place together with sales of bills depress only slightly the long-term rate of interest? This, I think, is due to the fact that many of the deposit owners are willing to buy bonds when their yield increases in spite of the much greater increase in the rate on deposits. (If, e.g., the long-term rate increases from 4 to 4·2, while the rate on deposits from 2 to 3.) The reason for such behaviour on the part of this type of deposit owners is as follows:

Consider a capitalist with a "non-speculative outlook," who faces the alternatives of holding his reserves in bonds or deposits. There is the advantage of a stable and generally higher income on the side of bonds: on the other hand, deposits are constant in value, while the price of bonds, in the case of an emergency which may necessitate their sale in the indefinite future cannot be foreseen, and the risk of loss is always present. Thus it is clear that the stimulus to keep bonds is the margin between the *present* long-term rate and the anticipated *average* short-term rate over a long period. Now it is very likely that the change in the present rate on deposits does not greatly affect the expectations of its average over a long period. Thus it is plausible that a deposit owner of the type considered may be induced to buy bonds though the rate on deposits has increased much more than the yield of bonds.

STATISTICAL ILLUSTRATION AND GENERAL REMARKS

1. The relative stability of the long-term rate of interest is generally known. But perhaps it is not fully realized how small are in fact its "purely cyclical" fluctuations. This can be seen from the table on p. 114, in which we have computed the difference between the yield of Consols and the 9-year moving average for the period 1853–1932.[1]

Only in the World War, early post-war years, and 1932 does the "cyclical deviation" of the long-term rate of interest exceed 0·2.

These facts are of great importance in the investigation of the business cycle. It seems likely that changes in the long-term rate of interest of the order of those noticed, say from 3·0 to 3·2, can hardly influence investment activity[2] to a great extent. Thus it will be a justifiable simplification if we assume in the analysis of the business cycle that the long-term rate of interest is constant. This assumption may be contested on the ground that it is the yield of industrial bonds which matters in investment activity, and that this yield increases (sometimes appreciably) in deep depressions because of

[1] The yields of Consols over the period considered are taken from the article "The Future of the Rate of Interest," J. Stafford, *The Manchester School*, VIII, No. 2, p. 137.

[2] See for that point Harrod, *The Trade Cycle*, p. 112.

the decline in lenders' confidence. The omission of this factor, however, does not distort the picture of the business cycle because it works in the same direction as the fall of the rate of profit, and therefore only aggra-

TABLE 10

Deviations of the yield of Consols from the 9-year moving average

1853	– 0·11	1873	+ 0·04	1893	+ 0·08	1913	– 0·16
54	+ 0·11	74	+ 0·05	94	+ 0·04	14	– 0·28
55	+ 0·14	75	+ 0·03	95	– 0·06	15	– 0·07
56	+ 0·04	76	– 0·02	96	– 0·14	16	+ 0·18
57	+ 0·06	77	– 0·01	97	– 0·18	17	+ 0·28
58	– 0·13	78	+ 0·03	98	– 0·16	18	– 0·06
59	– 0·07	79	– 0·01	99	– 0·10	19	+ 0·06
60	– 0·03	80	– 0·01	1900	+ 0·02	20	+ 0·70
61	+ 0·04	81	– 0·04	01	+ 0·10	21	+ 0·57
62	– 0·02	82	– 0·03	02	+ 0·02	22	– 0·21
63	– 0·03	83	– 0·04	03	+ 0·04	23	– 0·35
64	+ 0·06	84	+ 0·02	04	+ 0·07	24	– 0·26
65	+ 0·07	85	+ 0·12	05	– 0·04	25	– 0·12
66	+ 0·13	86	+ 0·12	06	– 0·04	26	+ 0·07
67	– 0·06	87	+ 0·12	07	+ 0·04	27	+ 0·13
68	– 0·09	88	– 0·18	08	– 0·08	28	– 0·05
69	– 0·03	89	– 0·12	09	– 0·07	29	+ 0·08
70	0·00	90	– 0·05	10	– 0·02	30	0·00
71	+ 0·01	91	+ 0·04	11	– 0·04	31	+ 0·08
72	+ 0·03	92	+ 0·10	12	– 0·07	32	– 0·37

vates the crises, but is not of fundamental importance for the mechanism of the trade cycle.

2. The fact of the stability of the long-term rate of interest stated above is particularly important for the analysis of the last stage of the boom. It excludes these theories of the business cycle which attribute the break-

down of prosperity to the increase of the rate of interest. For the rate of interest can stop the boom only by hampering investment, and it is chiefly the long-term rate which matters in investment activity.

Moreover, the fact of the stability of the long-term rate of interest shows indirectly that the boom ends in general before full employment is reached. When the system comes to the point of full employment, wages must rise sharply. But as shown above, this does not tend to reduce employment directly (see p. 89). Thus wages and prices continue to climb up, the demand for bank advances steadily increases, causing a strong rise in the short-term rate and—at least after a certain time —an appreciable increase in the long-term rate. Only this can overcome "inflation" by hampering investment and stopping the rise in wages and prices.

Since, however, no appreciable rise in the rate of interest usually occurs in the boom, it can be concluded that something like full employment is approached only in exceptional cases. In general unemployment (manifest or disguised) is sufficient to permit the boom to develop, and it is not the scarcity of labour which brings it to an end.

6

A THEORY OF THE BUSINESS CYCLE[1]

METHODOLOGICAL REMARKS AND SIMPLIFYING ASSUMPTIONS

1. The character of this essay is to a great extent different from that of the preceding ones. In the latter we frequently used simplified models, but only in order to solve some basic problems in their pure form, returning afterwards to the complexities of the real world. Here, however, we confine ourselves to the consideration of the business cycle only under simplifying assumptions, some of which may seem drastic. This is partly due to the peculiar character of the subject. The business cycle as such exists only as a tendency which in conjunction with what we call more or less vaguely "secular trend," "structural changes," etc., creates the extremely complex dynamic process we observe in the real world. Thus to pass from a simplified model to reality is to undertake a thorough analysis of this process as a whole, which is clearly beyond the scope of this essay.

[1] This essay is an altered version of the article published in *Review of Economic Studies*, February 1937. The essential ideas in it were developed already in my "Essai d'une Théorie du Mouvement Cyclique des Affaires," *Revue d'Economie Politique*, March–April 1935, and in mathematical form in "A Macrodynamic Theory of the Business Cycle," *Econometrica*, July 1935.

We cannot even find consolation in the idea that the mechanism of the business cycle, which we attempt here to construct, may be simply superimposed on the "secular trend," etc. On the contrary, the latter certainly affects the course of the business cycle as such.

This does not mean, however, that the consideration of the trade cycle in simplified models is a waste of time. To approach the dynamic process in all its complexity is certainly a hopeless task; so that the first step must consist in constructing elementary mechanisms of the "business cycle" or "secular trend." Only it must be kept in mind that these simple schemes are the beginning and not the end of economic dynamics.

2. We make the following simplifying assumptions. (1) We assume a closed economic system and a balanced State budget.[1] (2) We suppose the increase or decline in the volume of inventories (working capital and stocks) to be negligible. (3) We are dealing with an economy with no secular trend. The first assumption makes both the balance of expenditure of foreign countries and that of the Government equal to zero. Consequently investment I (as defined on p. 48), which is equal to private saving S, now becomes identical with private investment in fixed capital, working capital, and stocks. Thus bringing in assumption (2) about the constancy of inventories, we shall have in our model the equality between investment I and the output of fixed capital

[1] The doles for unemployed are financed by taxation or by the reduction of other State expenditure.

equipment.[1] However, before we proceed further, some explanation of the assumptions (2) and (3) is necessary.

3. There are various reasons why we abstract changes in inventories from our argument. The statistical evidence on this subject is very poor: the only series ranging over many years is that constructed by Dr. Kuznets for the U.S.A. during the period 1919–35.[2]

Except for this, we know very little about changes in inventories; while our knowledge of fluctuations in output of fixed capital equipment is considerably greater. (Steel production—the data on which are accessible for many countries over long periods—is a good indicator of the general output of fixed capital.)

Further, if we look at the changes in inventories and private investment in fixed capital in the U.S.A. in the period mentioned (see Fig. 9), we see at a glance that the former series is much less regular than the latter: indeed, one cannot properly speak of regular cyclical fluctuations in the changes in inventories. Nor is this surprising, for the latter are influenced by factors which are much more heterogeneous than those affecting investment in fixed capital. It follows that it is difficult to account for changes in inventories in a simple scheme, and, further, that they are not of primary importance in the explanation of the trade cycle. So far we have shown the desirability of keeping the changes in inven-

[1] Equipment in the course of construction is here *not* included in inventories. The change in the volume of equipment in the course of construction is contained in the "output of fixed capital equipment."

[2] *National Income and Gross Capital Formation, 1919–1935*, p. 40.

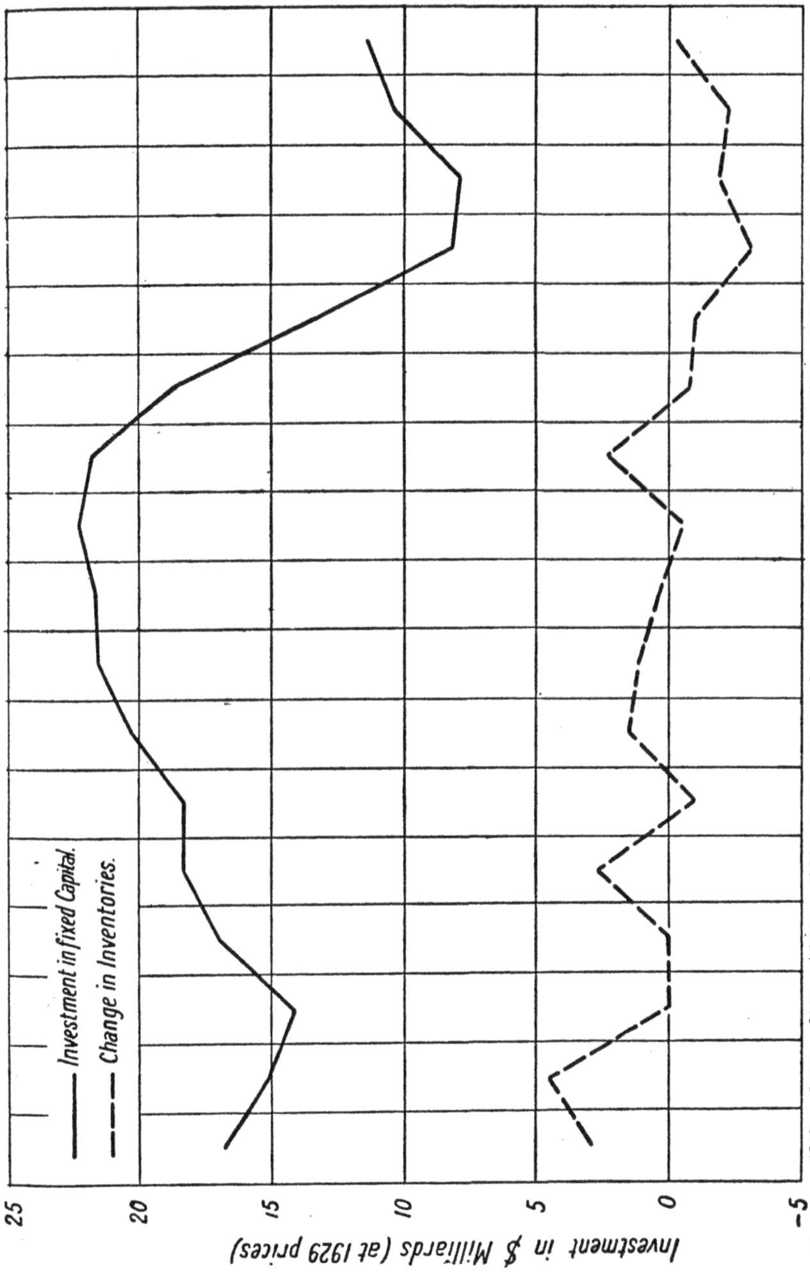
Investment in fixed Capital.
Change in Inventories.
Investment in $ Milliards (at 1929 prices)
25
20
15
10
5
0
−5
1919
1920
1921
1922
1923
1924
1925
1926
1927
1928
1929
1930
1931
1932
1933
1934
1935
FIG. 9.

tories out of our model. But how to "remove" them? i.e. how to construct our model in such a way as to keep the volume of inventories constant?

It is sometimes thought that the volume of inventories tends to vary proportionately with output, on the assumption that inventories are identical with working capital, which is regarded as bearing a constant relation

TABLE 11

The Volume of Inventories and Output in the U.S.A.

1929 = 100

	Inventories	*Output*		*Inventories*	*Output*
1919	72	71	1928	98	97
1920	81	73	1929	100	100
1921	87	69	1930	102	91
1922	87	74	1931	100	78
1923	90	82	1932	95	61
1924	92	83	1933	89	63
1925	93	86	1934	83	73
1926	96	92	1935	80	78
1927	98	92			

to output. Neither assumption is correct. Inventories contain besides working capital *sensu stricto* "stocks" in the form either of reserves or of accumulated unsold goods; and these move often in the opposite direction to working capital. Further working capital in trade—in particular in the retail trade changes much more slower than sales; for dealers during a depression try to attract custom by stocking a greater variety of goods. As a result the volume of inventories is much more stable than that of output. On the basis of Dr. Kuznets' data on changes in inventories and of the level of inventories in 1922 as given by Census of Production, we have computed the *level* of inventories in U.S.A. in the period 1919–35 (at 1929 prices).[1]

We see that inventories are very "sticky"; it is, for instance, surprising to learn that their volume in 1932 was only slightly lower than in 1928. Now one can easily imagine an economic system in which this tendency operates to the point of almost full stability of working capital and stocks, each fluctuating to the same extent but in opposite directions. Such a state of affairs need not seem fantastic in the light of the above figures.

4. We are next going to make some comments on the assumption of a "trendless" economy. We mean by this a system which can attain a state of long-run equilibrium, i.e. that there exists some position at which no change whatsoever occurs in the system.

It is clear that we cannot simply postulate a "trendless" economy, but we must attribute to our system characteristics which will render it trendless. This will be done largely in the course of the argument. At present we make only the following assumption. We suppose that not only manual workers (see p. 51) but also salary earners and rentiers do no saving. Obviously a contrary state of affairs is incompatible with "trendless" economy. Indeed, if salary earners and rentiers do save they may be expected in view of the relative stability

[1] Exclusive of the estimated value of movable equipment under construction, which we consider as fixed capital.

of their income to make some positive net saving in all circumstances. This, however, makes impossible the existence of a long-run equilibrium. For in such a state not only must there be no net saving, but in addition the net saving of salary earners and rentiers on the one hand and that of entrepreneurs on the other must each be equal to zero. For otherwise a shift of capital from entrepreneurs to salary earners and rentiers would take place, which would change the economic situation quite appreciably, as we shall see below (see p. **132**).

Thus, if we want to deal with a "trendless" economy we must assume that all saving is done by entrepreneurs.

ASSUMPTIONS RESTATED

1. The consequences of our assumptions so far established are as follows:

(1) In our system the sole type of investment is private expenditure on fixed capital equipment (the consequence of the assumptions of a closed system, a balanced budget, and constant inventories).

(2) The workers and rentiers are supposed not to save, and thus all saving is done by entrepreneurs (the necessary conditions of a trendless economy).

2. Besides these assumptions, some of the conclusions of the preceding essays are used.

On the basis of the first essay we take for granted that the prices of finished investment goods change more or less proportionately to those of consumption goods (see pp. 37–40).

The argument of the second essay (p. 60) enables us

to assume that capitalists' incomes are determined by the national income Y (both expressed in stable values). We shall also use the equation established there (p. 67).

$$Y_t = f(I_{t-\lambda}) \quad . \quad . \quad . \quad . \quad . \quad (10)$$

which describes the functional relation between the national income Y at time t and investment I at time $t - \lambda$ (both expressed in stable values).

Further, we shall use the connection between the level of "commitments" contracted by entrepreneurs and the difference between the marginal rate of profit and the rate of interest—which was developed in the fourth essay (on the basis of the principle of increasing risk).

Lastly, in accordance with the results arrived at in the fifth essay, the long-term rate of interest will be assumed stable throughout the cycle.

INVESTMENT DECISIONS AND INVESTMENT

1. Investment in our model is solely in fixed capital, i.e. deliveries of finished capital goods plus the increase in fixed capital in the course of construction (the latter was *not* included in inventories). Thus investment is here equivalent to the work actually performed in the industries producing fixed capital equipment. And I (expressed in stable values) is equal to the volume of their output.[1]

[1] In the second essay in order to express investment, saving (which is equal to the former), and national income in stable values, we divided them by the index of prices of all finished

2. Since investment coincides in our system with the output of fixed capital, its actual level at any time is the result of past investment decisions which objectively took the form of orders for machines, buildings, etc.

Let us consider first the connection between the flow

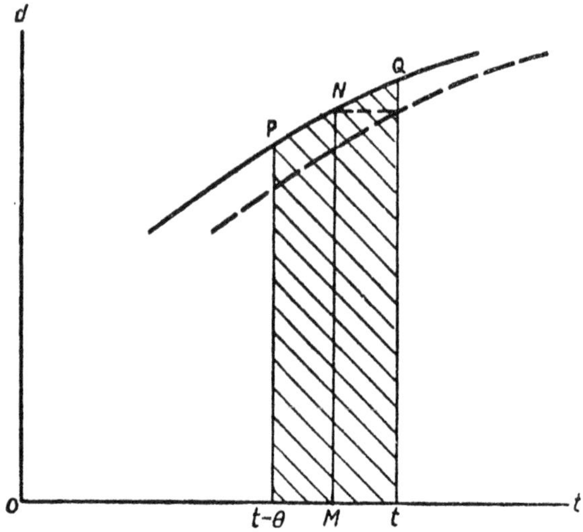

FIG. 10.

of decisions—orders for, and of output of, a particular type of investment goods. We denote the rate of investment orders for this type of goods by d, the output in

goods. Since, however, prices of finished investment goods (fixed capital equipment) and prices of finished consumption goods (cost of living) move almost proportionately (see pp. 37–40), I expressed in stable values coincides practically with the volume of output of investment goods industries.

the industry constructing them by i, and the construction period by θ.

All orders in the process of execution at the time t (Fig. 10) were given in the period from $t - \theta$ to t for previous orders were completed before $t - \theta$, while orders given after $t - \theta$ are still unfinished at time t. The volume of these outstanding orders is represented by the shaded area.

On the other hand, since all orders must be executed within a time θ, work corresponding to $\frac{1}{\theta}$ of each of the orders under execution must be performed per unit of time by the investment goods industry under consideration. And since the volume of all outstanding orders is given by the shaded area, the output i in this industry at the time t is equal to:

$$i = \frac{\text{shaded area}}{\theta}$$

It is easy to see from the diagram that this quotient is approximately equal to the median line MN. (This equality is perfect if PQ is a straight line.) Consequently the output i of our industry at time t is approximately equal to the rate of investment orders at the time $t - \frac{\theta}{2}$. Or the time-lag between d and i is approximately equal to half the construction period.

3. In reality we have of course not one type of investment goods, but many types with different construction periods. We shall call the volume of all types of investment orders per unit of time the rate of investment

decisions D; and the volume of the output of all types of fixed capital the rate of investment I.

The construction period of the various types of investment goods are different, but we can define the average construction period $\bar{\theta}$ as the ratio of the volume of all investment orders under execution (at a certain moment) to the total output of investment goods I. The average construction period is not constant, but if the distribution of orders between different types of investment does not undergo very great changes, which seems to be the case, variations in $\bar{\theta}$ will be slight. We shall assume that $\bar{\theta}$ is constant.

The argument developed in the preceding paragraph for d, i, and θ also applies approximately for D, I, and $\bar{\theta}$, and thus the time-lag between the rate of investment decisions and the output of investment goods is approximately equal to $\frac{\bar{\theta}}{2}$. Consequently we have that investment at time t is equal to the rate of investment decisions at time $t - \frac{\bar{\theta}}{2}$.

$$I_t = D_{t-\frac{\bar{\theta}}{2}} \quad . \quad . \quad . \quad . \quad . \quad . \quad (12)$$

(The available statistics show that the average construction period is probably between half a year and a year; thus $\frac{\bar{\theta}}{2}$ may be regarded as 3–6 months.)

4. We established in the second essay (p. 67) that the national income Y and investment I are connected by the equation

$$Y_t = f(I_{t-\lambda}) \quad . \quad . \quad . \quad . \quad . \quad (10)$$

Since investment at time $t - \lambda$ must be equal to the rate of investment decisions at time $t - \lambda - \frac{\bar{\theta}}{2}$, we have:

$$Y_t = f(D_{t-\lambda-\frac{\bar{\theta}}{2}}) \quad . \quad . \quad . \quad . \quad . \quad (13)$$

This means that since national income is lagging behind investment by λ and investment behind investment decisions by $\frac{\bar{\theta}}{2}$, income is lagging behind investment decisions by $\lambda + \frac{\bar{\theta}}{2}$. If we denote $\lambda + \frac{\bar{\theta}}{2}$ by τ we can write the last equation in the form:

$$Y_t = f(D_{t-\tau}) \quad . \quad . \quad . \quad . \quad . \quad (13a)$$

It may be mentioned that if we take $\frac{\bar{\theta}}{2}$ as 3–6 months and λ (see p. 73) as 4 months, τ amounts to 7–10 months.

The equation (13*a*) has important implications. It shows that past investment decisions determine the present national income, which of course influences current investment decisions; and these will in their turn influence the national income in the future. This conception is the basis for the type of treatment which Mr. Lundberg has called "model sequencies."[1]

Let us consider in each period the average level of investment decisions and the national income. Then the income in, say, period two is a function of investment

[1] *Studies in the Theory of Economic Expansion*, Erik Lundberg, London, 1937. It was applied also in my paper in *Review of Economic Studies*, February 1937, which appeared about the same time.

decisions in period one. Now the income in period two, as we shall see below, determines in conjunction with some other factors the investment decisions in this period, and they in turn the national income in period three, and so on.

So far we have established precisely only the connection between investment decisions and income. Now we shall inquire more closely into the determinants of investment decisions.

THE INDUCEMENT TO INVEST

1. Our argument about the inducement to invest, i.e. about the factors determining investment decisions, is based on some of the results arrived at in the essay on "The Principle of Increasing Risk."

We concluded there that the "commitments" which an entrepreneur is willing to enter at any time are an increasing function of net profitability, i.e. of the difference between the marginal rate of profit and the rate of interest. The same holds good for entrepreneurs as a whole.[1]

"Commitments" were defined as follows:

Commitments = Capital equipment (valued at cost)
+ Investment orders in execution (or just given)
− Private capital (inclusive of amortization funds)

[1] It is clear that in general the marginal rates of profit in various industries are not equal. But we can define the general marginal rate of profit as such a rate which, if it were to prevail in all industries, would affect the "commitments" in the same way as the given set of marginal rates of profit.

We can now add all such equations relating to individual entrepreneurs, and thus obtain a similar equation for entrepreneurs as a whole.

One may divide outstanding investment orders into the part already produced and the part yet to be completed. If, e.g., one-third of a factory whose total cost of construction is £1,500,000 has already been constructed, the value of the former part is £500,000, and of the latter £1,000,000. The former part is nothing else than capital in the course of construction. Thus the equation of "commitments" may be written as follows:

Commitments = Capital equipment + Capital in the course of construction + The uncompleted part of outstanding orders − Private capital.

or:

Commitments = (Capital equipment + Capital in the course of construction − Private capital) + The uncompleted part of outstanding orders.

It is easy to see that in our model the expression in brackets is constant. Indeed, in a unit of time the sum of capital equipment and capital in the course of construction increases by the value of the output of fixed capital equipment, i.e. by the value of investment. On the other hand, the private capital of entrepreneurs increases by the value of the total saving, for according to our simplifying assumptions entrepreneurs are the only savers in our system. As investment equals saving,

129 I

the sum of capital equipment and capital in the course of construction minus the private capital of entrepreneurs remains constant through time. Consequently "commitments" vary only because of changes in "the uncompleted part of outstanding investment orders." Thus since "commitments" are an increasing function of the gap between the marginal rate of profit and the rate of interest, the same must also be true of the uncompleted part of investment orders.

However great *actual* investment, i.e. the output of investment goods, may be, it cannot increase aggregate "commitments," for entrepreneurs (being the only savers) must save as a body always just as much as they invest. Thus increasing risk cannot charge "actual investment." The point where it does exert its pressure is on the unexecuted investment decisions. For an investment decision taken, but as yet unexecuted, has no counterpart in saving. And an increase in the uncompleted part of investment decisions—the only way in which aggregate "commitments" may increase in our system—thus requires a higher gap between the rate of profit and the rate of interest.

2. So far we have stated the functional connection between the *stock* of the uncompleted parts of investment orders and the difference between the marginal rate of profit and the rate of interest. Our real aim, however, is to find out what are the determinants of the *rate* of investment decisions. There is obviously a close connection between these two problems. The flow of new investment decisions must be such as to keep the stock

of the uncompleted parts of investment orders at the level corresponding to the prevailing net profitability. Now the period of turnover of this stock is $\frac{\bar{\theta}}{2}$, the time-lag between D (the rate of investment decisions) and I (the output of investment goods). Thus approximately the stock of unexecuted investment orders is equal to $D \cdot \frac{\bar{\theta}}{2}$. It follows that the rate of investment decisions D is also a function of the difference between the prospective rate of profit and the rate of interest.[1]

3. Some readers may regard this discussion about the functional relation between the rate of investment decisions and net profitability as labouring the obvious. This theorem has indeed been often used (more or less implicitly), but so far as I know it has not been satisfactorily demonstrated. To make, e.g., a statement that net profitability is an incentive to invest does not

[1] "Commitments" we have considered as measured in terms of money, while D is the *volume* of investment decisions per unit of time. The money value of D is Dp_i where p_i is the index of prices of investment goods. Thus it may seem that it is $Dp_i \cdot \frac{\bar{\theta}}{2}$ and not $D \cdot \frac{\bar{\theta}}{2}$ which is the function of net profitability. While $D \cdot \frac{\bar{\theta}}{2}$ would then be equal to this function divided by the price index p_i. But, e.g., if p_i rises, entrepreneurs are inclined to evaluate their wealth higher and to enter greater commitments. This may be roughly accounted for by assuming not $Dp_i \cdot \frac{\bar{\theta}}{2}$ but $D \cdot \frac{\bar{\theta}}{2}$ to be a function of net profitability.

establish that the *rate* of investment decisions is a function of net profitability.

Further, our argument shows that this theorem holds good only under special assumptions. We assumed in our simplified model that rentiers and workers do not save. If they do, entrepreneurs' "commitments" increase permanently by the amount saved "outside enterprises" (for the saving of entrepreneurs falls short of investment by this amount).

If in an economy the steady accumulation of "non-entrepreneurial" savings is accompanied by a secular growth of wealth the ratio of "commitments" to private capital of enterprises may not rise, and the investment activity may not be impaired by saving "outside enterprises."

If, however, we consider a system having no secular trend, the accumulation of savings "outside enterprises" must cause a "structural slump" of investment activity which is not due to the change in net profitability. For with a given net profitability the rate of investment decisions must decline because otherwise the marginal risk would increase.

This is the reason why, in order to construct a system tending neither to grow nor to shrink in the long run, we assumed the salary earners and rentiers not to save.

TWO DETERMINANTS OF INVESTMENT DECISIONS

1. We have shown that in our system the rate of investment decisions D is an increasing function of the difference between the marginal rate of profit and the

rate of interest. Since it is the long-term rate that matters here, and this was assumed constant, D is an increasing function of the marginal rate of profit. We are now going to show that the marginal rate of profit at a given time—by which is meant the marginal *prospective* rate of profit (see p. 96)—is determined *grosso modo* by the level of the national income Y and the stock of capital equipment. And thus these two factors are together the determinants of the rate of investment decisions. We shall first consider the effect of changes in the national income with a given capital equipment, and afterwards allow for changes in the latter.

2. As follows from the considerations on p. 60, the level of national income Y (expressed in stable values) determines approximately its distribution between various classes. In particular Y determines more or less closely the total capitalists' income Q (expressed in stable values).

Let us denote now by p the index of prices of finished (investment and consumption) goods by which we deflated the money income in order to obtain "income in stable values." The money national income is of course Yp, and total money capitalists' income Qp.

The greater Qp is with a given capital equipment, the greater will be the capitalists' income qp, which can be obtained at present from a given new investment (q is this income expressed in "stable values"). We now denote the index of prices of investment goods by p_i. It is easy to see that the capitalists' income per unit of newly-invested capital is proportionate to $\frac{qp}{p_i}$. But since, according to the result arrived at in the first essay, the prices of finished investment goods vary in approximately the same way as those of finished consumption goods, the ratio $\frac{qp}{p_i}$ is practically equal to q, which with given capital equipment is the greater, the greater is the actual capitalists' income expressed in stable values. And as this latter is determined by the national income Y, it follows that the rate of capitalists' income which can be obtained under current conditions from a new investment is the greater the greater is the national income Y (with a given capital equipment).

The rate of capitalists' income which can be obtained now from a new investment is not a sufficient basis for the estimate of the prospective rate of profit, for future developments must be taken into account. But since conjectures on this subject are extremely vague, present affairs have a predominant influence upon long-term expectations. Knowing so little about the future, entrepreneurs are inclined to be optimists when present trade is good and pessimists when it is bad. Thus as a good approximation we may assume that the rate of profit is a function of q, and thus with given capital equipment is the greater the greater is the national income Y. And since the rate of investment decisions D is an increasing function of the marginal rate of profit we have finally the equation

$$D = \phi_e(Y) \quad . \quad . \quad . \quad . \quad . \quad (14)$$

where ϕ is an increasing function and the index e means that it is determined only with a given capital equipment.

3. There are good reasons to believe that the curve representing the function ϕ is **S**-shaped (see Fig. **11**). For when things are improving entrepreneurs become more optimistic about their future, and the rate of investment decisions increases strongly; but after a certain point doubts begin to arise as to the stability of this development, optimism ceases to keep pace with the boom, and the rate of investment decisions tends to increase less rapidly. In the slump a symmetrical development is likely to occur.

The function ϕ represents the dependence of the rate of investment decisions at time t on the national income Y at the same time:

$$D_t = \phi_e(Y_t) \quad . \quad . \quad . \quad . \quad . \quad (14a)$$

We have, however, established another connection between these variables; the national income at time t is determined by the rate of investment decisions at time $t - \tau$, where τ is the time-lag depending both on the construction period and on the lag between income and consumption. In other words, the national income at time $t + \tau$ is a function of investment decisions at time t:

$$Y_{t+\tau} = f(D_t) \quad . \quad . \quad . \quad . \quad . \quad (13b)$$

Both functions are represented on Fig. **11**. The ordinate of the **S**-shaped ϕ curve shows the rate of investment decisions D_t corresponding to national income Y_t;

while the abscissa of the f-curve (which is taken here to be a straight line[1] corresponding to D_t gives $Y_{t+\tau}$, i.e. the national income at the time $t + \tau$. Owing to the ϕ-curve being **S**-shaped, it must cut the f-curve in some point B. We shall see at once that from these two curves we can find out how the system moves.

Let us imagine time to be divided into τ periods.

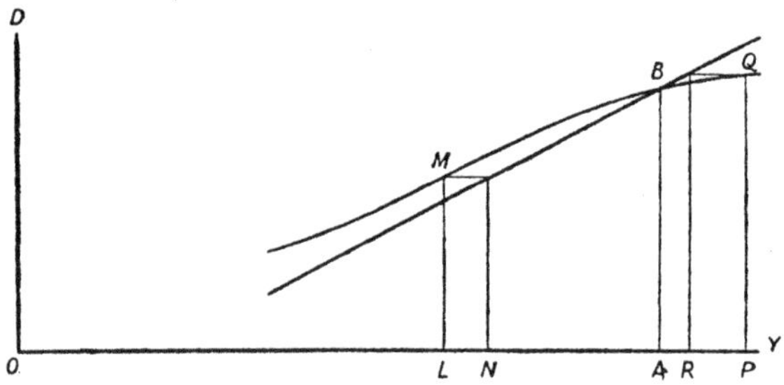

FIG. 11.

Suppose that in an initial τ period the national income has the value OL.

The rate of investment decisions in this period is determined by the ordinate of the ϕ-curve LM. These investment decisions, however, determine in turn the national income in the next τ period, which is equal to the corresponding abscissa of the f-curve ON. Thus the national income is increasing.

On the other hand, if the national income in the initial period has the value OP, investment decisions in this period are equal to PQ, and the national income in

[1] As we have seen in the first essay, the diagram of the function f for the U.S.A. was a straight line. (See p. 73.)

the next period is OR. Thus the national income is here diminishing.

While if Y is equal to OA, the abscissa of the point of intersection B of the ϕ- and f-curves, the national income tends neither to rise nor to fall.

To sum up: If the point Y, D lies above the f-curve, i.e. if the present investment decisions are higher than investment decisions in the preceding τ period, which have determined the present national income, this increases. If the point Y, D lies below the f-curve, i.e. if the present investment decisions are lower than those which have determined the present national income, this falls off. While if the point Y, D coincides with the point of intersection B of the ϕ- and f-curves, i.e. if the present investment decisions are equal to those which have determined the present national income, this is stationary. Thus the point Y, D either moves towards B, or remains stationary if it coincides with it.

4. A problem concerning the upward movement of the system towards the point B must yet be touched upon.

It is theoretically possible that before point B is reached employment might rise so much as to absorb the total available labour supply. In other words, the abscissa of point B might exceed the level of the national income at which full employment is attained. If, however, there exists at the point of full employment a tendency for a further rise in investment (expressed in stable values), the system must come into a state of "inflation" characterized by a violent rise in wages and prices, while no further increase in the "real" national income can occur.

The "inflation" would eventually be checked by an "automatic" rise in the rate of interest (see p. 115). The rise in wages and prices would cause a strong increase in the short-term rate of interest, and a much smaller but still appreciable one in the long-term rate. Thus

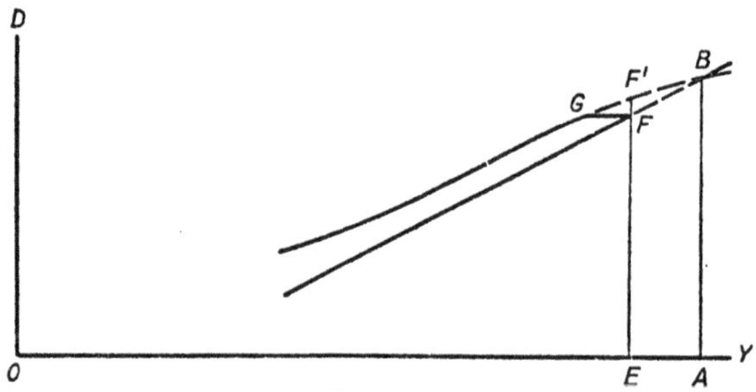

Fig. 12.

under "inflationary" conditions our assumption of a stable long-term rate would not hold good; for under such conditions it would increase until investment activity fell to a level compatible with the existing supply of labour. This may be very clearly represented on our diagram of the ϕ and f functions (Fig. 12). Suppose that full employment is reached at a point E, which lies to the left of point A. In order to prevent inflation, the rate of interest must increase so as to keep the rate of investment decisions at the level EF, for this rate determines the level of the national income equal to OE at which all available labour is absorbed. The rate of investment decisions is *not* equal to EF′ because of the rise in the rate of interest. The rise in the rate of interest as the system approaches full employment causes the curve ϕ, determining the rate of investment decisions in terms of income, to flatten out along GF instead of rising to F′, so that its point of intersection with the f-curve is F instead of B. In this way the case when full employment is reached may easily be accounted for in our analysis. We have already indicated, however (p. 115), that such a situation is rather exceptional; thus as a rule point B lies to the left of point F′.

5. B represents a conditional equilibrium in the sense that at this point the system has no tendency to change provided that there is no change in capital equipment (which has so far been assumed constant). However, as investment is generally not at the level of wear and tear, equipment *does* change, and, as will be shown in detail below, the state of "conditional equilibrium" cannot be permanent.

Many writers[1] who have constructed simplified models of the Keynesian theory have focussed their attention on the "equilibrium" represented by the point B. This was due to the fact that they did not distinguish between investment decisions and investment. They were there-

[1] J. E. Meade, "A Simplified Model of Mr. Keynes's System," *Review of Economic Studies*, February 1937.

J. R. Hicks, "Mr. Keynes and the Classics," *Econometrica*, April 1937.

Oskar Lange, "The Rate of Interest and the Optimum Propensity to Consume," *Economica*, February 1938.

fore unable to conceive of the system being in a position different from that presented by the point B.

In addition they did not consider the influence of changes in capital equipment.

It is true that—as shown above—the system always moves towards the point B, but it may, of course, take several τ periods to come close to it. Thus the time of adjustment is considerable (τ is more than half a year).

When at last "equilibrium" is reached, it cannot last long because of the change in capital equipment. Thus the position of "conditional equilibrium" is rather exceptional. As we shall see, it is attained only at the top of the boom and at the bottom of the slump.

6. We have so far examined the dependence of the rate of investment decisions D on the national income Y under the assumption of a given capital equipment. We must now analyse the influence of changes in equipment on investment decisions with a constant national income. In this way we shall be able to describe D as a function of both national income Y and capital equipment.

It is easy to see that if the capacity of equipment increases while Y is stationary, the "state of affairs" becomes worse. Capitalist's income Q (expressed in stable values) is, with constant Y, still approximately constant. Thus the capitalists' income "per factory" must diminish. The new plants compete with the "old" ones, and draw from them a part of the total sales. In this way a part of aggregate profits is transferred to "new" factories.

This deterioration in the "state of affairs" clearly influences adversely the prospective rate of profit. Thus we can conclude that the greater the equipment with constant national income the smaller the rate of investment decisions. Consequently the curve representing the function

$$D = \phi_e(Y)$$

is shifted downwards when equipment increases. D is

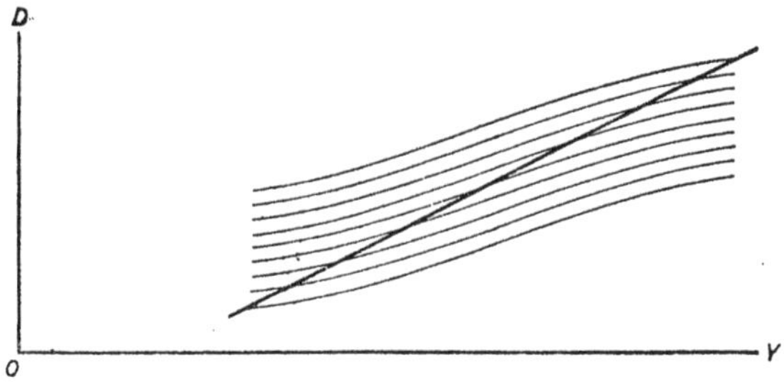

FIG. 13.

in this way a function of two determinants, the national income and capital equipment. It is represented by a family of ϕ_e-curves.

THE BUSINESS CYCLE

1. With the results arrived at in the preceding section, we are now able to describe the dynamic process in our system. The time is supposed to be divided into τ periods. To simplify the exposition, we will examine this process in two stages: in the first we abstract the changes in capital equipment; in the second stage we

allow for the effect of these changes which result from investment and wear and tear.[1]

Suppose the level of national income (expressed in stable values) in the first τ period to be Y_1 (see Fig. 13). The corresponding ordinate of the curve ϕ, which represents the dependence of the rate of investment decisions on national income (with given capital equipment), is

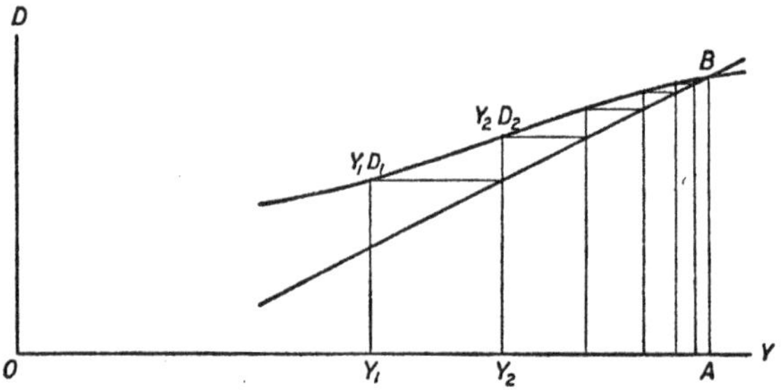

FIG. 14.

the rate of investment decisions D_1, in the first period. In turn D_1 defines the national income Y_2 in the second τ period, which causes in the same period a rate of investment decisions D_2, etc. The point Y, D moves along the ϕ-curve, and, strictly speaking, it never reaches the point B, or, in other words, reaches B only after the lapse of an infinite number of periods. It is clear, however, that after a relatively small number of

[1] In the first stage we can imagine, for instance, that both investment and wear and tear are very small in relation to equipment; thus equipment changes only a little in the course of the process considered.

periods the difference between Y, D and Y_B, D_B is negligible, i.e. the position of equilibrium is practically reached. For in succeeding τ periods the increase in Y and D is negligible.

Starting from the position represented by a point Y, D lying above the f-curve we obtain an upward "self-stimulating" process in which D and Y tend to reach the level D_B and Y_B. It is easy to see that if the initial position is represented by a point Y, D, lying below the f-curve, this process is reversed, and the system travels downwards towards B. As already mentioned the position Y_B, D_B is that of equilibrium only on the assumption of a constant equipment. We shall see in the next paragraph that it is the change in equipment which disturbs this equilibrium.

2. We come to the second stage of our argument: we have now to consider the influence exerted upon the dynamic process by changes in the capacity of equipment.

To every state of capital equipment there corresponds a certain level of investment necessary for the maintenance of its capacity, i.e. to make good wear and tear.

If the upward self-stimulating process described in the preceding paragraph starts from a position in which deliveries of investment goods are lower than the "level of maintenance," so that capacity is shrinking, the rise of investment is thereby stimulated. The ϕ-curve, up which the point Y, D moves, itself shifts upwards. But the situation alters when the deliveries of investment goods begin to exceed the level of maintenance. From then onwards capital equipment keeps expanding, and the upward process is retarded. The point Y, D moves farther up the ϕ-curve, but now the latter shifts downwards. Similarly a downward "self-stimulating" process (which is represented by a downward movement of the point Y, D along the ϕ-curve) is initially strengthened by the expansion of capital equipment, but afterwards hampered by its shrinkage. The point of intersection of the ϕ- and f-curves B is now *not* a position of equilibrium. If investment decisions D_B are greater than the maintenance level of equipment, so also will be the deliveries of investment goods; thus capital equipment will increase and the ϕ-curve shift downwards. If D_B is less than the "maintenance level" the reverse must occur.

We shall see in the next paragraph that the "self-stimulating process" (represented by the movement of point Y, D along the ϕ-curve), and the change in the capital equipment (represented by the shift of the ϕ-curve), create together an automatic business cycle.

3. Imagine that in the initial position income and investment decisions are represented by the point E in the Y, D plane (Fig. 15), and that at this point the deliveries of investment goods are just equal to the maintenance level of equipment. Thus as equipment is neither expanding nor shrinking, the ϕ-curve is stationary in the period considered. The point Y, D tends to move up this curve, but in succeeding periods investment activity increases, and the ϕ-curve shifts downwards. As a result the moving point Y, D has the

trajectory EF, which is the resultant of its movement up the downward shifting ϕ-curve. (At E this trajectory is tangential to the ϕ-curve, since Y, D is there moving along ϕ while the latter is stationary.) After point F, in which the national income Y ceases to grow, has been reached, the ϕ-curve still shifts downwards, consequently point Y, D moves vertically downwards. Thus it

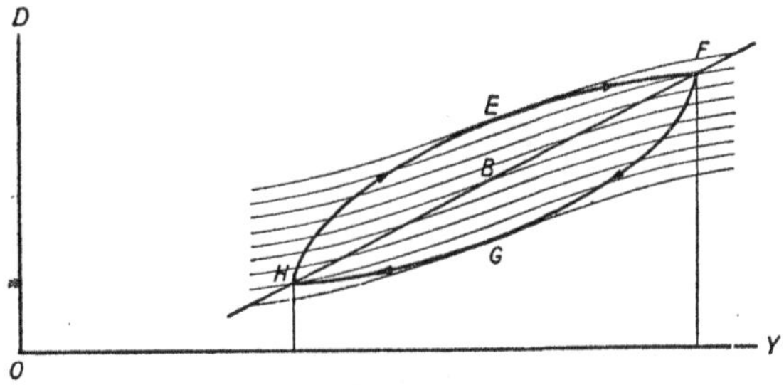

FIG. 15.

The cracs of the curve EFGH in F and H are due to the discontinuity introduced by division of the process into τ periods.

falls below the f-curve and begins to move down the ϕ-curve, which itself shifts downwards because investment activity still exceeds the maintenance level of capital equipment. But after a certain time the steady fall in investment decisions brings the system to the position G, in which deliveries of investment goods just cover wear and tear. The ϕ-curve now ceases to shift downwards, and the trajectory becomes tangential to it, as it was before in E. In succeeding periods investment activity is lower than the level of maintenance, so that the ϕ-curve begins to shift upwards, but as the point Y, D is still below the f-curve, it continues to move down the ϕ-curve. At point H income Y ceases to fall, while the ϕ-curve continues to shift upwards. Consequently point Y, D rises vertically. As the point Y, D comes in this way above the f-curve its movement along the ϕ-curve is now upward, while ϕ-curve itself continues to shift upwards. Thus the moving point comes back to point E and a new cycle begins.

We now see clearly that a business cycle is inherent in our model. This may be summarized shortly as follows:

4. We start from a position in which the requirements of wear and tear are just covered by investment activity, and in which investment decisions are at such a level that they tend to cause a higher level of income in the future (point E). Thus equipment is initially stationary while national income tends to rise. The result is a further rise in investment decisions, and later in income, and so on cumulatively. However, capital equipment also expands, because investment activity increases above the level of maintenance. This hampers the "self-stimulating" process of the rise in investment decisions and national income. After a certain time a position is reached in which national income ceases to grow (point F). But investment activity, which is now at its maximum, continues to add to the stock of capital equipment. Income being stationary, this brings the first fall in investment decisions, and thus breaks the boom. The fall of investment decisions causes a fall in

income, which in turn depresses investment decisions. So long as investment activity is higher than the level of maintenance, the downward movement is aggravated by the continued expansion of capital equipment. The effect of the latter is reversed when investment activity falls below the level of wear and tear (point G), i.e. capital equipment shrinks, and thus hampers the downward movement. Eventually the position is reached at which national income ceases to fall (point H). The shrinkage of capital equipment continues, however, and, as income is stationary, this starts a rise in investment decisions. Thus the bottom of the slump is passed. The rise in investment decisions causes a rise in income, which in turn further stimulates investment decisions. This upward process is accelerated by the shrinkage of capital equipment until investment activity reaches the level of maintenance (point E), and a new cycle begins.

5. We are now going back for a moment to our diagram. It is clear that the moving point cannot stop anywhere on the trajectory. At E and G equipment is stationary, but investment decisions are such as to cause in the next period a level of income which is higher or lower respectively than the present one, and thus to start a "self-stimulating" process. At F and H there is no tendency for "self-stimulating" process, but the amount of equipment is changing. There exists, however, on the f-curve somewhere between F and H a point B, at which investment activity just covers wear and tear. This point corresponds to a long-run equilibrium. For since it lies on the f-curve there is no tendency for a

self-stimulating process to begin; investment decisions, and therefore deliveries of finished investment goods, tend to be stable; while since they are both at the level of maintenance there is no change in equipment. If in its initial position the moving point does not coincide with B, it must move around B, and a business cycle arises.[1]

6. We see that the question, "What causes periodical crises?" could be answered shortly: the fact that investment is not only produced but also producing. Investment considered as expenditure is the source of prosperity, and every increase of it improves business and stimulates a further rise of investment. But at the same time every investment is an addition to capital equipment, and right from birth it competes with the older

[1] Clearly it is an arbitrary and even unlikely assumption that the moving point comes back to its initial position E—the trajectory may well be a spiral and not a closed curve. If the fluctuations produced by our mechanism have a tendency to subside, this means that the spiral converges towards point B, and in this way the system tends to attain long-run equilibrium. But as shown by the investigations of Professor Frisch ("Propagation problem and impulse problems in dynamics," *Economic Essays in honour of Gustav Cassel*, London, 1933, and unpublished works), this is prevented by the existence of "erratic shocks." Since the relationships represented by f and ϕ are in reality not quite stable functions, the actual dynamic process may be imagined as the resultant of the operation of the mechanism described above and of random shocks. Now Professor Frisch has shown that if the basic mechanism produces slightly damped fluctuations the existence of shocks establishes a state of relatively regular undamped fluctuations with an average period similar to that of the fluctuations created by the "basic mechanism."

generation of this equipment. The tragedy of investment is that it causes crisis because it is useful. Doubtless many people will consider this theory paradoxical. But it is not the theory which is paradoxical, but its subject —the capitalist economy.

INDEX

STATISTICAL INDEX

(Numbers refer to numbers of tables)

Studies in Economic Dynamics

by

M. KALECKI

LONDON
George Allen & Unwin Ltd

Foreword

THESE five interconnected essays present the results of further research into the subjects which I discussed in my *Essays in the Theory of Economic Fluctuations*. In particular, more attention has been paid in the present studies to the long-run aspect of the problems considered.

Although frequent use is made of formulæ, the mathematics involved is of elementary character (elementary algebra and the beginnings of differential calculus).

The following essays are reprinted (with important alterations) by permission of the editors concerned :

" The Short-Term and the Long-Term Rate of Interest," partly from the *Review of Economic Statistics*, May 1941, partly from *Oxford Economic Papers*, No. 4 ; and " A Theory of Profits " from *Economic Journal*, June–September 1942.

I am very much indebted to Mr. F. Burchardt, Mr. J. Steindl and Mr. G. D. N. Worswick of the Oxford Institute of Statistics for valuable comments and suggestions, and to Mr. J. Goldmann for reading the proofs.

This work was started with the assistance of a grant from the National Institute of Economic and Social Research, and I take this opportunity to express due acknowledgement.

M. KALECKI.

OXFORD INSTITUTE OF STATISTICS,
November 1942.

Contents

PART ONE

Prices, Interest, and Profits

PART TWO

Business Cycle and Trend

Part One

PRICES, INTEREST, AND PROFITS

1. COSTS AND PRICES

The Percentage Gross Margins and Monopolistic Competition.

1. The purpose of this essay is to discuss the relation between prime costs and prices of an industry under conditions of market imperfection and oligopoly. By an "industry" is meant here manufacturing and selling of a certain group of products which fulfils the following conditions: (i) The price fixing for a product by a firm is influenced mainly by the prices of other products in the group and the expected price reactions of firms manufacturing them, and only to a much lesser degree by prices and price reactions outside the group. (ii) The proportionate changes of the unit prime costs (unit costs of materials and wages) of the various products of an "industry" are not very divergent.

It is obvious that this definition is not clear cut. The broader the group the better condition (i) is fulfilled, and the worse in general condition (ii). The group must thus be formed so as to achieve a compromise between these two requirements and therefore the scope of the industry is within certain limits arbitrary.

Before proceeding with our discussion we shall make certain assumptions as to the average prime costs of the products in question. We assume that—as is usually the case in manufacturing—the average prime cost changes little as output expands, and that the entrepreneur takes the average prime costs as a crude approximation to the marginal costs. The latter seems to be borne out by recent inquiries which showed that entrepreneurs are really not familiar with the *exact* concept of marginal cost. In what follows we shall assume for the sake of simplicity that the average prime cost a_k of any product is *strictly* constant when output fluctuates. The marginal cost is equal to a_k and thus also constant until the firm reaches its maximum capacity. At this point the marginal cost has no definite value and the price of the product is determined by the condition that output cannot be increased.

2. Imagine that in an industry a short-period equilibrium of the price system has been reached, and that no firm works up to capacity. The average prime costs of the relevant products are $a_1, a_2 \ldots a_n$. The firms fix the prices of their products, taking into consideration the mobility of customers (market imperfection) and the influence of their own prices on those of their rivals (oligopoly). Each firm is satisfied that the price p_k fixed is more advantageous than a higher or a lower level.

Imagine now that a fall in material prices and wage costs reduces all average prime costs $a_1, a_2 \ldots a_n$ in the same proportion. It will be seen that this creates for entrepreneurs an inducement to cut their prices. For the fall of average costs $a_1, a_2 \ldots a_n$ with unchanged prices $p_1, p_2 \ldots p_n$ increases the profit + overheads margins $p_k - a_k$ (we shall call them gross margins) in relation to prices p_k, and thus a cut of the price p_k by a certain percentage means a smaller percentage cut of $p_k - a_k$ than in the initial position. Consequently, if the firms stick to their previous views about what are the expected percentage increases in their sales caused by a percentage cut in prices, they must consider it profitable to reduce them. Now as long as $\frac{p_k - a_k}{p_k}$ remain greater than in the initial position the price fall goes on. For $p_k - a_k$ is then less affected by a given percentage cut in prices than in the initial position and, consequently, the state of affairs is more favourable for price cutting than it was before the fall of average prime costs. The price system returns to equilibrium when prices have fallen in the same proportion as average prime costs because at this point $\frac{p_k - a_k}{p_k}$ reach their initial level.[1]

[1] In terms of individual demand curves this process may be described as an iso-elastic downward shift of these curves reducing their ordinates in the proportion in which the unit prime costs have fallen.

It has been assumed throughout that the conditions of market imperfection and oligopoly were unchanged. This may, however, not be the case. Indeed, if, for instance, the market imperfection is due to transport costs and these remain unaltered while prime (production) costs decline, the fall in prices in relation to transport costs increases market imperfection. As a result prices will fall here *less* than proportionately to prime costs. For if they *did* fall proportionately to prime costs a given percentage rise in prices would increase the gross margin $p_k - a_k$ by the same percentage as in the initial position, while the expected fall in firms' sales would be smaller; consequently the firms would consider it profitable to raise prices. Thus the increased market imperfection caused by the rise in the relation of transport costs to prime costs is here reflected in the increase of percentage gross margins $\frac{p_k - a_k}{p_k}$.

3. It follows from the above argument that with a given relation of average costs within the industry, and on condition that no firm is working up to capacity, the percentage gross margins $\frac{p_k - a_k}{p_k}$ reflect the changes in the state of market imperfection and oligopoly.

Let us now form a weighted average μ of the percentage gross margins, using as weights the respective values of sales $Q_k p_k$. We thus have

$$\mu = \frac{\Sigma Q_k p_k \frac{p_k - a_k}{p_k}}{\Sigma Q_k p_k} = \frac{\Sigma Q_k (p_k - a_k)}{\Sigma Q_k p_k}.$$

It may be seen at once that $\Sigma Q_k (p_k - a_k)$ represents aggregate profits + overheads of the industry, and $\Sigma Q_k p_k$ its aggregate value of sales. μ is thus equal to the ratio of profits + overheads to sales of the "industry."

We may, according to the above, say that μ reflects the changes in the degree of market imperfection and oligopoly of an industry provided: (i) the relations of average costs $a_1, a_2 \ldots a_n$ remain unchanged; (ii) no firm is working up to capacity. Thus, for instance, we may expect μ to fall when customers become more sensitive to price differences between suppliers (fall of market imperfection) and to rise when transport costs rise relative to prime production costs (rise in market imperfection, see preceding subsection). On the other hand, if technical progress reduces the average prime costs of all firms in the same proportion, it does not affect μ (unless it alters the conditions of market imperfection and oligopoly). For the argument of the preceding subsection applies whatever the cause of the fall in prime costs, provided it is uniform.

It has been stressed throughout the argument that the percentage gross margins $\frac{p_k - a_k}{p_k}$ reflect changes in the state of market imperfection and oligopoly only under the assumption that the ratio of prime costs $a_1, a_2 \ldots a_n$ remains unaltered. If this condition is not fulfilled $\frac{p_k - a_k}{p_k}$ may change, although nothing happens to alter the state of market imperfection and oligopoly. If, for instance, only the average cost a_1 falls, a_2, $a_3 \ldots a_n$ remaining unaltered, the price p_1 will be reduced for the same reason as in the case considered above when the fall in average prime costs is uniform; but in general the price p_1 will *not* fall here proportionately to a_1. For the fall of p_1 changes its relation to other prices $p_2, p_3 \ldots p_n$, and this in general affects the position with regard to the expected reaction of the sales Q_1 in response to a change in price p_1. Consequently the eventual level of $\frac{p_1 - a_1}{p_1}$ need not be the same as in the initial position, although no changes in conditions of market imperfection and oligopoly have occurred.[1]

[1] The theory of price formation when the average prime costs of firms of an "industry" do not change proportionately may be developed as follows: Let us start from a certain basic position where average prime costs are $a_1, a_2 \ldots a_n$ and prices $p_1, p_2 \ldots p_n$. Let us denote the cost and price indices in any position related to the basic position by $a'_1, a'_2 \ldots a'_n$ and $p'_1, p'_2 \ldots p'_n$ respectively. For the basic position we have thus $a'_1 = a'_2 \ldots = a'_n = 1$ and $p'_1 = p'_2 \ldots = p'_n = 1$.

It follows that the percentage gross margins $\frac{p_k - a_k}{p_k}$ are affected not only by changes in the state of market imperfection

Let us further denote the average of p'_k weighted according to the values of firms' sales in the basic position by $\bar{p}'$.

In accordance with the argument in the text it may be assumed that, with a given state of market imperfection and oligopoly, p'_k the price index of the firm k is a function of a'_k and $\bar{p}'$. As a first approximation we shall assume, moreover, that it is a linear function over the relevant range of changes of a'_k and $\bar{p}$, and thus we have

$$p'_k = \alpha_k a'_k + \beta_k \bar{p}' + \gamma_k. \qquad \text{(i)}$$

If prime costs of all firms change in the same proportion we have $a'_k = \bar{a}'$, and it follows from the text that with a given state of market imperfection and oligopoly $p'_k = \bar{p}' = \bar{a}'$ because then all prices change in the same proportion as prime costs. It follows for this case from the above equation (i)

$$\bar{a}' = \alpha_k \bar{a}' + \beta_k \bar{a}' + \gamma_k$$

whatever the value of $\bar{a}'$, which means that provided the state of market imperfection and oligopoly does not alter,

$$\gamma_k = 0 \text{ and } \alpha_k + \beta_k = 1.$$

Consequently the equation for p'_k may be written

$$p'_k = \alpha_k a'_k + (1 - \alpha_k)\bar{p}'. \qquad \text{(ii)}$$

Imagine now that a'_k increases while prime costs and prices of all other firms remain unchanged; it is then plausible to assume that p'_k increases, but in a lesser proportion than a'_k. As all prices but p'_k are assumed to be unchanged, p'_k increases in a higher proportion than $\bar{p}'$. Such a state of affairs, i.e. that p'_k increases less than a'_k but more than $\bar{p}'$, is compatible with the equation (ii) only if $a_k > 0$ and $1 - \alpha_k > 0$. It follows

$$0 < \alpha_k < 1. \qquad \text{(iii)}$$

Let us now form an average weighted according to the values of firms' sales in the basic position of both sides of equations (ii) for all firms. We obtain

$$\bar{p}' = \overline{\alpha a'} + (1 - \bar{\alpha})\bar{p}' \qquad \text{(iv)}$$

where $\overline{\alpha a'}$ is the weighted average of $\alpha_k a'_k$ and $\bar{\alpha}$ the weighted average of α. Hence we obtain the formula

$$\bar{p}' = \frac{\overline{\alpha a'}}{\bar{\alpha}}. \qquad \text{(iv')}$$

After substituting this value of $\bar{p}'$ into equation (ii) we have

$$p'_k = \alpha_k a'_k + (1 - \alpha_k)\frac{\overline{\alpha a'}}{\bar{\alpha}}. \qquad \text{(ii')}$$

In this way price indices of all firms are fully determined by the indices of the average prime costs a' and the coefficients α.

It may be shown that the price equilibrium determined by equations (iv') and

and oligopoly, but also by those in the relation between average prime costs $a_1, a_2 \ldots a_n$. However, the influence of these changes upon the *average* percentage gross margin μ is most probably relatively small.[1] As further, according to our definition of industry (cf. p. 9), the relative changes in average prime costs $a_1, a_2 \ldots a_n$ are kept in rather narrow limits, it is plausible to assume that in the movement of μ there are mainly reflected

(ii) is stable Indeed, imagine that prices deviate from the equilibrium values determined by (ii′) and as a result the average price index $\overline{p'}$ differs by Δ from the value determined by formula (iv′). It follows from the equations (ii) that this leads to price indices p'_k differing from the equilibrium level determined by the equations (ii′) by $(1 - \alpha_k)\Delta$; and from this results a new $\overline{p}'$ which differs from the equilibrium level by $(1 - \bar{\alpha})\Delta$. As according to equation (iii) $1 - \bar{\alpha} < 1$ the average price index $\overline{p'}$ will converge to its equilibrium level determined by equation (iv′)

[1] This may be corroborated by a transformation of equation (iv′) of the preceding footnote. From a known formula for the correlation coefficient it follows that

$$\overline{\alpha a'} = \bar{\alpha}\,\bar{a}' + r\sigma_\alpha\sigma_{a'}.$$

$\overline{\alpha a'}$ is the weighted average of $\alpha a'$; $\bar{\alpha}$ and $\bar{a}'$ are the weighted averages of α_k and a'_k respectively; r the coefficient of correlation between α_k and a'_k; σ_α and $\sigma_{a'}$ the standard deviations of α_k and a'_k respectively. By substituting this value of $\overline{\alpha a'}$ into equation (iv′) we obtain

$$\bar{p}' = \bar{a}' + r\frac{\sigma\alpha}{\bar{\alpha}}\sigma_{a'} \quad . \quad . \quad . \quad . \quad . \quad (v)$$

or

$$\frac{\bar{p}'}{\bar{a}'} = 1 + r\frac{\sigma_\alpha}{\bar{\alpha}}\frac{\sigma_{a'}}{\bar{a}'}. \quad . \quad . \quad . \quad . \quad . \quad (v')$$

Now there is no particular reason for a positive or negative correlation between a'_k which is the average cost index in relation to the basic position and the coefficient α_k; thus r is likely to be rather low. If it is equal to nought $\frac{\bar{p}'}{\bar{a}'} = 1$ and then the changes in the average price $\bar{p}'$ are independent of the relative changes of average prime costs a: the average price index $\bar{p}'$ is equal to the average prime cost index $\bar{a}'$.

In general, of course, r is not equal to zero. But it is likely to be lower in absolute value than, say, 0·30; further, even assuming a very wide dispersion in the coefficients α_k it is unlikely that $\frac{\sigma_\alpha}{\bar{\alpha}}$ would be higher than, say, 0·5. On these assumptions the absolute value of $r\frac{\sigma_\alpha}{\bar{\alpha}}\frac{\sigma_{a'}}{\bar{a}'} < 0{\cdot}15\frac{\sigma_{a'}}{\bar{a}'}$, and thus

$$1 - 0{\cdot}15\frac{\sigma_{a'}}{\bar{a}'} < \frac{\bar{p}'}{\bar{a}'} < 1 + 0{\cdot}15\frac{\sigma_{a'}}{\bar{a}'}.$$

changes in the degree of market imperfection and oligopoly. This, however, is still subject to the qualification that the firms do not work up to capacity.

4. Let us start from a position for which this condition is fulfilled and imagine that the effective demand for the products of the " industry " increases. As long as firms do not reach the point of full capacity the percentage gross margins remain unaltered unless the rise in demand has some effect upon the state of market imperfection and oligopoly.[1] If, however, the increase in demand continues, one firm after another will reach its maximum capacity beyond which it is unable to increase its output. It is obvious that if the demand for the firm's product rises while the supply is limited by the existing capacity, the prices charged by the firm will increase so as to bring into equilibrium the increased demand with the fixed supply—even though the average prime costs and the state of market imperfection and oligopoly are unaltered. This will result in the increase of the average percentage gross margin μ. We may thus conclude that in the movement of μ are mainly reflected changes in the degree of market imperfection and oligopoly and bottlenecks in the manufacturing of the products of the " industry," appearing as the demand for these products increases in relation to available capacities.

5. In all the above argument we have abstracted from selling costs and we must now allow for them. It may be assumed that the entrepreneur apportions a certain part of his selling costs to " investment or overhead selling costs " (a considerable part of advertisement is probably treated in this way) and the rest to " prime selling costs." The first may be included in overheads and profits while the second plays in price formation a rôle similar to prime production costs.

The entrepreneur may now be imagined to fix his price on the assumption that it is profitable for him to spend a certain percentage of the proceeds σ on prime selling costs. σ may be called the rate of prime selling costs. It is easy to see that in

[1] In terms of individual demand curves this means an iso-elastic shift of these curves to the right.

our argument on pages 10-11, attempting to establish that (with qualifications stated there) in the movement of $\frac{p_k - a_k}{p_k}$ are reflected changes in the state of market imperfection and oligopoly, $\frac{p_k - a_k}{p_k}$ must now be replaced by $\frac{p_k - a_k}{p_k} - \sigma$. It follows that if selling costs are allowed for, the average percentage gross margin μ reflects not only the changes in the degree of market imperfection and oligopoly and the bottlenecks in available capacities, but also changes in the rates of prime selling costs.

To summarise: in the movement of the average percentage gross margin μ are mainly reflected changes in the degree of market imperfection and oligopoly, changes in the rates of prime selling costs, and bottlenecks in available manufacturing capacities. (To a minor degree μ is influenced also by changes in the relation of prime production costs $a_1, a_2 \ldots a_n$ within the "industry.")

6. As shown on page 11, the ratio of profits + overheads to proceeds is equal to the average percentage gross margin μ. It is easy to see that μ determines the distribution of the net output (or value added) between wages on the one hand and profits + overheads on the other, if in addition the ratio of the cost of materials to that of wages is given. If we denote the wage bill by W and the ratio of the material bill to the wage bill by m, the aggregate prime costs are $(1 + m)W$. As the ratio of overheads + profits to proceeds $= \mu$, the ratio of overheads + profits to prime costs $= \frac{\mu}{1 - \mu}$. It follows that overheads + profits $= \frac{\mu}{1 - \mu}(1 + m)W$. Further, the net output (or value added) is equal to the sum of overheads + profits and the wage bill, and thus we have

$$\text{net output} = \frac{\mu}{1 - \mu}(1 + m)W + W.$$

Thus the relative share of wages w in the net output is

$$w = \frac{W}{\frac{\mu}{1-\mu}(1+m)W + W} = \frac{1-\mu}{1+\mu m}.$$

It may be seen at once that w is a diminishing function of both μ and m. That means that if, e.g., a change in the state of imperfect competition and oligopoly, in the rates of prime selling costs or in the "bottleneck factors" presses down the ratio of overheads + profits to proceeds μ, it tends to increase the relative share of wages in the net output w. But apart from this w depends on the ratio of material costs to wage costs m: it falls when the cost of materials rises in relation to that of wages and conversely.

Changes in the Percentage Gross Margin of an Industry

1. It has been shown above that changes in the average percentage gross margin of an "industry," i.e. of the ratio of its overheads + profits to its proceeds μ, are determined chiefly by changes in the state of market imperfection and oligopoly, changes in the rate of prime selling costs, and by the bottleneck factors. It is proposed to examine in this section how μ is affected through these channels by the business cycle and the long-run economic development. We shall deal first with the business cycle.

2. If market imperfection depends partly on transport costs, and the average prime costs a_k fall while transport costs remain unchanged or fall in a lesser proportion, the market imperfection and consequently the average percentage gross margin μ increases.[1]

Now it is a rather frequent case that prime production costs fall more strongly than transport costs in the slump. Thus under this influence μ will tend to rise in the slump and to fall in the boom.

There exists, however, a reason for cyclical changes in market imperfection, and thus in μ in the opposite direction, which has been indicated by Mr. Harrod. He calls attention to the fact

[1] Cf. p. 11.

that buyers are more careful in comparing prices charged by various sellers in the slump than in the boom. This would tend to cause a fall in market imperfection and the gross profit percentage margin μ in the slump and its rise in the boom. It should be added perhaps that if the slump is deep the market imperfection is likely to be relatively low in the subsequent recovery also, because the habit of more careful buying acquired during depression may persist for a certain time.

Probably more important than the effect of cyclical changes in market imperfection upon μ is the influence of " tacit agreements " in a deep slump which may be classified as changes in the degree of oligopoly.

Imagine a deep slump in which the average prime costs in an " industry " have fallen considerably. If the percentage margins were unchanged there would be an even stronger fall of what is left for overheads and profits of a single producer because output is reduced as well. The resulting deterioration in his financial position induces him to increase his percentage gross margin in the hope that other producers will act likewise. If they do not he is lost, but so he would be if he reduced his prices proportionately to average prime costs. If such is the prevailing attitude, a " tacit agreement " is established and μ is higher than it otherwise would be.

It is important to note that the rise in a percentage gross margin does not mean here a high measure of profit because it only compensates partly for the fall in average prime costs and output. The existing firms need not be afraid therefore that new enterprises will emerge; and even many " high cost producers " must close down in spite of the " tacit agreement."

When the slump is over, the degree of oligopoly will fall for various reasons. First, the rise in average prime costs and output removes the very basis of the tacit agreement, the more so that in the meantime a certain cut in " overhead expenditure " has probably been achieved; second, because of the fear of newcomers, and even more so to prevent the reopening of establishments closed down in the slump.

On the basis of the above analysis it seems probable that in a cycle showing no deep and prolonged slumps the changes of μ caused by fluctuations in the state of market imperfection and oligopoly or in prime selling costs are not likely to be important.

The position will be different in a deep and prolonged slump and also in the subsequent recovery. The most important factor in the slump is likely to be then the "tacit agreement" and thus μ may rise significantly. On the other hand, in the subsequent recovery μ is likely to fall below what would be its level after a moderate slump. Two factors will contribute to it: the "careful buying" which persists for a certain time after a deep and prolonged slump, and the tendency of the entrepreneurs to prevent reopening of numerous establishments closed down in the slump.

3. We have yet to deal with the influence upon the percentage gross margin of the "bottleneck factors" which come into the picture when the volume of sales of an "industry" increases in relation to its capacity beyond a certain point. The resulting rise in the percentage gross margin is likely to be significant only close to the top of the boom when the utilization of equipment is high. And in the light of the data we give in the next section it does not seem usually important even then for manufacturing industry as a whole. (It must be noted, however, that these data relate to the twentieth century only.)

It looks as if the influence of bottlenecks in manufacturing in a modern capitalist society becomes predominant only in "abnormal" times, during wars or after-war periods. In such periods total employment, and, consequently, the wage bill, expressed in terms of wage units, remains unaltered or even increases. At the same time the production of consumption goods is strongly curtailed, chiefly owing to the scarcity of raw materials and labour in the industries concerned. As a result, if the consumption of non-wage earners is not reduced sufficiently by increased propensity to save, taxation, and rationing to offset this divergency, prices will rise in relation to wage rates, i.e. the real wage rate will fall. This may happen in two ways: by the increase in prices of raw materials relative to wage rates and by the rise in the percentage gross margins of the manufactured products. Usually both these changes go hand in hand, although, if prices of raw materials are controlled and they are distributed among enterprises by a quota system, the equilibrium between demand for and supply of consumption goods is achieved only by the rise in percentage gross margins. The rise in money wage rates enforced by the workers who try to restore the " old " real wages cannot remedy the situation, and results only in a new rise in prices; for at the root of the trouble lies the fall in the ratio of production of consumption goods to total employment. It is this that is the actual cause of the " vicious spiral."

The position in an " ordinary " boom is different in that bottlenecks in plant and labour are not very significant. True, the supply of basic raw materials is sometimes inelastic and their prices increase considerably in relation to wage rates. This, however, results only in a rather slight increase in the prices of finished goods relative to wage rates because, usually, the basic raw materials are a much smaller cost item than wages. And even this tendency of real wages to fall is often counterbalanced (1) by the institutional rigidity of certain items in the cost of living (rents, bus and railway fares, etc.), which often causes their fall relative to wage rates when these increase, and (2) by technical progress which reduces the labour cost per unit of product relative to wage rates. As a result the fall in real wage rates in an " ordinary " recovery is small if any, and does not initiate, therefore, a " vicious spiral."

4. We shall now consider briefly the influence of long-run economic development upon the percentage gross margin μ.

As to the imperfection of the market, it will tend to diminish as a result of the fall of transport costs in relation to prime production costs, standardization of goods, spreading of commodity exchanges, etc.; the higher standard of living may tend to cause less careful buying (the " Harrodian factor "), but this will probably be fully offset by a higher degree of knowledge and more free time for buying; finally, at a certain late stage of capitalist development the expansion of advertisement may in many cases create an " artificial " market imperfection. With regard to oligopoly, the progressive concentration of industry is likely to enhance its degree. The rates of prime selling cost are also likely to rise in the long run, particularly at a certain late stage of capitalist development.

As to the influence of "bottleneck factors," it seems that at least in the twentieth century they are effective in "normal times" only close to the top of the boom and even then are not very significant for manufacturing industry as a whole. Thus "bottleneck factors" are probably not important in the long-run analysis of recent economic developments. This does not, however, exclude a possibility of significant long-run changes in μ caused by these factors.[1]

On balance it is impossible to say *a priori* how μ changes in the long run. But it follows clearly from the above that (if we abstract from bottleneck factors) it is more likely to rise in the later than in the earlier stage of capitalist development.

Application to the U.S.A. Manufacturing Industry

1. Apart from the causes of changes in the percentage gross margin of an "industry" discussed in the preceding section, there will be a variety of other factors influencing it. However, the above analysis gives a more or less comprehensive list of important factors which affect the gross profit percentage margins of *all* industries simultaneously as a result of the business cycle or long-run economic development. If we consider the percentage gross margin of the manufacturing industry as a whole (i.e. the ratio of its aggregate overheads + profits to its aggregate proceeds), it is these influences that will be most important while particular factors affecting percentage gross margins of thousands of industries will most probably cancel out. We therefore apply the results of the preceding discussion to the U.S.A. manufacturing industry as a whole.

Two problems arise here, however. The first depends on the existence of industries which are dominated by one firm or a cartel. To such a case our analysis, which was concerned with

[1] Cf. p. 30, below.

an industry working in conditions of imperfect competition and oligopoly, does not apply. It may be said, however, (i) that the predominant form of a manufacturing industry *is* that working under conditions of imperfect competition and oligopoly, (ii) that even " pure monopolists " must count with potential outsiders and this makes their behaviour broadly similar to that of oligopolies. It is therefore likely that the existence of cartels, etc., does not invalidate the application of the apparatus built up above for the examination of the percentage gross margin of the U.S.A. manufacturing industry as a whole.

The second difficulty is that changes in the ratio of aggregate overheads + profits of manufacturing industry to its aggregate proceeds are influenced not only by changes in such ratios of the particular industries but also by changes in the proportions of proceeds of these industries ; indeed μ may have different values for various industries and thus, for instance, the increased weight for industries with high μ may increase the ratio of overheads + profits to proceeds for the manufacturing industry as a whole although such ratios for the component industries have not changed. As far, however, as it could be ascertained by considering the changes of μ for industrial groups, this influence upon μ of the U.S.A. manufacturing industry as a whole was of no importance.

2. We give below the ratio of overheads + profits of the U.S.A. manufacturing industry to its proceeds in the period 1899-1937, calculated from the Census of Manufactures.[1]

[1] As given in the *Statistical Abstract of the United States*, 1939 To make, however, the figures for various years comparable, the following adjustments had to be made : (i) Prior to 1931 the tax on tobacco manufactures has been deducted from overheads + profits, where it was included by the Census (ii) Prior to 1935 the cost of work given out has been subtracted from overheads + profits, where it was included by the Census. Up to 1923 this has been done according to Census data ; from then onwards the percentage of the cost of work given out in terms of total prime costs has been assumed the same as in 1923. (iii) In 1929, 1931 and 1933, in which years the work and shop supplies were included by the Census in overheads + profits as opposed to other years, a corresponding correction has been introduced In 1904 the work and shop supplies were—according to the Census data—0·7 per cent. of total prime costs. In accordance with the rise of the value of capital equipment taken from Professor Douglas, *The Theory of*

TABLE I

The Percentage Gross Margin μ in the U.S.A. Manufacturing Industry

	%		%		%
1899	23·1	1919	22 4	1929	26·7
1904	23 3	1921	21 9	1931	28·1
1909	23·3	1923	23 2	1933	27 9
1914	22 5	1925	24 2	1935	25 0
		1927	25 3	1937	24 8

Figure 1 represents the time curve of μ. It may be seen at once that in the period 1899-1929 all points of it lie on a smooth

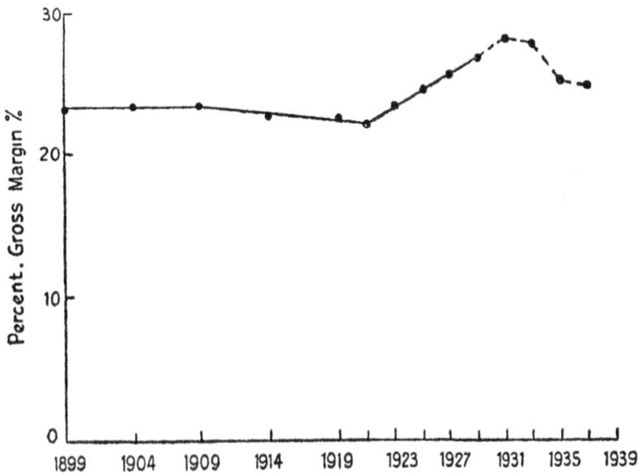

FIG. 1.—Percentage Gross Margin of U.S. Manufacturing Industry, 1899-1937.

curve formed by three straight lines: 1899-1909, 1909-21, and 1921-29. This may be interpreted as showing the absence of any business cycle effects upon μ, inclusive of the influence of "bottleneck factors." The long-period trend of μ, as represented by the curve 1899-1909-21-29 shows stability of μ in the period 1899-1909 and a slow fall in 1909-21. This may be accounted for as a balance between conflicting tendencies, described in the last section (pp. 20-21) We see then a rather

Wages, as compared with the value of prime costs, this percentage has been assumed 1 per cent for the years 1929, 1931 and 1933. (iv) The change in the scope of the Census in 1914 is accounted for by linking up the series.

sharp rise in μ in the period 1921-29. This is probably caused by what may be called a "commercial revolution" which took place in that period. The violent development of modern selling methods (advertisement, "invention" of new products, etc.) caused both an increase in prime selling costs and created an "artificial" market imperfection.

The changes of μ in the period 1929-37 show quite a different pattern from those in the period 1899-1929. While cyclical changes were not noticeable in the latter period, after 1929 we see a strong increase in μ in the slump (1931, 1933) and a still stronger fall in the subsequent recovery (1935, 1937). This may be explained by the effects of a deep and prolonged slump as described in the preceding section: "tacit agreement" in the slump, and in the recovery its reversal strengthened by the tendency to prevent the reopening of establishments closed down in the slump and by the habit of "careful buying" persisting for a certain time as an after-effect of the slump.

In this connection it is interesting to notice that changes in the percentage gross margins μ (i.e. the ratios of overheads + profits to proceeds) in the wholesale and retail trade in the U.S.A. show a similar pattern as in manufacturing in the period 1929-37.

TABLE II

The Percentage Gross Margin μ in Manufacturing Industry, Wholesale Trade, and Retail Trade in the U.S.A.

Year.	Manufacturing. Industry.[1]	Wholesale Trade.[2]	Retail Trade.[2]
	%	%	%
1929	26 7	14·3	29·6
1931	28·1	15·0	30 9
1933	27·9	15 2	32·8
1935	25 0	12·5	29 0
1937	24 8	12 9	28·7

[1] Taken from Table I.

[2] Difference between sales and purchase costs of goods sold expressed as a percentage of sales. Thus prime costs are here identified with purchase costs of goods, which is approximately correct. Source, B. M. Fowler and W. H. Shaw, "Distributive Costs of Consumption Goods," *Survey of Current Business*, July 1942. The figures relate to wholesale and retail trade in consumption goods only.

The above cannot, of course, provide a full proof of the correctness of our theory. It shows only that this can supply a plausible interpretation of changes in pricing in the U.S.A. manufacturing industries (and wholesale and retail trade in that country in the period 1929-37). It will therefore be useful to examine to what extent the alternative theories of price formation are capable of explaining the phenomena in question.

3. We may distinguish two theories of price formation alternative to ours: (i) the perfect competition theory, (ii) the "full cost" theory.

The supporters of the perfect competition theory do not deny in fact the existence of market imperfection and oligopoly. But they consider them to be factors of minor importance and thus maintain that the assumption of perfect competition is justified to the first approximation.[1]

One of the important corollaries of the free competition theory is that the relative share of wages in the value added (net output) falls in the boom and rises in the slump. Indeed, price being equal to short-period marginal costs, the average value added (i.e. price — average cost of materials) is approximately equal to the marginal wage cost, since it may be assumed that the average cost of materials is independent of the firm's output and the marginal cost of salaries and depreciation is small. Further, under perfect competition the relevant branch of the marginal wage cost curve is upward sloping; also the average wage cost increases from a point onwards but (unless the shape of its curve is very peculiar) it increases in a smaller proportion than the marginal wage cost; so that the ratio of average to marginal wage cost falls when the utilization of plant increases. It follows

[1] Cf., for instance, J. R. Hicks, *Value and Capital:* "If we can suppose that the percentages by which prices exceed marginal costs are neither very large nor very variable, and if we can suppose (what is largely the consequence of the first assumption) that *marginal* costs do generally increase with output at the point of equilibrium (diminishing marginal costs being rare), then the laws of an economic system, working under perfect competition, will not be appreciably varied in a system which contains widespread elements of monopoly" (p. 84). The only justification of these assumptions is that "a universal adoption of the assumption of monopoly must have very destructive consequences for economic theory" (p. 83).

directly that the relative share of wages in the value added falls in the boom when the utilization of the plant increases, and rises in the slump when the utilization of the plant diminishes. This consequence of free competition theory may be tested by statistical data. In Table III we give the relative share of wages w in the value added for the U.S.A. manufacturing industry in the period 1919-37.[1]

TABLE III

The Relative Share of Wages w *in the Value Added by the U.S.A. Manufacturing Industry*

	%		%
1919	41·8	1929	37·5
1921	45·0	1931	37·4
1923	42·9	1933	36 7
1925	40·4	1935	39 4
1927	39·8	1937	40·2

The only instance when the theory accords with fact is the slump year 1921, when the relative share of wages in the value added is higher than in 1919 and 1923. It falls, however, after 1923 in 1925 and 1927, although in both these years the degree of utilization of equipment was definitely lower than in 1923. (1923 was the year of highest degree of utilization in the period 1921-37.) Further, in the slump years 1931 and 1933 w remains at the level of the boom year 1929 and rises in the subsequent recovery in 1935 and 1937. Thus the facts are rather against the perfect competition theory.

It should be added that changes in the relative share of wages in the value added w are fully determined by those in the gross profit percentage margin μ and the ratio of the material bill to the wage bill m (see p. 17). Thus if the above interpretation (pp. 23-24) of changes in μ in the U.S.A. manufacturing in terms of our theory is accepted, this theory provides *eo ipso* an explanation for changes in w.

[1] Based on the data of " Census of Manufactures," as given in the *Statistical Abstract of the U.S.A.*, 1939, with the same adjustments as described in the footnote to p. 22. The comparable figures for the period 1899-1914 are:

1899	42·7	1909	41·0
1904	42·5	1914	42·1

4. The full cost theory in its familiar version maintains that the firm fixes its price by adding to average prime cost the overheads per unit of actual output or per unit of " standard " output (i.e. per unit of output corresponding to what is considered reasonably full employment of firms' plant) and " something " for profit. This statement has no precise theoretical meaning because the amount that is added for profit makes quite a lot of difference to the price and more still to the gross margin.

The full cost theory has been actually derived from the replies of entrepreneurs to the inquiries about their pricing methods.[1] But it is not unlikely that the procedure described by them is not the actual process of fixing prices but only a check applied to prices fixed in another way to see whether they make any net profit. Indeed, if the " something " which is the difference between price and the full cost calculated per unit of actual output is positive the firm knows that it makes a net profit on the product in question. If overheads are calculated per unit of " standard " output the positive difference means that losses if any are due to the fall in output only, and if the slump is not too deep and prolonged they have no importance from a longer point of view; while if the slump *is* deep and prolonged the " standard " output is being appropriately reduced. Both in the case of calculation with actual and with " standard " output the calculator seems not so much to fix the price as to translate the price fixed by other considerations into the " full cost language." In a modern cotton spinning mill the manager described once to me at great length the work of their calculating department. To my question, however, how the results are used to fix the prices, he replied: " Oh, the prices are fixed by the market."

Nevertheless, in certain circumstances the calculator's analysis may have some bearing upon fixing of prices. In a deep slump it helps to realize the precarious position of the firm and thereby it initiates the attempts to increase the percentage gross margin, and so may lead to the establishment of a " tacit agreement."

[1] See, for instance, R. L. Hall and C. J. Hitch, " Price Theory and Business Behaviour," *Oxford Economic Papers*, May 1939.

Percentage Gross Margin and Capital Intensity

1. We have shown in the preceding sections that both short-term and long-term changes in the ratio of overheads + profits to proceeds μ are determined chiefly by changes in the state of market imperfection and oligopoly by changes in the rates of prime selling costs, and by "bottleneck factors." True, μ is influenced also by relative changes in the average prime costs as between firms, but this influence is likely to be not very important. It follows that if in the long run the state of market imperfection and oligopoly and the rates of prime selling costs remain stable and "bottleneck factors" do not come into the picture, the ratio of profits + overheads to proceeds μ is more or less constant.

This is in contradiction with the widely accepted view that in the long run the relative share of overheads and profits in the price increases owing to the rising capital intensity of production. We must therefore analyse the basis of this contention and then examine also what effect the increase of capital intensity has upon the percentage gross margin according to our theory.

2. The argument in favour of μ rising with capital intensity of production runs roughly as follows. As a result of technical progress more capital is used per unit of output, and therefore the value of capital (at reproduction prices) rises relatively to the value of production. Now the rate of depreciation being stable or increasing, and the rate of profit more or less stable, profit + depreciation, must rise in relation to the value of production. The salary bill usually rises with capital intensity in relation to wage bill + material bill. Hence the relative share of overheads +profits in the value of production μ must be expected to increase. Two objections may be raised, however, against this argument.

First, the assumption that the rate of profit in the long run is rather stable is, in fact, quite arbitrary. It is based on the idea that the rate of profit in long periods tends to be equal to the long-term rate of interest + "normal profit" and that both these components change rather slowly. But this long period equilibrium approach is not justified because the long-run economic development is a complicated dynamic process, and the rate of profit may very well fall in the long run, although the long-term rate of interest remains constant (or even increases).[1] Thus the ratio of overheads + profits to proceeds may remain constant in spite of the fall of the value of production in relation to the value of capital. A striking example of such a situation is provided by the developments in the U.S.A. manufacturing industry in the period 1899-1914:

TABLE IV

The Ratio of the Value of Production to the Value of Capital and the Percentage Gross Margin in the U.S.A. Manufacturing Industry

Year.	(1) Reproduction Cost of Fixed Capital.[2]	(2) Value of Products [3]	(3) Ratio (2):(1).	(4) Long-Term Rate of Interest.[4]	(5) Percentage Gross Margin μ.[5]
	(1899 = 100)			%	%
1899	100	100	100	3·1	23·1
1904	137	130	95	3·5	23·3
1909	216	182	84	3·6	23·3
1914	280	212	76	4·0	22·5

There is, however, still another objection against the argument on which the statement is based that the percentage gross margin μ increases with capital intensity of production. The rise in the latter means that capital contained in equipment increases relative to its maximum productive capacity. The ratio of actual output to capital depends in addition on the degree of

[1] The determinants of the rate of profit are discussed below in the essay "A Theory of Profits."

[2] Obtained by multiplying the index of real fixed capital by the price index of investment goods. Both series are taken from Professor Douglas, *The Theory of Wages*, p. 121. Douglas' series extends to 1922, but his post-war figures are not quite reliable because he did not take into account the possible revaluation of capital by firms in connection with the "price revolution." I am indebted for this point to Mr. E. Rothbarth.

[3] Taken from the "Census of Manufactures" (the changes in the scope of the Census in 1914 are accounted for by linking up the series).

[4] Douglas, *op. cit.*, p. 469.

[5] Cf. p. 23.

2

utilization of equipment, i.e. the ratio of actual output to maximum capacity. If, therefore, the rise in capital intensity is accompanied by an increase in the degree of utilization, the value of production does not necessarily fall relative to the value of capital.

It follows that rising capital intensity, even if the rate of profit remains stable, is compatible with a constant percentage gross margin μ : the rise in the degree of utilization of equipment may offset the influence of the increase in capital intensity. It should be noticed, however, that if this increase lasts for a certain time there will be reached a point of the degree of utilization where " bottleneck factors " appear and then μ starts to rise.

We may thus formulate the interrelation between μ and the rise in capital intensity according to our theory as follows : Let us start from a situation where " bottleneck factors " are absent, and thus μ is determined by the state of market imperfection and oligopoly (and by the rates of prime selling costs). If there is a rise in capital intensity of production and the degree of utilization does not increase, the rate of profit falls, while the percentage gross margin is stable.[1] If, however, the degree of utilization increases sufficiently to offset the influence of increased capital intensity, the rate of profit can be maintained ; and if the rise in the utilization of equipment has not brought " bottleneck factors " into the picture the percentage gross margin is also stable here. But if this development—rising intensity of capital, stable rate of profit, rising utilization of equipment—continues for some time, a point will be reached where bottlenecks do appear. It is only after this stage has been reached that increasing capital intensity must cause either a fall of the rate of profit or a rise in the percentage gross margin.

3. On page 17 we have deduced the following formula for the relative share of wages in the value added by manufacturing :

$$w = \frac{1 - \mu}{1 + \mu m}$$

[1] This situation corresponds roughly to that assumed by Marx in his law of the falling rate of profit.

where μ is the percentage gross margin and m the ratio of the material bill to the wage bill. Now, as long as " bottleneck factors " do not come into the picture changes in μ depend chiefly on changes in the state of market imperfection and oligopoly (and in the rates of prime selling costs). Thus if these determinants are unchanged technical progress can affect w only by influencing the ratio of the material bill to the wage bill. A fall in the wage cost, for instance, in relation to the raw material cost will raise m and thus reduce the relative share of wages in the value added. But if technical progress reduces in the same proportion the cost of labour and the prices of raw materials, w remains unchanged—provided that " bottleneck factors " do not cause any change in μ.

2. THE SHORT-TERM AND THE LONG-TERM RATE OF INTEREST

The Short-Term Rate

1. Before we discuss the problem of the formation of the short-term rate of interest it is necessary to establish first a functional connection between the short-term rate of interest and the velocity of cash circulation. By the latter we mean the ratio of turnover, T, to the stock of cash (current accounts or notes), M. It is clear that the smaller, with a given turnover, is the amount of cash possessed, say, by a firm, the greater the convenience derived from the marginal unit of cash in managing transactions. Moreover, after cash holding is reduced to a certain level, its further curtailment involves a very strongly rising marginal inconvenience. On the other hand, if cash is very plentiful with a given turnover, the marginal convenience falls to nought and remains at this level if the amount of cash, M, increases further. The marginal convenience of holding cash, therefore, is an increasing function of the velocity of circulation, T/M, and may be represented by a J curve.

The short-term rate of interest is closely connected with the marginal convenience of holding cash. Indeed, if the short-term rate is higher than this marginal convenience, there is an inducement for lending additional cash; if the short-term rate is lower, it becomes profitable to withdraw from short-term assets and acquire cash. Thus equilibrium is reached when the short-term rate of interest is equal to the marginal convenience of holding cash.

The above requires a certain qualification. The operation of short-term lending as such involves some costs and inconveniences, or "investment costs." The short-term rate is thus equal to the sum of the marginal convenience of holding cash + "investment costs." Thus when the marginal convenience of cash holding falls to nought the short-term rate is equal to investment costs. As a result we may say that *a priori* grounds exist for postulating a connection between the short-term rate and the velocity of circulation of the shape represented by the curve in Figure 2.[1] That this curve must not be assumed to be absolutely stationary through time is obvious. Habits of cash holding, etc., may change in the long run, and a financial panic may cause

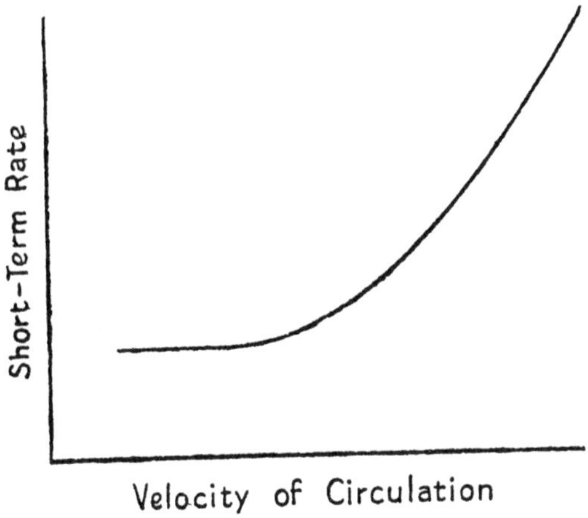

FIG. 2.—Hypothetical Relationship between Velocity of Circulation and the Short-Term Rate of Interest.

higher requirements for cash at the same turnover and the same short-term rate; this will be reflected in a shift of the curve.

2. We shall now try to verify statistically the relationship under consideration. Since 1930 the London Clearing Banks have published figures of turnover (debit entries to current accounts). The ratio of these figures to current accounts may

[1] There arises here the problem whether in this context the short-term rate of interest must be understood gross or net of income tax. If the marginal inconvenience of curtailment of the cash holding is supposed by a manager to be finally reflected in a corresponding reduction of profits, then it is the interest gross of tax which should be taken into account. This seems likely to be the case. However, the subsequent empirical inquiry which relates to the U.K. in the period 1930-38 is independent of this assumption because the rate of income tax was fairly stable over that period.

seem to be just what we need for our investigation, but unfortunately the case is not so simple.

The turnover consists of two parts, each of a very different character: of financial and of non-financial transactions. For 1930 the latter were estimated to have constituted only 15 per cent of the total turnover.[1] On the other hand, the financial current accounts are unlikely to be more than one-third of the total.[2] This disproportion reflects the obvious fact of the much greater velocity of circulation of financial, compared with non-financial, accounts. As a result changes in the velocity of circulation of financial accounts are reflected in the ratio of turnover to current accounts too heavily in relation to the share of financial accounts in the latter. This defect can be remedied in the following way. We divide the turnover into the non-financial and financial components; we reduce the financial component in a proportion which brings its ratio to financial accounts in the base year 1930 to the level of the ratio of the non-financial component to non-financial accounts, i.e. to the level of the non-financial velocity of circulation. Finally, we add the "reduced financial component" to the non-financial component and divide the sum by total current accounts. This ratio may be considered an adequate index of changes in the velocity of circulation.

The calculation is described in detail in my paper on "The Short-Term Rate of Interest and the Velocity of Circulation."[3] The results obtained there[4] are given in Table V and plotted in Figure 3.

As we see, all points except 1931 lie around a curve of a shape which we deduced on *a priori* grounds in the preceding paragraph. Point 1931 is considerably above the curve. This is explained by the financial crisis in the second half of that year which caused

[1] E. H. Phelps Brown and G. L. S. Shackle, *Statistics of Monetary Circulation in England and Wales, 1919-1937* (Royal Economic Society, Memorandum No. 74), p. 28.

[2] *Ibid*, p. 33.

[3] *Review of Economic Statistics*, May 1941.

[4] Slightly revised; allowance having been made for: (1) a change in the working practice of Town Clearings in November 1932 which increased the volume of total clearings by about 2 per cent; (2) a change in the scope of current accounts in January 1938 which caused an increase by about 2 per cent.

TABLE V

Index of Velocity of Circulation and Rate on Treasury Bills

Year	Velocity of Circulation (1930 = 100).	Rate on Treasury Bills (%).
1930	100	2·48
1931	95	3·59
1932	93	1·49
1933	83	0·59
1934	88	0·73
1935	85	0·55
1936	82	0·58
1937	84	0·56
1938	80	0·61

an upward shift of the curve considered, i.e. increased the amount of cash required at a given turnover and a given short-term rate

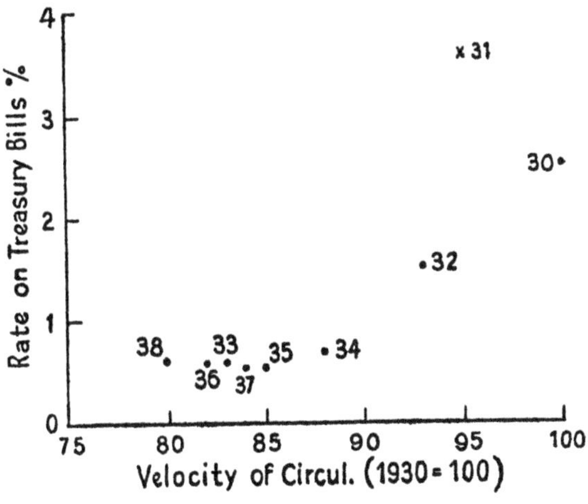

FIG. 3.—Velocity of Circulation and Rate on Treasury Bills, 1930-38.

of interest.[1] The period examined is rather short, and further inquiries are necessary to confirm the theory.

[1] The point for the year 1938 is also slightly raised by the increase of the short-term rate in the autumn, due to political events.

3. The relation examined above may be written

$$T/M = V(\rho) \quad . \quad . \quad . \quad . \quad (1)$$

where T is the money volume of transactions (turnover), M the stock of cash and $V(\rho)$ the velocity of circulation, being an increasing function of the short-term rate of interest ρ. Formula (1) may also be written

$$M\,V(\rho) = T. \quad . \quad . \quad . \quad (1a)$$

In this form it is nothing else but the quantity of money equation.[1] The significance of it is, however, quite different here than in the quantity theory of money. It shows simply that with a *given* volume of transactions T an increase in the supply of cash M by the banking system causes a fall in the short-term rate of interest. One can, of course, argue that this fall tends to increase the rate of investment, and thus through this channel it influences T. But, as we shall see in the following sections of this essay, changes in the short-term rate have a rather small immediate effect upon the long-term rate; and it is chiefly the latter which is relevant for investment activity. Thus, only after the new level of the short-term rate of interest has been maintained for a rather prolonged time will it affect appreciably the rate of investment. Therefore the *immediate* influence of the increase in the supply of cash will be not to raise the money volume of transactions but to reduce the velocity of circulation and the short-term rate of interest.

4. It is still interesting to discuss the mechanism of the increase in the supply of current accounts by the banking system. Imagine that banks decide to reduce their cash ratio (the ratio of the amount of their notes and accounts in the Central Bank to deposits, i.e. current and deposit accounts) and buy bills. Let us first assume that the rate on deposit accounts follows the discount rate. Thus when the discount rate starts to fall there will be no inducement to sell bills and open deposit accounts instead. The rate of discount must consequently fall to such a level at

[1] T is the *money* volume of transactions and thus stands for PT in the Fisher equation.

which people will be prepared to add to their current accounts the amount for which the banks buy bills. With a given turnover T_0 this level of the short-term rate may be obtained easily by means of formula (1*a*). Indeed, if the initial state of current accounts is M_0 and the banks bought bills for the amount B, then

$$(M_0 + B)V(\rho) = T_0.$$

If the rate on deposit accounts remains unchanged, the process is more complicated. For a fall in the discount rate then induces some people to sell bills and acquire deposit accounts. The fall in the discount rate is therefore smaller than in the case previously considered: it will fall to the level at which the sum of the increases in current *and* deposit accounts is equal to the amount B of bills bought by the banks.

The Short-Term Rate and the Long-Term Rate

1. It has been shown in the preceding section that the short-term rate of interest is determined by the volume of transactions and the supply of cash by the banking system. We shall now examine the problem of the determination of the long-term rate.

In order to establish a connection between the short-term and the long-term rate, we shall examine the problem of substitution between a representative short-term asset, say a bill of exchange, and a representative long-term asset, say a Consol. Imagine a person or enterprise considering how to invest its reserves. It will be, I think, a frequent case that the security holder compares the result of holding one or the other type of security over a few years. Thus in comparing the yields he takes into account the expected average discount rate over this period, which we denote by ρ_e and the present long-term rate (yield of Consols) r. We must now consider the advantages and disadvantages of both types of securities which account for the difference $r - \rho_e$.

There is first to be considered the possibility of a capital loss if at some time Consols will have to be converted into cash. It should be taken into account, however, that the holder need not actually sell bonds in order to obtain the cash required: he may

2 *

take bank credits against their security up to a high percentage of their value.[1] There still remains the disadvantage, as compared with bills, that this percentage is less than 100 per cent and that the interest on such credits is slightly higher than the rate of discount. (When the holder converts bills into cash his income is reduced by the interest which the bills yield; when he borrows against the security of bonds, by the interest he pays on bank credit.) On the other hand, the holding of bills which must be re-bought every three months involves various inconveniences and costs, and this often causes money to be invested on short term not in bills but in loans to the discount market.[2] If, therefore, we denote by β the value corresponding to the net disadvantages of bond holding from this point of view, it follows from the above that β is not necessarily positive and that it is normally small, say of the order of $\frac{1}{2}$ per cent.[3]

There is, however, yet another more important factor contributing to the difference $r - \rho_e$. The holding of bills guarantees the integrity of the principal. On the other hand, bonds may depreciate during the period for which the results of investment are considered. Short-period fluctuations of the value of securities owned may be disregarded[4] by the holder, but if the capital loss proves to have a permanent character it must be reckoned as such. Therefore a provision for the risk of depreciation γ must be taken into account when the yields r and ρ_e are compared. We thus have

$$r - \rho_e = \beta + \gamma. \qquad (2)$$

[1] I am indebted for this point to Mr. P. W. S. Andrews.

[2] In other words, "costs of investment" in bills (cf. p. 32) are relatively high.

[3] The margin between the rate on loans to the discount market and the discount rate is, say, $\frac{1}{2}$-1 per cent; that between discount rate and the rate on credits against the security of bonds, say, 1-2 per cent. It does not, however, follow that β is necessarily, or even normally, positive; because the latter margin, unlike the first, applies only to the periods during which the purchaser expects to be using his assets to obtain cash. β may therefore be regarded as tending to equal a fraction of the second margin *minus* the first.

[4] In so far as short-period fluctuations affect the amount of cash obtainable on the security of the bonds they will tend to raise the value of β.

2. We may still say something more about the value of γ. If the present price of Consols is p and the holder has a certain more or less definite idea based on past experience about the minimum to which this price may fall, $p_{\min}$, it is plausible to assume that γ is proportionate to $\frac{p - p_{\min}}{p}$, i.e. to the maximum percentage by which the price of Consols is considered apt to fall. We thus have

$$\gamma = g\frac{p - p_{\min}}{p} = g\left(1 - \frac{p_{\min}}{p}\right). \quad (3)$$

If the period for which the calculation is made is one year and the depreciation was considered certain, g would be equal to 100. But since the period is normally longer and the maximum depreciation not very probable, g may be expected to be rather small as compared with one hundred.

As the price of Consols is in inverse proportion to their yield, the expression (3) may be written

$$\gamma = g\left(1 - \frac{r}{r_{\max}}\right) \quad (3a)$$

where $r_{\max}$ is the yield corresponding to the "minimum price" $p_{\min}$. By substituting this expression for γ in the equation (2) we obtain, after simple transformations,

$$r = \frac{\rho_e}{1 + \frac{g}{r_{\max}}} + \frac{\beta + g}{1 + \frac{g}{r_{\max}}}. \quad (4)$$

If the coefficients β, g, and $r_{\max}$ are stable, this equation expresses the long-term rate r as a linear function of the expected short-term rate ρ_e. It is easy to see that (g, β, and $r_{\max}$ being stable) r always changes by a smaller amount than ρ_e, since $1 + \frac{g}{r_{\max}} > 1$. This is the result of our assumption that as r increases the risk of the depreciation of Consols declines (equation 3*a*).

We have thus *two* factors explaining the stability of the long-term rate as compared with the short-term rate of interest.

(1) The short-period changes of the short-term rate ρ are only partly reflected in the estimates of ρ_e. (2) The long-term rate r changes by a smaller amount than the average short-term rate ρ_e expected over the next few years.

3. It is important to notice that the "risk coefficient" (which is a marginal concept) may increase not only when the depreciation of bonds is considered more likely but also when the proportion of long-term assets held to short-term assets + cash rises. For then with the same probability of bond depreciation the latter, if it happens, means a greater loss relative to the value of all liquid assets. This "increasing risk" is accounted for by a higher g. Thus if, *ceteris paribus*, the amount of long-term assets relative to all liquid assets held by the public rises, g tends to increase. Moreover, if income tax—from which we have so far abstracted—is in existence, g is not a pure risk coefficient, but depends on the rates of income tax as well. Indeed, the difference between the long-term rate and the short-term rate is subject to tax, but the depreciation in bonds is not allowed for in tax assessment.[1] Thus if g were the pure risk coefficient $\gamma = g\left(1 - \frac{r}{r_{max}}\right)$ would cover only the difference $r - \rho_e$ after taxation. To cover the *actual* difference $r - \rho_e$, the coefficient g must be correspondingly higher.[2] If, for instance, the tax is 5s. in the £ and there is no surtax, $g = \frac{4}{3}$ of the pure risk coefficient. If surtax exists it is not possible to establish such a simple relation because the tax incidence is then not even.

Application to the Yields of Consols, 1849-1938

1. We shall now apply the results arrived at in the last section to the analysis of yields of Consols in the period 1849-1938.

[1] This is true of the U.K.; in the U.S.A., however, a part of the loss from sales of bonds *is* allowed for in income tax assessment and therefore our subsequent argument does not apply strictly to that country.

[2] This problem does not arise with regard to β because this represents a loss in income which is allowed for in taxation.

Their time curve is given in Figure 4. It may be seen that it is possible to subdivide this period into ten very unequal intervals, in each of which the long-term rate undergoes relatively small fluctuations round the average as compared with the changes between the intervals: 1849-80; 1881-87, 1888-93, 1894-1900, 1901-09, 1910-14, 1915-18, 1919-21, 1922-31, 1932-38. This may be accounted for by an hypothesis that within each of these intervals the expected short-term rate ρ_e and the coefficients g, r_{max}, and β fluctuated rather slightly around certain values while

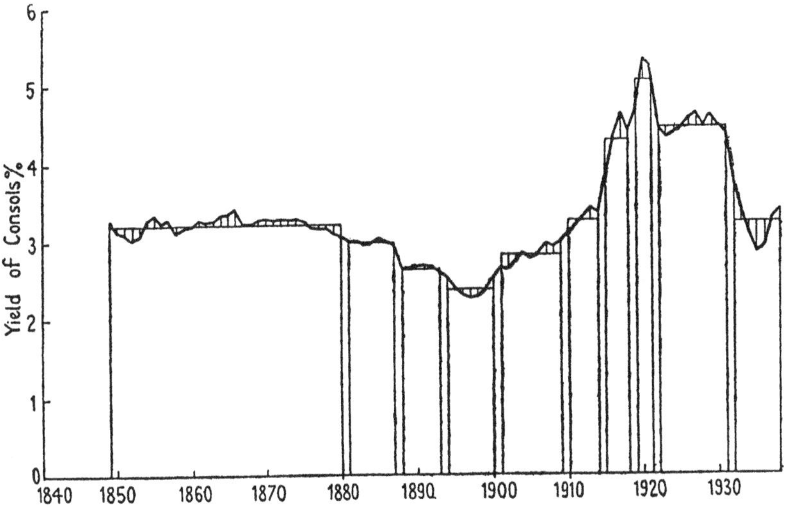

FIG. 4.—Yield of Consols, 1849-1938.

they underwent long-run changes from interval to interval. Let us turn our attention to such changes of the expected average discount rate ρ_e. Within each of our intervals the discount rate ρ underwent in fact strong fluctuations which did not, however, cause important fluctuations of ρ_e. This may be accounted for by the following hypothesis: the investors disregarded to a great extent in their estimates of ρ_e the "high" and "low" levels of the discount rate within the intervals, classifying them as temporary, and based their expectations chiefly on the last "medium" position; and the spread of these "medium values" was rather small within each period. If this hypothesis is correct, it follows that the average ρ_e in each period does not differ much from the average of the actual rate of discount ρ in that period. This is very important for our inquiry. For on this assumption we may take the average discount rate in each period to be the first approximation of the average ρ_e. Thus we may correlate the average yields of Consols and average discount rates in our periods and analyse the regression equations by means of our formula (4).

2. The data are given in Table VI:

TABLE VI

Yield of Consols and Discount Rate

Interval.	Average Yield of Consols (%)	Average Discount Rate (%)
1849-80	3·21	3·66
1881-87	2·98	2·82
1888-93	2·63	2·68
1894-1900	2·38	2·18
1901-09	2·82	3 09
1910-14	3·27	3·4
1915-18	4·30	4·3
1919-21	5·07	5·09
1922-31	4 48	3·76
1932-38	3·25	0 82

We now plot these figures on a scatter diagram (Fig. 5). It will be seen that most of the points lie very close to two straight lines AB and A_1B_1. The points corresponding to the intervals before the last war lie close to AB except those corresponding to 1881-87 and 1910-14. The points corresponding to the post-war periods lie close to the line A_1B_1, which is considerably above AB. Finally, the war period 1915-18 is represented by a point lying between AB and A_1B_1. It must be noticed at once that the position of the point 1881-87 above AB is fully accounted for by the fact that the yield of Consols in this period did not reflect the level of the "pure long-term rate," being "too high" because of the expected conversion.[1]

The results obtained may be plausibly interpreted in terms of our formula (4). In the period 1849-1909 the coefficients g, r_{max}, and β were more or less stable, and therefore we have a linear functional relation between r and ρ_e represented by AB. After this period these coefficients underwent a strong change,

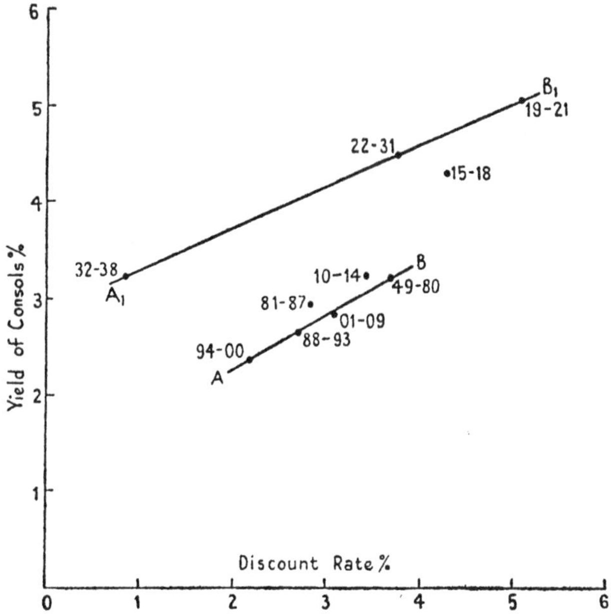

FIG. 5.—Discount Rate and Yield of Consols, 1849-1938.

chiefly during the last war, and then became stable again in the post-war period, so that the points ρ_e, r are in this period again situated on the straight line A_1B_1. The points 1910-14 and 1915-18 lying between AB and A_1B_1 represent the period during which the shift from AB to A_1B_1 occurred.

3. From the equations of the lines AB and A_1B_1 the coefficients g and β may be now obtained for the pre-war and post-war period respectively.

[1] See R. G. Hawtrey, *A Century of Bank Rate.*

The equation of AB (pre-war period) is

$$r = 0{\cdot}550\rho_e + 1{\cdot}17.$$

If we compare it with our formula (3),

$$r = \frac{\rho_e}{1 + \frac{g}{r_{\max}}} + \frac{\beta + g}{1 + \frac{g}{r_{\max}}},$$

we obtain two equations

$$\frac{1}{1 + \frac{g}{r_{\max}}} = 0{\cdot}550 \quad \text{and} \quad \frac{\beta + g}{1 + \frac{g}{r_{\max}}} = 1{\cdot}17.$$

Now as to the expected maximum long-term rate we may assume that it is approximately 3·4, for this was the maximum rate in the period in question and the level of r at the beginning of it was not much lower. It is then possible to obtain from the last equations the coefficients g and β. We have $g = 2{\cdot}78, \beta = -0{\cdot}65$.

The equation for the post-war period is

$$r = 0{\cdot}425\rho_e + 2{\cdot}90,$$

and consequently

$$\frac{1}{1 + \frac{g}{r_{\max}}} = 0{\cdot}425 \quad \text{and} \quad \frac{\beta + g}{1 + \frac{g}{r_{\max}}} = 2{\cdot}90.$$

Here $r_{\max}$ may be assumed equal to 5·1, this being the level reached at the beginning of the period and never exceeded afterwards. Thus we obtain $g = 6{\cdot}9$, $\beta = -0{\cdot}07$.[1]

We may now put together the results of our calculation :

Period	g.	$r_{\max}$.	β.
1849-1909	2·78	3·40	− 0·65
1919-38	6 90	5·10	− 0·07

[1] It is perhaps more correct to assume that in the interval 1932-38 $r_{\max}$ was lower than 5·1, say 4·5. We then obtain for this interval $g = 6$ 03, $\beta = 0{\cdot}73$. The positive value for β in this interval is quite plausible in view of the unusually low margin between the discount rate and the rate on loans to the discount market (cf. p. 38).

From the point of view of the confirmation of our theory the most important result is that β (the balance of disadvantages and advantages of bonds as compared with bills apart from the risk of depreciation) is small, as we expected it to be for theoretical reasons. If the coefficient of ρ_e in the post-war period had been not 0·425 but, say, 0·25, we should, *ceteris paribus*, have obtained for β the value $-3{\cdot}7$, which would be obviously absurd and so disprove our theory.

The coefficient g is—again in accordance with *a priori* argument—small as compared with 100, both in the pre-war and the post-war periods. (The " pure " risk coefficient is even smaller because g is inflated by income tax, cf. p. 40.) The tremendous rise in g (about 2·5 times) between these two periods is explained by the much stronger fluctuations in r after 1914 and by the rise in income tax and surtax. The strong rise in g in combination with the increase in r_{max} accounts for the shift of the line AB to the position A_1B_1.

4. It is interesting to notice that during this war the movement of the long-term rate conforms to the 1919-38 formula. The average discount rate ρ was 1·04 per cent in 1940 and 1·03 per cent in 1941. This was probably also the level expected for the next few years. Substituting these values into the 1919-38 formula,

$$r = 0{\cdot}425\rho_e + 2{\cdot}90,$$

we obtain about 3·34 per cent for both years. The actual average yields of Consols were: 3·40 per cent in 1940 and 3·13 per cent in 1941. The agreement between the calculated and the actual values is thus very close. This is the more surprising in that the increase in income tax tended to increase g.

It is necessary to take into account here that g depends *inter alia* on the ratio of long-term assets held to short-term assets + cash (see p. 40) and thus the Government borrowing policy determines within certain limits the long-term rate of interest. If the Government borrows a part of the amounts required on long-term at a certain fixed rate and the rest on short-term—as it was in fact the case during this war—the long-term rate is actually fixed by the Government. This is, however, only the case if this rate is chosen so that the Government is able to sell *some* amount of its long-term issues. If the Government long-term rate of borrowing is so low that nobody is prepared to lend at this rate, the Government must finance all the Budget deficit by floating debt. It loses then the control of the long-term rate unless it is prepared to borrow short over and above the deficit requirements and buy long-term securities from the public.

3. A THEORY OF PROFITS

The Determinants of Profits

1. In this essay we attempt to investigate the determinants of profits in short and long periods. The short-period analysis will consist in relating the profits in a given short period to certain factors operating in the preceding periods. From this we shall pass to the examination of the level of the rate of profit in long periods, in particular in relation to the rate of interest.

We abstract in our argument from the influence on profits of the balance of foreign trade and the Budget deficit (or surplus). We therefore assume a closed system and a balanced State Budget. It is, consequently, quite clear that our conclusions are by no means applicable to a war economy. Our aim is, on the contrary, to examine the problem of profits in a closed *laissez-faire* system. In concert with abstracting from the Budget deficit we also assume that no interest on the National Debt is paid.

By gross profits we shall mean depreciation and maintenance, net undistributed profits, dividends, interest, rent and also managerial salaries, all *after payment of direct taxes.*[1] The receivers of this type of income we call capitalists. The rest of incomes (also taken net of direct taxes) are wages, small salaries (for the sake of brevity we shall use below " salaries " for small salaries), and doles. The saving out of these incomes is assumed to be small as compared with total saving, and is neglected for the sake of simplicity—i.e. equated to nought.

2. We shall now establish the fundamental equation between profits on the one hand and capitalists' consumption and private investment on the other. We must, however, first define certain concepts. By gross investment we shall mean the value of all sales of newly produced fixed capital equipment + increase in working capital and stocks ; and by gross national income the

[1] However, taxes accruing but not yet paid—i.e. increase in tax reserves *are* included in profits.

47

sum of total personal consumption and gross investment. We shall distinguish private and Government investment (armaments, Government buildings, etc.). The gross national income so defined is, as may easily be seen, also equal to profits gross of depreciation and net of direct taxes + wages, salaries and doles (also net of taxes) + Government investment. For the proceeds of sales of consumption and investment goods [1] will be received by capitalists and workers employed by them, or passed by means of indirect and direct taxes to the Government, which will, in turn, spend the revenue either on wages and salaries of Government employees and doles or Government investment. We thus have the following "balance sheet" of national income and expenditure:

Gross profits (gross of depreciation but net of direct taxes)	Total gross investment
Wages, salaries and doles (net of direct taxes)	Capitalists' consumption
Gross Government investment	Workers' consumption
Gross national income	Gross national income.

Now, since wages, salaries and doles are, as assumed above, fully spent on consumption, and total gross investment − gross Government investment = gross private investment, it follows directly that

Gross profits = Gross private investment + Capitalists' consumption. . . . . (1)

What is the proper meaning of this equation? Does it mean that profits in a certain period determine capitalists' consumption and investment, or the other way round? The answer to this question depends on which of these items is directly subject to the decisions of capitalists. Now, it is clear that they may decide to consume and to invest more in a certain short period than in the preceding period, but they cannot decide to earn

[1] The latter inclusive of the increase in working capital and stocks. When this type of investment does not actually involve a sale, it may be considered as a firm's sale to itself.

more. It is therefore their investment and consumption decisions which determine profits, and not vice versa.

If the period which we consider is short, we may say that capitalists' investment and consumption are determined by decisions formed in the *past*. For the execution of investment orders takes a certain time, and as to the capitalists' consumption, it is only with a certain delay that the capitalists' standard of living reacts to the change of factors which influence it.

If capitalists decided always to consume and to invest in a given period what they have earned in the preceding period, the profits in the given period would be equal to those in the preceding one. In such case they would remain stationary, and the problem of how to read the above equation would lose its importance. But such is *not* the case. Although profits in the preceding periods are one of the important determinants of capitalists' consumption and investment, capitalists in general do *not* decide to consume and invest in a given month what they have earned in the preceding one. This explains why profits are *not* stationary, but fluctuate in time.

3. The above argument requires a certain qualification. The past investment decisions may not fully determine the volume of investment in a given period, owing to unexpected accumulation or running down of stocks. The importance of this factor seems, however, to have been frequently exaggerated.

A second qualification arises out of the fact that these decisions will usually be in real terms, and in the meantime prices may change. For instance, a piece of ordered capital equipment may cost more than at the period when the order was given. To get over this difficulty it will be convenient to deflate both sides of the equation by appropriate price indices. We thus obtain an equation between real gross profits and real capitalists' consumption + real gross private investment.

We may now conclude that the real gross profits in a given short period are determined by decisions of capitalists as to their consumption and investment formed in the past, subject to the correction for unexpected changes in the volume of stocks.

There arises here the problem what will be the place of the factors determining the distribution of the national income in this theory. Since profits in a given short period are determined by capitalists' decisions as to their consumption and investment formed in the past, the factors determining the distribution of income will affect not real profits but the real wage and salary bill—and consequently the national output. If, for instance, the degree of market imperfection or oligopoly increases, and, as a result, so does the ratio of profits to wages, real profits do not change, but the real wage bill falls, first, because of the fall in real wage rates, and secondly, because of the consequent reduction in demand for wage goods, and thus of output and employment in the wage-good industries. (If salary rates do not rise relative to wage rates the real salary bill falls as well.) Percentage gross margins increase, but the national output falls just so much that, as a result, the real total profits remain the same. However great the margin of profit on a unit of output, the capitalists cannot make more in total profits than they consume and invest (inclusive of accumulation of unsold goods).[1]

4. The above analysis obviously cannot answer the question why the rate of profit taken as an average for longer periods is higher than the rate of interest. It only relates profits in a given short period to capitalists' consumption and investment in this period determined by factors which operated in the preceding periods. To say something about the actual level of profits it is necessary to apply a different type of analysis.

The Rate of Profit in the Long Period

1. The long-run analysis is often conducted under the assumption of long-run equilibrium *sensu stricto* (i.e. in the sense that the system is at rest). This is entirely unjustified, because we *know* that apart from cyclical fluctuations the economic system is subject to a complex process of long-run development. We shall

[1] The theory of profits presented here is closely allied to Lord Keynes' theory of saving and investment. It has been, however, developed independently of Lord Keynes in my "Essai d'une théorie du mouvement cyclique des affaires," *Revue d'économie politique*, Mars-Avril 1935, and "A Macrodynamic Theory of Business Cycles," *Econometrica*, July 1935.

therefore approach the problem from a different angle: we shall simply consider connections between averages of variables in a period extending over a full business cycle and chosen so that its beginning and end are positions half-way between boom and slump.

We shall assume that the average change of any variable per year of our period is small as compared with the average of this variable over this period. That means that if the period considered consists of years 1, 2, 3, . . . n, and is preceded by a year 0, we assume for any variable X that $\frac{X_n - X_0}{n}$ is small as compared with $\frac{X_1 + X_2 + X_3 + \ldots + X_n}{n}$. This condition is likely to be fulfilled in reality, since our period covers a full cycle and the economic development after elimination of the trade cycle is usually "slow."

The assumption of the "slowness" of long-run economic development is of great significance for the long-period analysis. Indeed, when short periods are considered, any relation between two variables involves time lags. For instance, investment at a given moment is a function of factors which operated some time ago. Now, if these time-lags are short—say, not greater than of an order of a year—they may be disregarded in our long-period analysis. For, since $\frac{X_n - X_0}{n}$ is small as compared with $\frac{X_1 + X_2 + \ldots + X_n}{n}$, the latter differs little from $\frac{X_0 + X_1 + \ldots + X_{n-1}}{n}$; thus, when the influence of X upon the situation in a given long period is examined, we shall make only a small error by taking into consideration the former instead of the latter.

2. In every year of our period gross profit is equal to capitalists' consumption + private gross investment. (For the sake of brevity we shall use below "investment" for private investment.) Thus the average gross profit is equal to the average capitalists' consumption + average gross investment. If we deduct from

both sides of this equation the average depreciation and maintenance, we find that the average net profit $\bar{P}$ is equal to the average capitalists' consumption $\bar{C}$ + the average net investment $\bar{I}$,

$$\bar{P} = \bar{C} + \bar{I} \quad . \quad . \quad . \quad . \quad (2)$$

where $\bar{C}$ and $\bar{I}$ are understood here to be expressed in real terms —namely, calculated at prices prevailing at the beginning of the period considered, and also $\bar{P}$ is the average "real" profit.

We may make the following assumption, plausible as a first approximation, about the "real" capitalists' consumption C_t in a given year: that it consists of a stable part A and a part proportionate to the real profit $P_{t-\psi}$ of some time ago:[1]

$$C_t = A + \lambda P_{t-\psi}. \quad . \quad . \quad . \quad (3)$$

ψ indicates thus the delay of the reaction of capitalists' consumption to the change in their current income; it is probably of an order of a year or less. λ is positive and < 1.[2] Finally, A is the result of habits acquired by capitalists as a result of past long-run development. It changes, therefore, slowly in time, also in the period considered, but the time lags involved are very long, and therefore we shall assume A in the period considered (which, covering a full cycle, is about 10 years long) to be determined by factors which operated prior to it. We take now the average of both sides of our equation (3) over our period. Since the time-lag ψ is relatively short, it may be neglected according to the argument of the preceding section. We thus obtain

$$\bar{C} = \bar{A} + \lambda\bar{P}, \quad . \quad . \quad . \quad . \quad (4)$$

and from this equation and equation (2) it follows

$$\bar{P} = \frac{\bar{A} + \bar{I}}{1 - \lambda} \quad . \quad . \quad . \quad . \quad (5)$$

[1] We neglect the influence of the rate of interest upon capitalists' consumption as not very important.

[2] A tentative estimate of λ for the U.S.A. in the period 1925-35 suggests that it was $< 0 \cdot 33$. (Undistributed profits were, of course, included in capitalists' incomes.)

where $\bar{A}$ depends on the development preceding the period considered.[1]

3. In order to obtain a formula for the average *rate* of profit in our period, we shall now consider the average volume of total capital in this period. Let K_0 be the value of total capital equipment at current prices of investment goods at the beginning of this period. Since $\bar{I}$ is the average net "real" investment in our period at prices prevailing at the beginning of our period, the "real" capital at the end of the period is $K_0 + n\bar{I}$, where n is length of the period.

Now, the deviations of the annual rate of investment from the average annual rate of investment $\bar{I}$ throughout the period may be assumed small (say, of the order of 2 or 3 per cent) as compared with the initial volume of capital equipment K_0. It may be shown that if this is the case then with $n = 10$ years, say, the average volume of capital $\bar{K}$ will differ little from the average of its volume at the beginning and at the end of the period. We have thus as a good approximation

$$\bar{K} = K_0 + \frac{n}{2}\bar{I}. \qquad (6)$$

4. We shall now obtain a formula for the average rate of profit in our period which we may determine as the ratio of average *money* profit to average *money* value of capital at current prices. Thus, before dividing $\bar{P}$ by $\bar{K}$, which are "real" values calculated at prices at the beginning of the period, they should be multiplied by appropriate price indices. It is, however, easy to see that this correction will be important only if the average of the price index of consumption goods related to the beginning of the period as basis differs considerably from that of investment

[1] It must be noticed that equation (3), and consequently equations (4) and (5), cease to be plausible in the case where taxation is heavy, and its system is such that the tax on profits increases much quicker than profits (for instance, Excess Profits Tax). For although profits $P_{t-\psi}$ are net of taxes paid, they include taxes accruing but not yet paid—i.e. the increase in tax reserves; and if this part of profits is considerable it may affect capitalists' consumption decisions. Now, as long as the tax is on a proportionate basis, our formula, it may be shown, still holds good approximately, although λ and ψ will have then a more complex meaning. However, if taxation is strongly disproportionate, the formula becomes invalid.

goods. Since, however, the beginning of the period has been chosen in such a way that it represents a half-way position between boom and slump, this is unlikely to be the case, and therefore $\bar{P}/\bar{K}$ may be taken as a first approximation to the average rate of profit π in our period. We thus obtain

$$\pi = \frac{1}{1-\lambda} \frac{\bar{A}+\bar{I}}{K_0 + \frac{n}{2}\bar{I}}. \qquad (7)$$

If we denote $\bar{A}/K_0$ by α, and $\bar{I}/K_0$ by i, we have after simple transformations

$$\pi = \frac{2}{n(1-\lambda)} \frac{\alpha + i}{\frac{2}{n} + i}. \qquad (7a)$$

Since both $\bar{A}$ (the average of the stable part of capitalists' consumption) and K_0 (the value of capital at the beginning of the period) are fully determined by development prior to this period, $\alpha = \frac{\bar{A}}{K_0}$ may be considered given. Thus the average rate of profit π is represented as a function of i—i.e. of the ratio of average investment $\bar{I}$ to the initial value of capital K_0.[1]

As will be seen in the last essay, $\bar{I}$ depends on a variety of factors. We shall try to arrive here at certain results from the discussion of the formula (7*a*) without going into the problems of the determination of i.

The Rate of Profit and the Rate of Interest in the Long Period

The problem which concerns us here is what causes the rate of profit to be higher than the rate of interest in the long period and whether this must be the case under all circumstances.[2]

[1] It may seem from equation (7) that π falls when the length of the full cycle n increases. But it must not be forgotten that, since A, the stable part of capitalists' consumption, changes within this period, its average $\bar{A}$ depends on its length. Therefore π may not be affected by the change in n.

[2] As profits are understood throughout the argument to be after taxation, the rate of interest, when compared with the rate of profit as given by formula (7*a*), must also be taken after deduction of income tax.

1. It may be seen directly from the formula (7*a*) that if $\alpha' \geqslant \frac{2}{n}$ the average rate of profit $\pi \geqslant \frac{2}{n(1-\lambda)}$. Since n is about 10 years, it follows at once that the rate of profit is greater than 20 per cent.

In this case the fact that the rate of profit is higher than the rate of interest would be very simply explained. The rate of profit, whatever the rate of investment, is above a certain level. The rate of interest determined by the volume of transactions and supply of cash by banks[1] is below this limit. The latter is subject to the qualification that no " over full employment " is then involved; for in such a state the increasing volume of transactions and thus increasing demand for cash may drive the rate of interest to a very high level. It is unlikely, however, that it should reach the level of the rate of profit because this would imply a very low rate of investment and thus most probably a low level of employment.

We shall now consider the case of $\alpha < \frac{2}{n}$ which is of much greater practical importance.

2. In this case the average rate of profit $\pi < \frac{2}{n(1-\lambda)}$. It is also easy to see from formula (7*a*) that π is an increasing function of i. For if i increases by a certain amount, the numerator of the fraction $\frac{\alpha + i}{\frac{2}{n} + i}$ increases if $\alpha < \frac{2}{n}$ in a higher proportion than the denominator.

It follows directly that to obtain the lower limit of the rate of profit we must substitute into the formula (7*a*) the lowest level to which i may fall. Now, i is the ratio of the average net investment in our period to the value of capital at its beginning. If investment activity is at a complete standstill $i = -d$, where

[1] These factors determine directly the *short-term* rate of interest (see p. 36). The *long-term* rate of interest is determined by the expected short-term rate and by certain risk factors and income tax (see pp. 39 and 40). It should be remembered that it is the interest *net* of tax which is relevant for our argument.

d is depreciation and maintenance in per cent of capital. But because some repairs are always carried out, $i_{min} > -d$.[1] We thus obtain the lowest limit for the rate of profit,

$$\pi \geqslant \pi_{min} = \frac{2}{n(1-\lambda)} \frac{\alpha + i_{min}}{\frac{2}{n} + i_{min}}. \quad \quad (8)$$

Let us assume now for the moment that the short-term rate of interest, and in consequence also the long-term rate of interest, is kept by banking policy at a certain definite level r. The condition for the rate of profit being always higher than the rate of interest is then

$$\frac{2}{n(1-\lambda)} \frac{\alpha + i_{min}}{\frac{2}{n} + i_{min}} > r. \quad \quad (9)$$

From this inequality may be obtained the level above which α must be in order that the rate of profit shall always be higher than the rate of interest. If, for instance, $\lambda = 0{\cdot}3$, $n = 10$, $i_{min} = -0{\cdot}04$ and $r = 0{\cdot}04$, we obtain from (9) $\alpha > 5{\cdot}0$ per cent. Thus if α is higher than 5·0 per cent, the average rate of profit is always higher than the long-term rate of interest, which is kept at the level of 4 per cent.

3. It follows from the argument in the last two paragraphs that if α is above the " critical level " the rate of profit is *always* higher than the rate of interest.

On the other hand, if α is at the " critical level " (which makes the expression on the left-hand side equal to the rate of interest) the rate of profit may fall to the level of the rate of interest if $i = i_{min}$. There arise here two problems : (1) Is it possible that investment activity may remain in our long period at the minimum level so that i is actually equal to i_{min} ? (2) If this happened in one of our periods, and thus the average rate of

[1] As capital consists not only of fixed capital but of working capital and stocks as well i_{min} may be lower than $-d$ if inventories are being run down at more than d per cent per annum.

profit was equal to the rate of interest in that period, can this position persist in the next long period?

Let us consider the first question. If investment activity is maintained throughout the period at its minimum level the average rate of profit is equal to the rate of interest. Investment I being stable (at the minimum level throughout the period) the rate of profit undergoes only small changes within the period because both the stable part of capitalists' consumption and the volume of fixed capital K change slowly. Therefore the rate of profit does not differ much throughout the period from the average and thus is close to the rate of interest. But if the rate of profit is close to the rate of interest throughout the period, investment activity is likely to be maintained at the minimum level because no margin to cover rent on land, management costs, and risk is provided. Thus $i = i_{min}$ *is* a possible state of affairs.[1]

Let us now consider the second problem. Imagine that α is at the "critical level" and in one of our long periods $i = i_{min}$; the average rate of profit in that period is consequently equal to the rate of interest. Do developments in this period prepare the ground for a higher rate of profit in the next full-cycle period? Certainly i, which $= i_{min}$ in the period considered, is negative, therefore the capital K_0 at the beginning of the next period will be smaller. And this will tend to increase α of the next period, which is the ratio of the average of the stable part of capitalists' consumption $\bar{A}$ to the capital K_0 at the beginning of the period. However, dis-saving, which takes place in the period considered, will certainly tend to depress the stable part of capitalists' consumption in the next period: the less wealthy the capitalists feel the less is the amount they are apt to consume irrespective of their current income. Also the persistence of a very low capitalists' income in the period considered will tend to press down the capitalists' customary standard of living, and this will be reflected in the fall in the stable part of their consumption A in the next period.

Thus not only will K_0 at the beginning of the next period be smaller, but so also is likely to be $\bar{A}$ in that period. It is thus

[1] In this case there are actually no cyclical fluctuations, cf. p. 75, below.

not at all certain that $\alpha = \frac{\bar{A}}{K_0}$ will increase. And if it remains at the same level as in the period considered, nothing has happened to push upwards the rate of profit, which may thus continue to be equal to the rate of interest.

If α falls *below* the " critical level " the rate of profit will be below the rate of interest when investment activity is at the minimum level. It may be demonstrated in the same way as above that this state of affairs is possible and may persist over a number of long periods.

4. So far we have assumed that the rate of interest is given. If, however, investment activity falls—as was assumed in the last section—to its minimum level, total output and employment must shrink considerably; the demand for cash for transactions is greatly reduced, and, as a result, the short-term rate of interest tends to fall, and is followed by the long-term rate. However, the short-term rate cannot fall below zero, and the long-term rate, because of the risk involved in the fluctuations of the price of bonds, below a positive value $r_{\min}$. Thus, if α is sufficiently low, the fall of the rate of interest cannot prevent the possibility of the rate of profit reaching the level of the rate of interest. Indeed, there is always such a value of α at which the lower limit of the rate of profit $\pi_{\min}$ is equal to the lower limit of the rate of interest $r_{\min}$.

5. In the light of the above argument, the relation between the rate of profit and the rate of interest in long periods depends to a great extent on the value of α (the ratio of the average of the stable part of capitalists' consumption over the period $\bar{A}$ to the volume of capital K_0 at the beginning of the period). If α is above the " critical level " (which depends on the rate of interest) the rate of profit is *always* higher than the rate of interest. If α is at the " critical level " (or below it), and investment activity is at its minimum level, the rate of profit is equal to the rate of interest (or falls short of it). Such a state of " long-period deadlock " is by no means excluded and may even last for a number of long periods.

Part Two

BUSINESS CYCLE AND TREND

4. THE "PURE" BUSINESS CYCLE

THE theory of the business cycle presented below is in many respects similar to that given in my *Essays in the Theory of Economic Fluctuations* and my earlier writings. The justification for this new version is that: (1) I now tackle the problem from a new angle and introduce new factors into the explanation of the business cycle; (2) with this new treatment it is possible to drop some of my simplifying assumptions and to achieve some new results; (3) I do not now consider only the problem of the "pure" business cycle, but deal in the last essay with the trend superimposed on the cycle.

Investment and Profits

1. We make the same assumptions as in the preceding essay, i.e. we consider a closed economic system with a balanced State Budget and abstract from working class savings. We thus have the equation

$$P = C + I \quad . \quad . \quad . \quad . \quad (1)$$

where P are net real profits, C real capitalists' consumption, and I real net investment. If we denote by R the real depreciation and maintenance (i.e. replacement required to maintain capital intact, which we shall call "required replacement"), $I + R$ is the real gross investment. As in the preceding essay we assume the following interrelation between capitalist consumption C and profits P (see p. 52):

$$C_t = A_t + \lambda P_{t-\psi}. \quad . \quad . \quad . \quad (2)$$

A_t, the stable part of capitalists' consumption, is the result of habits acquired by capitalists in the past long-run development.

(A_t changes slowly in time but is not subject to cyclical fluctuations. We shall consequently assume it constant for the discussion of the " pure " business cycle and reintroduce this factor only in the next essay where the trend problem will be considered.) λ, which is the capitalists' marginal propensity to consume, is positive and substantially less than 1. Finally, ψ indicates the delay of the reaction of the capitalists' consumption to the change in their current income.

2. From the equations (1) and (2) it follows

$$P_t - \lambda P_{t-\psi} = A_t + I_t. \quad . \quad . \quad . \quad (3)$$

Now it may be shown that if the change of P_t can be assumed approximately linear in a period of a length of the order of ψ, we may write

$$P_t - \lambda P_{t-\psi} = (1 - \lambda)P_{t+\kappa} \quad . \quad . \quad (4)$$

where κ is determined by the formula $\kappa = \frac{\lambda}{1 - \lambda}\psi$.[1]

It follows directly from equations (3) and (4)

$$P_{t+\kappa} = \frac{A_t + I_t}{1 - \lambda},$$

or, which amounts to the same,

$$P_t = \frac{A_{t-\kappa} + I_{t-\kappa}}{1 - \lambda}. \quad . \quad . \quad . \quad (5)$$

This is nothing else than the " multiplier equation " for profits in which there is involved a time-lag κ. The " multiplier " $= \frac{1}{1 - \lambda}$.

[1] Equation (4) is equivalent to

$$P_t = \lambda P_{t-\psi} + (1 - \lambda)P_{t+\kappa}.$$

Under the above assumptions κ fulfils approximately the condition

$$\lambda(t - \psi) + (1 - \lambda)(t + \kappa) = t,$$

from which follows $\kappa = \frac{\lambda}{1 - \lambda}\psi$. If ψ is shorter than a year and λ smaller than 1/3 (cf. footnote to p. 52), κ is shorter than half a year.

The Determinants of the Rate of Investment Decisions

1. We are now going to discuss the much more intricate problem of the determinants of the rate of investment decisions. Let us consider a short period *dt*. The investment plans undertaken before this period have been pushed up to a point where they cease to be profitable owing to the imperfection of the market for products on the one hand and to the imperfection of the capital market and "increasing risk"[1] on the other. What happens then in the period *dt* to cause new investment plans to emerge?

There may, of course, occur a rise in the prospective rate of profit (or a fall in the rate of interest) owing to the change in the economic situation in *dt*, and this would cause an expansion of the investment plans at the end of this period as compared with its beginning. We shall consider this reason for new investment later on in some detail. But provided that such a change has not occurred, will new investment decisions—taking the objective form of investment orders—not be forthcoming at all in the period *dt*? What is the factor which may cause new investment decisions in the absence of a change of the prospective rate of profit (or the rate of interest)? This factor is the inflow of new gross savings (i.e. of net saving + depreciation and maintenance) which will push forward the barriers set to investment plans by the limited accessibility of the capital market and "increasing risk."

2. Before we proceed to a detailed consideration of this influence it should be remembered that real gross savings in any period of time are equal to the real gross investment, i.e. required replacement R + real net investment I. Thus in the period dt real gross savings $= (R + I)dt$. (The rate of real gross investment $R + I$ in the period dt must not, of course, be confused with the rate of investment *decisions* in that period; the actual investment in *dt* is the result of *past* investment decisions.)

[1] See my *Essays in the Theory of Economic Fluctuations*, "The Principle of Increasing Risk," pp 95-106 According to this principle the larger the investment in fixed equipment undertaken by an entrepreneur with given own capital, the greater its marginal risk. See also J. Steindl, "On Risk," *Oxford Economic Papers*, No. 5.

3

A part of the new savings $(R + I)dt$ accrues to " entrepreneurs," i.e. to enterprises directly (undistributed profits) or to people ready to absorb the new issues of shares of enterprises. The rest of savings accumulates in the hands of " pure rentiers " holding their savings exclusively in deposits or bonds.[1] If we denote the real " rentiers " savings by s, the gross real savings of the entrepreneurs are $R + (I - s)$. Let us first consider a special case when $I - s = 0$. The gross saving of entrepreneurs in the period dt is then equal to the required replacement Rdt, and if they reinvest this amount in fixed capital they do not strike against the barriers of the limited accessibility of the capital market or " increasing risk " because they do not increase their commitments. Thus the rate of investment decisions is here R. We shall now consider the general case where $I - s$ is not equal to zero.

Prima facie it looks as if what was said about reinvestment of R remains true of $R + (I - s)$. For the entrepreneurs as a body when deciding to invest anew $[R + (I - s)]dt$ will not increase their indebtedness at the end of the period as compared with the level at its beginning. Two factors must, however, be taken into consideration. First, what is relevant is not absolute but relative commitments. If the ratio of the fixed entrepreneurs' capital to their own capital is δ they can invest $[R + \delta(I - s)]dt$ (where $\delta > 1$) without increasing their *degree* of commitment. Secondly, a decision to invest not only Rdt but also $\delta(I - s)dt$ means (when $I - s$ is positive) a decision to expand equipment Now if the objective factors determining the profitability of investment are unchanged and the investment is in the line of entrepreneur's production, this means, because of market imperfection for his products, a smaller prospective rate of profit although the economic situation has not changed. And shifting to new fields means a higher risk. Thus new investment decisions may be represented by a formula $[R + \eta\delta(I - s)]dt$ where $\eta < 1$ and $\delta > 1$. The same formula will hold good for the case when $I - s$ is negative.

[1] In fact there does not exist such a sharp line of division : what we consider here is rather a simplified model being a first approximation to the real world.

Since $\eta < 1$ and $\delta > 1$ it is uncertain whether $\eta\delta$ is higher or lower than 1. We shall make a plausible assumption that the degree of indebtedness of "entrepreneurs" towards "rentiers" is not very high and thus δ only moderately exceeds 1; and on the other hand that the limitation in reinvestment imposed on "entrepreneurs" savings by market imperfection and the high risk of investment in alien fields make for a rather low η. In these conditions $\eta\delta$ is likely to be lower than 1 and this will be assumed throughout the argument. We shall denote $\eta\delta$ by $1 - c$ where c is positive and < 1.

3. We have assumed so far that in the period dt there was no change in the economic situation which would influence the prospective rate of profit (or the rate of interest). We shall now consider this problem. The two most important determinants of the prospective rate of profit may be considered to be the real profits P and the volume of capital equipment. The larger P and the smaller the existing capital equipment the larger will be in general the prospective rates of profit on new investment.[1] The influence of the prices of new investment goods upon the prospective rates of profit is roughly accounted for by taking into consideration the *real* profits P. This allowance for changes in the prices of investment goods may prove insufficient for two reasons: (1) the prices of investment goods may not change in the same proportion as the prices which are used to deflate profits; (2) what is more important, the entrepreneur takes into account in his investment decisions not only the current situation but also the uncertain future; the present money profits cannot be expected to last over all the life of the investment, but only in the near future; but the price he pays for investment goods is a determinant of the prospective rate of profit which is fixed once and for all. Therefore the rise in prices of investment goods usually accompanying the rise in real profits will weaken the effect of the latter upon investment decisions.

If the real profits P increase in the period dt by dP we can say, according to the above, that this will push the investment plans by adP. a is here by no means a constant, but a positive

[1] Cf. my *Essays*, pp. 132-140.

3 *

co-efficient susceptible to various types of changes and reflecting, *inter alia*, the influence of changes in the prices of investment goods as discussed above.

Further, the rise in fixed capital equipment in the period dt is equal to Jdt where J is the rate of excess of deliveries of fixed capital equipment over the required replacement R; and the negative influence upon the volume of new investment decisions in dt may be represented by $-bJdt$ where b is again a positive, but not necessarily a constant, coefficient. Thus, in so far as we would take into account only the factors enumerated above, we could write for the volume of new investment decisions in the period dt: $[R + (1 - c)(I - s)]dt + adP - bJdt$.[1]

4. We have not yet taken into account the influence of the rate of interest which must be deducted from the prospective rate of profit in order to obtain the net profitability. The rise in the rate of interest in the period dt will thus clearly reduce the volume of investment decisions in that period. This influence can be accounted for in the same way as prices of investment goods in the coefficient a, but because of the stability of the long-term rate of interest[2] as compared with the rate of profit it seems to be not very important.

We may thus consider as an approximate formula for new investment decisions $Rdt + (1 - c)(I - s)dt + adP - bJdt$. And the *rate* of investment decisions (both for replacement and extension), which we shall denote by D, may be obtained by dividing this expression by dt. We must yet, however, take into account that the phenomena inducing investment decisions do so with a certain time-lag which we may denote ω. We thus have

$$D_{t+\omega} = R_t + (1 - c)(I_t - s_t) + a\frac{dP_t}{dt} - bJ_t$$

or

$$D_{t+\omega} - R_t = a\frac{dP_t}{dt} - bJ_t + (1 - c)(I_t - s_t). \qquad (6)$$

It must be stressed that all the above argument applied to investment decisions with regard to fixed capital, and thus D

[1] This formula has a close affinity with that arrived at in my "Principle of Increasing Risk," *Economica*, November 1937, p. 447.

[2] Cf. pp. 39-40.

represents the rate of this type of decisions only. J is the net addition to fixed capital equipment, i.e. the difference between deliveries of finished fixed equipment over required replacement. I is the total net investment and consequently it differs from J in that it includes also the increase in working capital (*inter alia*, in fixed capital under construction) and stocks.

The coefficients a, b, and $1 - c$ are positive. In the extreme case when $b = 0$ and $1 - c = 0$ equation (6) would amount to saying that the excess of the rate of investment decisions over the level of maintenance and depreciation is proportionate (if a is constant) to the rate of change in profits. That would be nothing else but the so-called "acceleration principle" in the narrow sense which has been definitely disproved by statistical inquiries.[1] The acceleration principle requires that the rate of investment decisions is highest when profits (or output) pass through their medium position in the cycle on the way upwards. The facts, however, show that the maximum of investment decisions is reached in a much more advanced stage of the boom. This state of affairs may be accounted for by formula (6) if the coefficients b and $(1 - c)$ fulfil a certain condition. Indeed, if $1 - c > b$ one can say that investment decisions are, roughly speaking, in a double positive correlation with the rate of change of profits and the level of investment. (Real rentiers' savings s_t are rather stable in the course of the trade cycle.) Further, through the "multiplier equation" (see p. 60) profits are—with a short time-lag—positively correlated with investment. Thus the rate of investment decisions is in a double positive correlation with the rate of change in profits and the level of profits, and that means that it reaches its maximum somewhere between the medium position of recovery and the top of the boom.

5. It may easily be seen that in equation (6) is involved what one can call a "trend component." For it follows from it that long-run equilibrium of the system is impossible unless special assumptions are made about the rentiers' savings s. Indeed, in

[1] See, for instance, J. Tinbergen, "Critical Remarks on Some Business-Cycle Theories," *Econometrica*, April 1942.

a long-run equilibrium profits P are constant and net additions to fixed capital J and total net investment I are constant and $= 0$. The rate of gross investment decisions D is constant and $=$ required replacement R. Thus equation (6) becomes in such a state

$$0 = -(1 - c)s_t.$$

Consequently long-run equilibrium is possible only if the latter equation is fulfilled, which need not in general be the case because rentiers' savings s_t do not fall automatically to nought if net investment is at a zero level. If rentiers do some saving the system will thus be subject to a negative trend. Thus to obtain a model of the pure business cycle we assume for the present that in a business cycle period considered the rentiers do no saving so that $s = 0$. However, we shall re-introduce this factor in the last essay where we consider the problem of trend. For the purpose of discussion of the pure business cycle equation (6) is thus

$$D_{t+\omega} - R_t = a\frac{dP_t}{dt} - bJ_t + (1 - c)I_t. \qquad (6a)$$

Fundamental Equation for a Simplified Model

1. In addition to equation (6*a*) we have the following relations between the variables entering it.

There exists first a simple relation between the rate of investment decisions D and the deliveries of finished capital equipment. The rate of the latter follows the former with a time-lag θ which is equal to the average period of construction.

Thus to the rate of gross investment decisions $D_{t+\omega}$ in the last equation there corresponds an equal rate of deliveries at time $t + \omega + \theta$. As the latter is the sum of required replacement and of the net investment in fixed capital at the time $t + \omega + \theta$, we have

$$D_{t+\omega} = R_{t+\omega+\theta} + J_{t+\omega+\theta}.$$

Taking into consideration that required replacement varies slowly in time, and that the combined time-lag $\omega + \theta$ is rather small (something like a year), we may write as a good approximation

$$D_{t+\omega} - R_t = J_{t+\omega+\theta} \quad . \quad . \quad . \quad (7)$$

where J is net investment in finished fixed capital (i.e. the excess of deliveries of finished fixed capital over the required replacement), the time-lag ω is related to the delay with which investment decisions are taken under the influence of inducements, and θ is the average construction period. From equations (6*a*) and (7) we obtain

$$J_{t+\omega+\theta} = a\frac{dP_t}{dt} - bJ_t + (1 - c)I_t. \quad . \quad . \quad (8)$$

2. As mentioned above I and J differ in that the latter represents the rate of net investment in finished fixed capital equipment only while I is the total rate of investment and thus includes the increase in working capital and stocks as well. Now while working capital rises with output stocks usually move in the opposite direction. As a first approximation we shall assume that these changes cancel each other and thus

$$I = J. \quad . \quad . \quad . \quad . \quad (9)$$

A second approximation, based on a more general assumption about the movement of working capital and stocks, will be given at the end of the essay.

Taking into account equation (9) we obtain from equation (8)

$$I_{t+\omega+\theta} = a\frac{dP_t}{dt} + (1 - b - c)I_t, \quad . \quad . \quad (10)$$

and after subtracting from both sides I_t,

$$I_{t+\omega+\theta} - I_t = a\frac{dP_t}{dt} - (b + c)I_t.$$

If the change of I_t over a period $\omega + \theta$ may be assumed not far from linear, the difference $I_{t+\omega+\theta} - I_t$ may be represented as the derivative of the medium value $\frac{dI_{t+\frac{\omega+\theta}{2}}}{dt}$ multiplied by the length of the period $\omega + \theta$. If we denote $\omega + \theta$ by 2ϵ we thus have

$$I_{t+\omega+\theta} - I_t = 2\epsilon \frac{dI_{t+\epsilon}}{dt}$$

and equation (9) may be written

$$2\epsilon \frac{dI_{t+\epsilon}}{dt} = a \frac{dP_t}{dt} - (b + c)I_t. \qquad (10a)$$

If we integrate this equation (assuming that a, b and c are constants or functions of P_t and I_t respectively) we find that investment I is an increasing function of the real profits P and a decreasing one of the volume of capital equipment some time ago, which is the basis of the business cycle theory presented in my *Essays in the Theory of Economic Fluctuations*.

It should be noticed, however, that the significance of the integral of the negative member $-(b + c)I_t$ is now different from that which it had in my theory in the *Essays*. The negative influence of the level of investment I upon the increase in investment in the subsequent period in the equation (10a) expresses: (i) the adverse influence of the increase in capital equipment (coefficient b); (ii) the effect of entrepreneurs reinvesting only a part of their current savings, even though the objective determinants of the profitability of investment are unchanged (coefficient c). In my theory in the *Essays*, however, the latter factor was abstracted and thus c was assumed to be nought.

The present theory includes as special cases the "acceleration principle" theory ($b = 0$; $c = 1$; cf. p. 65) and my old theory ($c = 0$).

3. The equation (10a) expresses the change in investment as a function of the change in real profits and of the level of investment some time ago. But according to the "multiplier" equation (5) profits are in turn a function of investment with a time-lag

$$P_t = \frac{A_{t-\kappa} + I_{t-\kappa}}{1 - \lambda}. \qquad (5)$$

From this follows, if the stable part of capitalists' consumption is assumed strictly constant for the "pure" business cycle dis-, cussion,

$$\frac{dP_t}{dt} = \frac{1}{1-\lambda}\frac{dI_{t-\kappa}}{dt}. \quad . \quad . \quad . \quad (5a)$$

By substituting this value of $\frac{dP_t}{dt}$ into the equation (10*a*) we obtain the fundamental equation

$$2\epsilon\frac{dI_{t+\epsilon}}{dt} = \frac{a}{1-\lambda}\frac{dI_{t-\kappa}}{dt} - (b+c)I_t$$

or

$$\frac{dI_{t+\epsilon+\kappa}}{dt} = \frac{a}{2\epsilon(1-\lambda)}\frac{dI_t}{dt} - \frac{b+c}{2\epsilon}I_{t+\kappa}. \quad . \quad (11)$$

This equation tells us that with a given a the change in investment to-day induces a proportionate change after a time $\epsilon + \kappa$ which, however, will be retarded by the positive level of investment I in the intermediate period ($t + \kappa$ lies between t and $t + \epsilon + \kappa$); while if this item is negative its influence will be accelerating.

The retarding influence of I reflects: (i) the adverse effect of the increase in capital equipment upon the rate of profit (coefficient b); (ii) the consequences of the fact that entrepreneurs reinvest only a part of their current savings even though the objective determinants of the profitability of investment are unchanged (coefficient c).

The Mechanism of the Business Cycle

1. Let us now divide the time into periods equal to the time-lag $\epsilon+\kappa$. The points 0, 1, 2 . . . in Figure 6 show the rate of real net investment I in successive "unit periods." (The horizontal distance between two successive points is $\epsilon + \kappa$.) The rate of change from one unit period to another is then given by the inclination of the segments 0-1, 1-2, etc. It follows directly from equation (11) that the change in the period 0-1, induces that in 1-2; the change 1-2 induces in turn that in 2-3, etc., and that the coefficient of this influence is $\frac{a}{2\epsilon(1-\lambda)}$. When dis-

cussing the process we must, of course, take into account: (1) variations in the coefficient a which measures the strength of the influence of the change in real profits upon investment and is *not* constant; (2) the retarding influence of the rate of net investment I when it is positive or its accelerating influence when it is negative. It follows from the equation (11) that the time-lag between the influence of I and the corresponding change in the rate of investment is ϵ. If one remembers that the periods 0-1, 1-2, etc., are of the length $\epsilon + \kappa$ the relevant I for the change of investment in the period 1-2 is somewhere between the middle

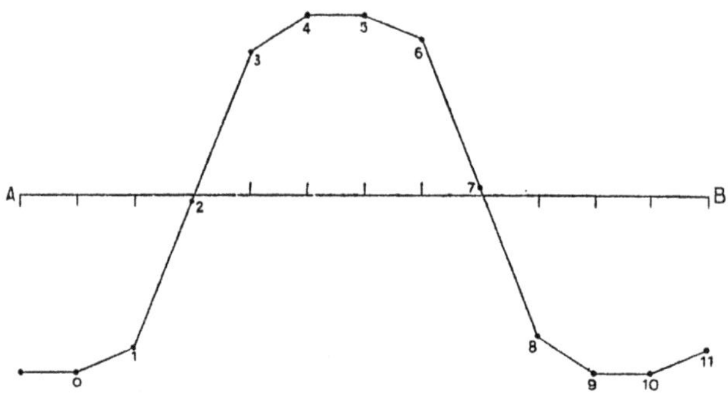

FIG. 6.—Hypothetical Time-Curve of Net Investment
(A-B corresponds to zero net investment)

of 0-1 and 1-2, for the change in investment in the period 2-3 somewhere between the middle of 1-2 and 2-3, etc.

2. Let us start our discussion of the mechanism of the business cycle from point 1 being the end of the period 0-1 in which a moderate recovery from the bottom of the slump has taken place. The positive change in investment in 0-1 induces a positive change in 1-2. The coefficient a may be assumed here very high. The entrepreneurs know that "the recovery is on." The change in profits is therefore an inducement to them not only because the rate of profit as calculated on the basis of current profits has increased, but also because they anticipate a further considerable rise in profits in the near future. Further, the relevant net investment I is negative here, which contributes to the increase in

the rate of change in 1-2 as compared with 0-1. As a result the rise in investment in the period 1-2 is considerably larger than in the period 0-1.

In the subsequent period a will fall sharply because the anticipations of entrepreneurs about a *further* rise in profits in the near future will be less optimistic: they have already a part of the boom behind them. This and the retarding influence of the positive I will finally reduce the rate of change. This need not, however, necessarily happen already in the period 2-3. If $\frac{a}{2\epsilon(1-\lambda)}$ for the period 1-2 was much higher than 1, then even after a has fallen considerably it may produce in 2-3 a greater or equal change in investment to that in 1-2. (On our graph it is assumed to be equal.) But after some time the rate of change in investment will slacken. (On the graph it is assumed to have happened in the period 3-4.) This leads finally to the stop of the rise in investment (on the graph in the period 4-5).

In the subsequent period 5-6 the rate of investment must begin to fall. For the change in investment 4-5 was nought, which without the influence of I would mean a stationary level of investment in 5-6; but the net addition to fixed capital equipment and the incomplete reinvestment of entrepreneurs' savings [1] cause a *reduction* in investment in 5-6.

Now the "slump is on" and a for the subsequent period 6-7 is very high because the entrepreneurs discount the *further* fall in profits in the near future while I is still positive, which accelerates the slump. The gradual reduction in a as these anticipations lose in strength and the negative value of I slackens the rate of fall in investment and finally brings it to a standstill in the period 9-10.

Next the negative I extricates the system from the slump just as its positive value made for the turning-point in the boom. We have thus a moderate recovery in the subsequent 10-11 which starts the boom in the next period as described above.

[1] The importance of the "incomplete reinvestment" factor for the explanation of the turning-point in the boom was emphasized for the first time by E Rothbarth in a lecture to the Economic Society of the London School of Economics in 1939

3 **

3. In this description of the mechanism of the business cycle we have left out of consideration the factor of changes in prices of investment goods. As mentioned above (p. 63), these should be accounted for in the variations of the coefficient a. The greater the change in the prices of investment goods accompanying the change in real profits dP the smaller a. It follows that in the advanced stage of the boom when raw materials and wages in investment goods industries rise rather sharply, a is likely to be reduced by this factor and so to contribute another reason for its fall from the high level it has at the beginning of the recovery.

The bottleneck in the existing capacities in investment goods industries may also contribute to the rise of prices of investment goods and thus hamper the advance of investment. Here, however, an even more important factor may be the " stretching " of orders, which will work as follows. The time-lag between investment orders and deliveries θ will increase and so, as a result, will the time-lag $\epsilon = \frac{\omega + \theta}{2}$ (ω is the delay in the influence of " inducements to invest " upon investment decisions). As the coefficient of influence of the change in investment in a " unit period " upon that in the next unit period is $\frac{a}{2\epsilon(1 - \lambda)}$, the rise in ϵ contributes to slowing down the increase of investment in the same way as the fall in a considered above.

It must be added that in the advanced stage of the boom investment decisions may be discouraged by the difficulty of finding suitable labour for employment in the new plant. This may be also accounted for in our scheme by the fall in the coefficient a. This factor will prevent investment from rising to the level at which full employment in the strict sense is reached.

4. The period of the trade cycle as described above depends on the time-lag $\epsilon + \kappa$ and on the values of the coefficients $\frac{a}{2\epsilon(1 - \lambda)}$ and $\frac{b + c}{2\epsilon}$ in the course of the trade cycle. One can say roughly that with a given time-lag $\epsilon + \kappa$ the cycle is the shorter (1) the more sharply a falls with the increasing level of

profits in the boom or with the decreasing level of profits in the slump; (2) the stronger the rise or fall in the rate of investment decisions at the beginning of the boom or slump (periods 1-2 and 6-7); (3) the higher the coefficient $\frac{b+c}{2\epsilon}$. For all these factors tend to shorten the duration of the boom and slump, and thus the period of the business cycle. (If $b = 0$ and $c = 0$ there would be no fall at all from the high level reached in the boom nor a rise from the low level reached in the slump.)

An important point about any trade cycle theory is whether the cycle may be damped down or not. Indeed, the course of the cyclical fluctuations as determined by the fundamental equation may be such that the amplitude diminishes from cycle to cycle so that the system gradually approaches a state of equilibrium. It is true that it has been shown that a combination of a damping mechanism with erratic shocks (due to the fact that the economic relations as represented by the fundamental equation are rather loose) produces cycles with an amplitude which has no tendency to decline.[1] But if damping is strong such cyclical movements would be of extremely irregular character. Thus, because it is difficult to prove why the coefficients of the fundamental equation should be such as to exclude strong damping, these theories have a serious loophole.[2] Our present theory is free of this difficulty. It may be shown that the type of variations assumed for the coefficient a prevents the cycle from being damped down.

In the period 1-2 after the beginning of recovery in 0-1 $\frac{a}{2\epsilon(1-\lambda)}$ is much greater than 1, and this accelerates the rise of investment in 1-2. If, however, the recovery in 0-1 was slight, the increase in investment in the period 1-2 may be not very considerable in spite of a high a. But then the entrepreneurs have not much of the boom behind them and therefore a does not fall strongly, and $\frac{a}{2\epsilon(1-\lambda)}$ still remains greater than 1. Thus

[1] Professor Frisch, "Propagation Problems and Impulse Problems in Dynamics," *Economic Essays in Honour of Gustav Cassel*, London 1933, and unpublished work.

[2] This may also be said of my theory in the *Essays*, see p. 148

the acceleration in the rise of investment continues, and so a high level of investment is reached. Then, however, $\frac{a}{2\epsilon(1 - \lambda)}$ does fall below 1, the increase of investment is slowed down and finally is brought to a standstill (by this variation of a and by the retarding influence of the positive I, i.e. by the rise in fixed capital equipment and incomplete reinvestment of entrepreneurs' savings). From this description it is clear that investment must rise appreciably above the zero line A-B because it is only at a relatively advanced stage of the boom that $\frac{a}{2\epsilon(1 - \lambda)}$ declines considerably below 1.

The amplitude of the cycle depends, therefore, chiefly on the level of investment at which $\frac{a}{2\epsilon(1 - \lambda)}$ begins to fall below 1, on how strongly it falls with the further rise of investment, and also on the coefficient $\frac{b + c}{2\epsilon}$ which measures the intensity of the retarding influence of the level of I. The higher the level of investment at which $\frac{a}{2\epsilon(1 - \lambda)}$ begins to fall below 1, the slower it falls with the further rise of investment, and the smaller the coefficient $\frac{b + c}{2\epsilon}$ the higher the amplitude.[1]

5. One query must still be answered. Our business cycle mechanism seems to imply that there is always recovery from a slump. On the other hand, it has been shown in the essay on

[1] With regard to the fact that the business cycle cannot be damped down and its amplitude is determined by the parameters of the system, the above theory has a certain affinity to that of Mr. Kaldor (*Economic Journal*, March 1940). He obtained his results by examining a special case of my theory in the *Essays* which I have failed to consider. His theory is therefore based on the assumption of a particular shape of the functional relation between income and the rate of investment decisions ; and it is difficult to advance any satisfactory *a priori* reasons for this shape's being necessarily such as he assumes. In my present theory the cycle is prevented from being damped down by variations in a (the coefficient of the influence of profits upon the rate of investment decisions), and the pattern of these changes in variations seems to me much better founded than the shape of Mr Kaldor's curve.

the theory of profits that investment activity can persist over long periods at its minimum level. How can this apparent contradiction be reconciled? The answer is that a situation is conceivable in which the factors causing a recovery from the slump in our business cycle model will prove inadequate.

With a given rate of interest—and the long-term rate of interest cannot fall below a certain minimum (see p. 58)—there will always be a level of the rate of profit at which all investment activity (both extensions and replacements except for necessary repairs) will stop because no investment plan appears profitable. If the rate of profit is at this level or below it, the rate of investment is at its minimum.

Imagine now that in a slump I has reached its minimum level $I_{\min}$. According to our formula (5) we may write for profits in this situation

$$P = \frac{A + I_{\min}}{1 - \lambda}.$$

Moreover, assume that the value of the stable part of capitalists' consumption in relation to the volume of capital equipment is such that the rate of profit is then appreciably *below* the level at which all investment plans become unprofitable. It is easy to show that the system is then unlikely to extricate itself from the slump. True, the volume of capital shrinks with lapse of time because depreciation is not made good, and thus the rate of profit increases because A is assumed here to be constant. But this rise is very slow, and it will take a number of years before the level of the rate of profit is reached at which any investment plans begin to become profitable. In such a situation, however, the assumption that A is constant cannot be upheld any more: the capitalists' "standard of living" will be adversely affected by the protracted slump and thus the system is likely never to reach the position where investment would start to recover from its minimum level.

6. So far we have dealt only with the fluctuations in net investment I. But since net "real" profits P are connected with I by equation (5),

$$P_t = \frac{A + I_{t-\kappa}}{1 - \lambda},$$

their fluctuations follow those of net investment. And as the required replacement R fluctuates only slightly in the course of the trade cycle, the changes in gross profits $P + R$ are also roughly determined by those in net investment I. Further, the fluctuations in the national output will be determined by those in gross real profits and by factors determining the distribution of the gross national income (cf. p. 50). However, the fluctuations in distribution are much smaller than those in gross profit $P + R$, and therefore output moves in the same direction as $P + R$.

The factors which cause a relative shift from gross profits to other incomes in the slump and from other incomes to gross profits in the boom tend to reduce the amplitude of output fluctuations, and conversely. For instance, if the salary bill rises relative to gross profits in the slump this tends to mitigate the decline in output. The fall in the ratio of material costs to wage costs in the slump tends to raise the relative share of wages in the national income (cf. p. 17) and thus works in the same direction. But the rise in the degree of oligopoly in a deep slump tends to reduce the relative share of wages in the national income (cf. p. 18) and thus to accentuate the fall in output.

The Problem of Stocks and Working Capital

1. All our argument so far has been based on the very special assumption that changes in working capital and stocks cancel each other. We shall now introduce a more general hypothesis.

Let us recall that before making any assumption about the movement of working capital and stocks we arrived on page 67 at the equation

$$J_{t+\omega+\theta} = a\frac{dP_t}{dt} - bJ_t + (1 - c)I_t. \qquad (8)$$

Now, however, we do *not* assume that total investment I is equal to the investment in finished fixed capital J, which is equivalent to changes in working capital being always just offset by that in stocks. Instead we shall assume that the balance of these influences is proportionate to the derivative of profits dP/dt; this is justified by the fact that the increase in working capital and the running down of stocks are caused by the increase in output, the movement of which is closely correlated with that of profits (see p. 76). We thus say that the change in working capital and stocks at time t is $e\frac{dP_t}{dt}$.[1]

The coefficient e (not necessarily a constant) is positive if the increase in working capital is less than offset by the running down of stocks and negative if it is more than offset by it. Statistical data suggests that it is the former case which is of practical importance. Now as the total investment I_t is equal to that in finished fixed capital J_t + the change in working capital and stocks, we have

$$I_t - J_t = e\frac{dP_t}{dt}, \qquad (12)$$

and from this and the equation (8) we obtain

$$I_{t+\omega+\theta} - e\frac{dP_{t+\omega+\theta}}{dt} = a\frac{dP_t}{dt} - b\left(I_t - e\frac{dP_t}{dt}\right) + (1-c)I_t,$$

or

$$I_{t+\omega+\theta} - I_t = (a+be)\frac{dP_t}{dt} + e\frac{dP_{t+\omega+\theta}}{dt} - (b+c)I_t.$$

After adding and subtracting $e\frac{dP_t}{dt}$ on the right-hand side we have

$$I_{t+\omega+\theta} - I_t = (a+be+e)\frac{dP_t}{dt} + e\left(\frac{dP_{t+\omega+\theta}}{dt} - \frac{dP_t}{dt}\right) - (b+c)I_t.$$

By applying the transformation described on pp. 67-68 to $I_{t+\omega+\theta} - I_t$ and to $\frac{dP_{t+\omega+\theta}}{dt} - \frac{dP_t}{dt}$ and denoting $\frac{\omega+\theta}{2} = \epsilon$, $a + be + e = a'$ we obtain

$$2\epsilon\frac{dI_{t+\epsilon}}{dt} = a'\frac{dP_t}{dt} + 2\epsilon e\frac{d^2P_{t+\epsilon}}{dt^2} - (b+c)I_t. \qquad (13)$$

[1] There may be involved here a short time-lag which we leave out of consideration for the sake of simplicity; this does not affect significantly the results of our subsequent argument.

Further, we have the "multiplier equation" for profits

$$\frac{dP_t}{dt} = \frac{1}{1-\lambda}\frac{dI_{t-\kappa}}{dt}. \quad . \quad . \quad . \quad (5a)$$

After substitution of this value of $\frac{dP_t}{dt}$ into equation (13) we arrive at

$$2\epsilon\frac{dI_{t+\epsilon}}{dt} = \frac{a'}{1-\lambda}\frac{dI_{t-\kappa}}{dt} + \frac{2\epsilon e}{1-\lambda}\frac{d^2I_{t+\epsilon-\kappa}}{dt^2} - (b+c)I_t,$$

or

$$\frac{dI_{t+\epsilon+\kappa}}{dt} = \frac{a'}{2\epsilon(1-\lambda)}\frac{dI_t}{dt} + \frac{e}{1-\lambda}\frac{d^2I_{t+\epsilon}}{dt^2} - \frac{b+c}{2\epsilon}I_{t+\kappa}. \quad (14)$$

2. This equation differs from the equation (11)—obtained on the basis of the special assumption of the changes in working capital and in stocks cancelling each other—only by the member $\frac{e}{1-\lambda}\frac{d^2I_{t+\epsilon}}{dt^2}$ and by a' having a different significance from a ($a' = a + be + e$). The business cycle mechanism described above was based on the fact that—according to the equation (11)—given the coefficient a and $b + c$, the rate of change of investment $\frac{dI_{t+\epsilon+\kappa}}{dt}$ is an increasing linear function of the rate of change of investment some time ago $\frac{dI_t}{dt}$, and a diminishing one of the level of investment in between, $I_{t+\kappa}$. (There were also made some plausible assumptions about the variation of the coefficient a.) At present the rate of change of investment $\frac{dI_{t+\epsilon+\kappa}}{dt}$ is in addition an increasing linear function of $\frac{d^2I_{t+\epsilon}}{dt^2}$, i.e. of the acceleration of the increase in investment in between ($t+\epsilon$ lies between t and $t + \epsilon + \kappa$). It follows that the acceleration of the increase in investment at the beginning of recovery in our mechanism and its slowing down in the advanced stage will now be accentuated because $\frac{d^2I_{t+\epsilon}}{dt^2}$ will be positive in the first stage and negative

in the second one. At the top of the boom $\frac{d^2I_{t+\theta}}{dt^2}$ will be negative and will thus contribute to the breakdown of the boom alongside with the adverse influence of the positive investment (member $-\frac{b+c}{2\epsilon}I_{t+\kappa}$). The position in the downward movement and at the bottom of the slump is symmetrical. Thus the pattern of the business cycle is not fundamentally changed by our new hypothesis about the changes in working capital and stocks.[1]

It must be stressed that even our second approximation to the movement of working capital and stocks is still very far from giving an accurate picture of the processes in question. From the scanty information we have, changes in working capital and stocks are much too complex to be accounted for by a simple formula. But it is likely that the deviations of the actual state of affairs from our second approximation are not sufficiently important to require fundamental changes in our pattern of the business cycle.

[1] This, however, is subject to a certain qualification. The member $\frac{e}{1-\lambda}\frac{d^2I_{t+\theta}}{dt^2}$ and the fact that $a' = a + be + e$ may cause, if e is not sufficiently low, the boom (or slump) in investment to continue in spite of the fall in the coefficient a and the retarding influence of the member $-\frac{b+c}{2\epsilon}I_{t+\kappa}$.

With regard to the *boom*, however, it may be shown that in this case a stage is finally reached where e falls to a very low level. Indeed the rate of change of working capital and stocks has been assumed $= e\frac{dP}{dt}$ because it is positively correlated with the change in output, and this in turn is positively correlated with the change in real profits P. Now if the system approaches the state of full employment the national output almost ceases to grow, even though investment and profits continue to rise. As a result the increase in working capital and stocks almost stops as well and thus e must fall to a very low level.

The argument does not apply to the *slump*, and here a sufficiently high level of e *could* cause a downswing of a cumulative character.

5. THE TREND

General Remarks on Trend

1. We shall now discuss the influence of factors which were abstracted in the preceding essay in order to obtain a " pure " business cycle in a trendless economy. We must, however, first deal shortly with the general problem of trend in relation to our " business cycle equation " :

$$\frac{dI_{t+\theta+\kappa}}{dt} = \frac{a}{2\epsilon(1-\lambda)}\frac{dI_t}{dt} - \frac{b+c}{2\epsilon}I_{t+\kappa}. \qquad (11)$$

(For the sake of simplicity we take as a basis of our inquiry into the problem of trend the equation which involves the assumption that the volume of working capital and stocks is constant. By this we abstract from the influence of the long-run changes in working capital and stocks upon the development of the system. This may be justified as a first approximation on the ground that in long-run development changes in working capital and stocks play a subordinate rôle as compared with the accumulation of fixed capital.)

Suppose that as a result of the preceding long-run development of the economy there will appear on the right hand of the above equation an additional member $L(t)$,

$$\frac{dI_{t+\theta+\kappa}}{dt} = \frac{a}{2\epsilon(1-\lambda)}\frac{dI_t}{dt} - \frac{b+c}{2\epsilon}I_{t+\kappa} + L(t), \qquad (15)$$

and thus the rate of change of investment $\frac{dI_{t+\theta+\kappa}}{dt}$ will have an additional determinant depending on the preceding evolution of the system. If such is the case the economy cannot be trendless any more. Moreover, this current trend, being the result of the preceding developments, contributes in turn to the future long-run development of the economy. It is in this way that a long-run dynamic process arises. We shall next examine briefly the influence of the features of the function $L(t)$ upon the character of the trend.

2. Let us assume first that over the period considered $L(t)$ is a constant which we shall denote by L. Our equation is then

$$\frac{dI_{t+\theta+\kappa}}{dt} = \frac{a}{2\epsilon(1-\lambda)}\frac{dI_t}{dt} - \frac{b+c}{2\epsilon}I_{t+\kappa} + L. \quad . \quad (15a)$$

Imagine now that over a certain business cycle the average of the rate of investment I is I_0 and that this value fulfils the condition

$$\frac{b+c}{2\epsilon}I_0 = L. \quad . \quad . \quad . \quad (16)$$

Let us further denote the deviations of I from its average by I' so that we have

$$I = I_0 + I'.$$

By substituting this value into the equation (15*a*) and taking into account the equation (16) we obtain

$$\frac{dI'_{t+\theta+\kappa}}{dt} = \frac{a}{2\epsilon(1-\lambda)}\frac{dI'_t}{dt} - \frac{b+c}{2\epsilon}I'_{t+\kappa}. \quad . \quad (17)$$

This equation means the same with regard to I' as equation (11) meant with regard to I. It follows that I' fluctuates now round the level I_0 in the same way as in the case of the "pure" business cycle it fluctuates round zero.

Now it may be seen that this is *the* solution of the business cycle and trend problem when $L(t)$ is a constant. Indeed, let us assume that the average of I over the cycle period, I_0, does *not* fulfil the condition (16). Imagine, for instance, that

$$\frac{b+c}{2\epsilon}I_0 < L.$$

Then, as it is easy to see, equation (17) would contain a positive trend component $L - \frac{b+c}{2\epsilon}I_0$. But that would mean that the average of I' over the cycle period could not be zero, and thus the average of I would be *not* equal to I_0. It follows that I_0 must fulfil the condition (16).

Consequently, if L is constant and positive, the rate of investment after elimination of the business cycle is positive (as $b + c > 0$) and stable. Capital accumulates but the rate of investment does not rise. If $L(t)$ is an increasing function the rate of investment also increases in the long run, while it falls if $L(t)$ is a decreasing function. Positive long-run investment may be thus rising, stable, or falling. The rising trend in the volume of capital need not be accompanied by a similar trend in the rate of investment. Statistics of net investment in fixed capital in

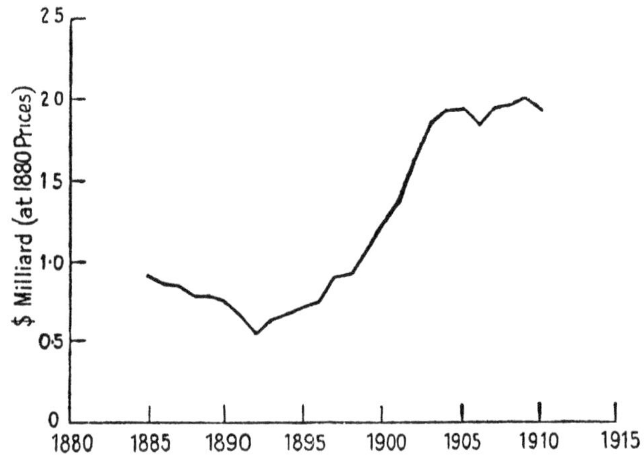

FIG. 7.—Nine-Year Moving Average of Net Investment in Fixed Capital (except Dwelling Houses) in the U.S.A. at 1880 Prices, 1881-1914 (Source: Professor Douglas, *The Theory of Wages*, p. 465).

the U.S.A. in the period 1881-1914 show a very good example of this state of affairs (see Fig. 7).

3. As long-run expansion of capital equipment may be accompanied by a fall in the rate of net investment, it is also uncertain whether net profits P will rise with the accumulation of capital. Indeed, according to equation (5), $P_t = \dfrac{A_{t-\kappa} + I_{t-\kappa}}{1 - \lambda}$ and thus, if I falls, P increases only if the stable part of capitalists' consumption A rises sufficiently to offset the decrease in I. The

gross profits $P + R$ have a greater chance to rise with the expansion of capital equipment than the net profits P, because the required replacement R rises in the long run more or less proportionately to the stock of capital. (For the same reason gross investment $I + R$ has a greater chance to rise with the volume of capital equipment than net investment I.)

The position of the salary bill is similar to that of required replacement. It will usually tend to increase with the volume of capital equipment. For this reason net profits + required replacement + salaries, i.e. profits + overheads, have a much greater chance to increase in their real value with the rise of the volume of capital equipment than net profits P.

Finally, the changes in the wage bill will be determined by changes in profits + overheads and in factors determining the distribution of the gross national income. For instance the long-run rise in the degree of oligopoly will make the wage bill fall relative to other incomes.

It follows from the above that it is not quite certain whether the gross national income or national output will increase in the long run with capital equipment. But, if there is no important change in the relative share of wages in the gross national income, such an increase is in any case much more likely than that in net profits. For the expansion in capital equipment tends to increase overheads (depreciation and maintenance, and the salary bill). And with no important changes in the relative share of wages the national output changes more or less proportionately to profits + overheads.

Long-Run Changes in Capitalists' Consumption

1. On page 60 we assumed, for the sake of the "pure business cycle" discussion, that the stable part of capitalists' consumption A_t is a constant, although in fact it varies slowly in time as a result of preceding long-run development which has influenced the capitalists' standard of living. We shall now remove this assumption and thus we must take into account that dA_t/dt is not in general equal to zero.

On page 69 we obtained from the formula

$$P_t = \frac{A_{t-\kappa} + I_{t-\kappa}}{1 - \lambda}$$

the derivative of profits

$$\frac{dP_t}{dt} = \frac{1}{1-\lambda} \frac{dI_{t-\kappa}}{dt}$$

under the assumption that A is constant. If $\frac{dA}{dt} \neq 0$ we have

$$\frac{dP_t}{dt} = \frac{1}{1-\lambda}\left(\frac{dA_{t-\kappa}}{dt} + \frac{dI_{t-\kappa}}{dt}\right).$$

It may be easily found from the argument on page 69 that as a result an additional member $\frac{a}{2\epsilon(1-\lambda)} \frac{dA_t}{dt}$ will appear on the right hand of the equation (11). In other words, we have here a trend component

$$L(t) = \frac{a}{2\epsilon(1-\lambda)} \frac{dA_t}{dt}.$$[1]

2. The trend component is here positive if $\frac{dA_t}{dt} > 0$, because the coefficient $\frac{a}{2\epsilon(1-\lambda)}$ is positive. Thus, according to the results arrived at in the last section, a positive change in the stable part of capitalists' consumption causes a long-run accumulation of capital. This is quite plausible because a positive dA/dt means a positive trend in profits P because $P_t = \frac{1}{1-\lambda}(A_{t-\kappa} + I_{t-\kappa})$. A system which we rendered stationary in the essay on "pure

[1] The problem is actually a little more complicated because of the fact that the coefficient a undergoes cyclical fluctuations. However, a may be represented as $a_0 + a'$, where a_0 is the average a over the cycle period and a' the deviation of a from a_0. Thus $\frac{a}{2\epsilon(1-\lambda)} \frac{dA_t}{dt} = \frac{a_0}{2\epsilon(1-\lambda)} \frac{dA_t}{dt} + \frac{a'}{2\epsilon(1-\lambda)} \frac{dA_t}{dt}$. The actual trend component is $\frac{a_0}{2\epsilon(1-\lambda)} \frac{dA_t}{dt}$. The member $\frac{a'}{2\epsilon(1-\lambda)} \frac{dA_t}{dt}$ is of cyclical character; it will have a certain influence upon the course of the trade cycle.

business cycle" by the assumption that $\frac{dA}{dt} = 0$ will be an expanding one—at least with regard to capital equipment—if dA/dt is positive.

Now what factors in the past long-run development cause the rise (or fall) of the stable part of capitalists' consumption A? A secular rise in wealth and income of capitalists tends to raise, with rather a long time-lag, their "standard of living," i.e. the amount they are apt to consume irrespective of the level of their current income. Thus an increase in capital and profits in the past tends to cause a positive dA/dt. But these are not the only factors in question. For the long-run rise in capital and profits may be associated with the concentration of both, and this tends to reduce A.

It follows that the trend caused by a positive dA/dt in a certain period need not be "self-continuing." True, a positive dA/dt causes an accumulation of capital which tends to cause A to increase in the future. It is, however, not certain if a positive dA_t/dt causes a rise in profits [1] which are the other link with the future changes in A. Moreover, the possible increase in the concentration of capitalists' wealth and income may induce a fall in A even though capital and profits were rising over the past long period.

Rentiers' Savings

1. To render our system trendless we also abstracted from rentiers' savings (see p. 66). If they are taken into consideration it follows from page 64 and the subsequent argument (pp. 66-69) that an additional member $-\frac{1-c}{2\epsilon}s_{t+\kappa}$ appears on the right-hand side of equation (11). We have thus a trend component,

$$L(t) = -\frac{1-c}{2\epsilon}s_{t+\kappa},$$

[1] We have for them the formula $P = \frac{A_{t-\kappa} + I_{t-\kappa}}{1-\lambda}$. Now if $\frac{dA}{dt}$ is positive so is the long-run rate of investment, but as shown in the preceding section, I may be constant, rising or falling. And thus in the latter case it is not certain that the profits P rise even though A increases.

where $s_{t+\kappa}$ is the " real " value of rentiers' savings. $L(t)$ is here always negative. Indeed, the coefficient $1 - c$ is positive (see p. 63); so, of course, is the time-lag ϵ, and the real rentiers' saving may be assumed always to be positive because their real incomes are rather steady (except in abnormal cases of hyper-inflation), and on the average sufficiently large to make them savers. Consequently, according to the preceding section, the existence of rentiers' savings causes a negative long-run investment, i.e. long-run shrinking of capital equipment. This is not surprising. By the assumption $s = 0$ we obtained in the essay on the " pure business cycle " a trendless system. But such a stationary situation (from the long-run point of view) is incompatible with positive rentiers' savings because this causes a continuous increase in the entrepreneurs' indebtedness towards rentiers which depresses investment activity (cf. pp. 61-62). Therefore the rentiers' savings—if taken in isolation from other trend factors—create a negative trend.

2. If prices are falling over a certain long period it causes the real value of rentiers' savings to increase over this period and thus accelerates the negative trend caused by them. If, because of the existence of positive trend factors, the total $L(t)$ is positive, the long-run fall in prices tends to decrease $L(t)$. But, as shown in the preceding section, a decreasing $L(t)$ causes a long-run fall in the rate of net investment I. It follows that the long-run fall in prices will, through this channel, affect adversely the long-run rate of net investment.

The Rise in Population and the Increasing Productivity of Labour

1. It is frequently maintained that the main reason for trend is the rise in population or the increase in productivity due to technical progress. No doubt one or the other is a *necessary* condition for a long-run expansion of output of an economy which has no large reserve army of unemployed. But are they also a *sufficient* condition? Does the rise in population or the increase in labour productivity due to technical progress *induce* the trend movement?

Let us first consider the influence of the rise in population. If population increases while output remains stable in the long-run there will be a secular increase in unemployment. This exerts a pressure on money wages which consequently tend to fall. The problem is thus reduced to the question: How will a long-run fall in money wages affect our trend analysis? Now money wages do not appear at all in our fundamental equations. That may be traced to the fact that real profits P are fully determined by past consumption and investment decisions of capitalists and that into their current decisions enter again current real profits and the volume of capital equipment (or changes in these elements). This is in line with the Keynesian theory of money wages. There is, however, one influence of money wages which should enter our fundamental equation and was abstracted only for our "pure business cycle" analysis. Indeed, a long-run fall in money wages causes a fall in prices and thus with stable output a fall in the money volume of transactions. If the supply of cash by banks is not proportionately reduced this leads in turn to a long-run fall of the short-term rate of interest which results in a fall of the long-term rate of interest. Now such a fall will make for the appearance of a positive member $L(t)$ on the right-hand side of our fundamental equation and cause a positive trend movement. The increase in output in such a movement cannot, however, be so great as to prevent the long-run increase in unemployment for in such a case the very cause of the trend would disappear.

2. Let us now consider the effects of the increase in the productivity of labour due to technical progress. The immediate effect, as in the case of a wage cut, is to reduce wage costs and prices. This causes a fall in turnover (money volume of transactions) and consequently a decline in the rate of interest, which creates a tendency for a positive trend. If as a result output increases in the same proportion as productivity of labour, no unemployment arises.

If, however, the increase in output is smaller, "technological unemployment" must appear. This (as in the case of the increase in population) will depress wages. As a result an additional fall in the rate of interest will ensue which will induce an additional positive trend. But the latter cannot lead to a full absorption of "technological unemployment" for then the very cause of the additional trend would cease to exist.

3. The functioning of the mechanisms described seems, however, to be of very doubtful character. The connection between the rise in unemployment and the fall of money wages is rather loose if strong trade unions are in existence. Even more uncertain is the connection between the fall in turnover and that in the short-term rate of interest in the long run. If the fall in turnover continues over a long period the banking policy may easily adapt itself to this secular fall in such a way that the supply of balances shrinks *pari passu* with turnover and thus no fall in the short-term rate of interest occurs. In any case if growth of population and increase in productivity of labour were the main causes of trend the turnover would have a secular tendency to fall, which is by no means generally the case. Moreover, as we have seen in the last section, the secular fall in the price level exerts a negative influence upon the expansion of the economy by increasing the real value of rentiers' saving, and this counteracts the positive effect of the pressing down of the rate of interest.

To conclude: although growth of population or increasing productivity are a necessary condition for the long-run expansion of output if no large reserves of labour are available, these factors seem not to play an important rôle in *inducing* the trend movement.[1]

[1] It is sometimes maintained that the increase in population encourages investment because the entrepreneurs anticipate a broadening market. What is important, however, in this context is not the increase in population but in purchasing power. The increase in the number of paupers does not broaden the market. For instance, increased population does not mean necessarily a higher demand for houses: without an increase in the purchasing power the result may well be crowding of more people into the existing dwelling space. On the other hand, it should be noticed that our conclusions are valid only if our simplifying assumptions that the system is closed and the State Budget balanced are fulfilled. In an open system the fall in wage rates resulting from unemployment growing as a result of the increase in population will stimulate exports and so contribute to the upward trend. The payment of doles for unemployed, if financed by Government borrowing, will constitute another channel through which the rise in population may cause a positive trend of the system.

It follows that growing population and increasing productivity of labour may well cause long-run unemployment without setting to work forces which would absorb it.

Innovations

1. We tried to show above that the increase in productivity of labour due to technical progress is not likely *as such* to be an important factor in creating a trend movement. This does not mean, however, that technical progress as a whole is an indifferent phenomenon in this respect. On the contrary, some aspects of technical progress, we mean innoviations, *are* probably one of the main forces behind the long-run economic development.

The influence of new inventions upon investment consists in making the profitability of a certain type of investment higher than it would be otherwise. A new invention will therefore be another factor—alongside the change in current profits and capital equipment (see pp. 63-64)—which causes the emergence of investment decisions in a given period. With the replacement of old equipment by modern, the additional profitability of investment caused by the invention is gradually reduced and this has a negative effect upon investment decisions. The appearance of new inventions has a similar effect in the sphere of investment activity as a rise in current profits ; the repercussions of the "spreading" of inventions by replacing old by modern equipment may be compared with those of a fall in current profits.

Thus in any period we have the positive influence of new inventions on the one hand, and the negative effect of the gradual "liquidation" of past ones on the other. We shall call the technical progress uniform with regard to investment if these two effects upon an economy of a given size cancel out. If the effect is on balance positive or negative, we shall speak of accelerated or retarded technical progress.

2. It may seem from the definition of uniform technical progress that the corresponding trend component $L(t) = 0$ because the effect of new inventions on investment are exactly

offset by the "liquidation" of past ones. That may be so, but need not necessarily be the case.

We stressed in our definition that the positive and negative effect cancel out with regard to an economy of a *given size*. Now the larger the economy the larger is the positive effect of new inventions upon investment; it may be considered roughly proportionate to the volume of capital equipment. Further, the negative effect of replacements "liquidating" the old inventions may be assumed roughly proportionate to the volume of old equipment at the time when the respective inventions emerged. It follows clearly that if we have a uniform technical progress, but if in the longer period preceding the period considered the equipment was steadily growing, the positive effect will be larger than the negative effect, i.e. $L(t) > 0$. And only in the case when the equipment was stationary in the preceding long period is $L(t) = 0$. Thus uniform technical progress will cause the development of the preceding long period to continue; for, as shown above, a positive trend component $L(t)$ causes a long-run accumulation of capital. While, if the system was stationary in the preceding long period, uniform technical progress will not induce expansion because then $L(t) = 0$.

A stationary economy is thus not incompatible with uniform technical progress. But if the economy expanded prior to the period considered, the uniform technical progress will cause this expansion to continue.

3. In the latter case the positive trend component $L(t)$ depends on two factors: (1) It is the greater the larger is the rate of capital accumulation, i.e. of net investment, in the preceding long-run period, because the stronger was the preceding expansion the greater the difference between the positive effect of new inventions and the negative effect of the liquidation of past inventions. (2) In addition $L(t)$ depends on the speed of the uniform technical progress, i.e. on the magnitude of the "investment effect" of new inventions. With the increase of the speed of the uniform technical progress both the positive and the negative effect rise in the same proportion and, consequently, so does $L(t)$, being the balance of these two effects.

From the latter it follows that the relation of the long-run net investment caused by $L(t)$ to the net investment in the preceding long period increases with the speed of technical progress. For $L(t)$ rises with the latter and net investment caused by $L(t)$ is the larger the greater is $L(t)$ (see p. 81). There will thus be a certain speed of technical progress which makes current long-run investment equal to the past long-run investment. The uniform technical progress then causes the capital accumulation of the past period to continue at the same rate. If the speed of technical progress is higher the current long-run investment will be higher than that in the past, and thus the technical progress causes here a secular growth of the rate of investment. Finally, if the speed of technical progress is lower than that necessary to maintain the rate of net investment, this will cause a long-run fall in the latter and the system will then approach asymptotically a stationary situation in which long-run net investment is zero.

4. So far we have discussed only technical progress uniform with regard to investment. According to our definition an accelerated technical progress takes place if the balance of the effect of new inventions and " liquidation " of past inventions on investment is positive for an economy of a given size. In such a case the trend component $L(t)$ is positive, and consequently so is the resulting net investment, even if in the preceding long-run period the system was stationary (i.e. the long-run net investment was equal to zero). While if the economy was previously expanding $L(t)$ consists of two components, one resulting from the acceleration of technical progress and the other from the preceding expansion of the system. If technical progress is retarded with regard to investment $L(t)$ is negative if the economy was stationary in the preceding long-run period; while if the economy was previously expanding $L(t)$ is the balance of the positive component resulting from this expansion and a negative one due to the slowing down of the technical progress.

Imagine now that in the initial long period technical progress is accelerated and this causes $L(t)$ and consequently net investment to be positive. Imagine further that after this period technical progress is uniform but the speed which it has reached is sufficient at least to maintain the rate of net investment of the preceding period. We shall then have a continuous trend created entirely by technical progress. *This pattern is likely to have played an important rôle in the development of capitalist economies.*

Imagine now on the other hand that after a period of expansion technical progress is slowing down (with regard to investment) over the period considered. This may occur, for instance, because of the formation of industrial monopolies which hamper the application of new inventions ; or it may be the result of concentrating of technical progress on " scientific organization " of labour. This retardation of technical progress with regard to investment depresses $L(t)$ and thus the net investment in the period considered. In addition, the speed of technical progress is reduced ; if it has fallen appreciably below the level which is necessary to maintain the rate of net investment in the future at the level of the period considered—net investment will rapidly approach zero in the subsequent period and the expansion of the system will come to a standstill.

5. There emerge out of our analysis, as the chief determinants of investment in the long run, changes in capitalists' consumption, rentiers' savings and innovations.

It should be noted that the limitations imposed on our analysis by simplifying assumptions prevented such factors as capital exports, budget deficits and gold production from being taken into consideration, although they definitely played a very important rôle in the development of single capitalist economies.

POLITICAL ASPECTS OF FULL EMPLOYMENT[1]

By M. KALECKI

I

A SOLID majority of economists is now of the opinion that, even in a capitalist system, full employment may be secured by a Government spending programme, provided there is in existence adequate plant to employ all existing labour power, and provided adequate supplies of necessary foreign raw materials may be obtained in exchange for exports

If the Government undertakes public investment (e g builds schools, hospitals, and highways) or subsidises mass consumption (by family allowances, reduction of indirect taxation, or subsidies to keep down the prices of necessities), if, moreover, this expenditure is financed by borrowing and not by taxation (which could affect adversely private investment and consumption), the effective demand for goods and services may be increased up to a point where full employment is achieved. Such Government expenditure increases employment, be it noted, not only directly but indirectly as well, since the higher incomes caused by it result in a secondary increase in demand for consumption and investment goods.

2.—It may be asked where the public will get the money to lend to the Government if they do not curtail their investment and consumption. To understand this process it is best, I think, to imagine for a moment that the Government pays its suppliers in Government securities. The suppliers will, in general, not retain these securities but put them into circulation while buying other goods and services, and so on until finally these securities will reach persons or firms which retain them as interest-yielding assets. In any period of time the total increase in Government securities in the possession (transitory or final) of persons and firms will be equal to the goods and services sold to the Government. Thus what the economy lends to the Government are goods and services whose production is "financed" by Government securities. In reality the Government pays for the services not in securities but in cash, but it simultaneously issues securities and so drains the cash

[1] This article corresponds roughly to a lecture given to the Marshall Society in Cambridge in the Spring of 1942

322

off; and this is equivalent to the imaginary process described above.

What happens, however, if the public is unwilling to absorb all the increase in Government securities? It will offer them finally to banks to get cash (notes or deposits) in exchange. If the banks accept these offers, the rate of interest will be maintained. If not, the prices of securities will fall, which means a rise in the rate of interest, and this will encourage the public to hold more securities in relation to deposits. It follows that the rate of interest depends on banking policy, in particular on that of the Central Bank. If this policy aims at maintaining the rate of interest at a certain level that may be easily achieved, however large the amount of Government borrowing. Such was and is the position in the present war. In spite of astronomical budget deficits, the rate of interest has shown no rise since the beginning of 1940.

3.—It may be objected that Government expenditure financed by borrowing will cause inflation. To this may be replied that the effective demand created by the Government acts like any other increase in demand. If labour, plant and foreign raw materials are in ample supply, the increase in demand is met by an increase in production. But if the point of full employment of resources is reached and effective demand continues to increase, prices will rise so as to equilibrate the demand for and the supply of goods and services. (In the state of overemployment of resources such as we witness at present in the war economy, an inflationary rise in prices has been avoided only to the extent to which effective demand for consumption goods has been curtailed by rationing and direct taxation.) It follows that if the Government intervention aims at achieving full employment but stops short of increasing effective demand over the full employment mark, there is no need to be afraid of inflation.[1]

[1] Another problem of a more technical nature is that of the National Debt. If full employment is maintained by Government spending financed by borrowing, the National Debt will continuously increase. This need not, however, involve any disturbances in output and employment, if interest on the Debt is financed by an annual capital tax. The current income after payment of capital tax of some capitalists will be lower and of some higher than if the National Debt had not increased, but their aggregate income will remain unaltered and their aggregate consumption will not be likely to change significantly. Further, the inducement to invest in fixed capital is not affected by a capital tax because it is paid on any type of wealth. Whether an amount is held in cash or Government securities or invested in building a factory, the same capital tax is paid on it and thus the comparative advantage is unchanged. And if investment is financed by loans it is clearly not affected by a capital tax because it does not mean an increase in wealth of the investing *entrepreneur* Thus neither capitalists' consumption nor investment is affected by the rise in the National Debt if interest on it is financed by an annual capital tax

II

1.—The above is a very crude and incomplete statement of the economic doctrine of full employment. But, I think, it is sufficient to acquaint the reader with the essence of the doctrine and so enable him to follow the subsequent discussion of the *political* problems involved in the achievement of full employment.

It should be first stated that although most economists are now agreed that full employment may be achieved by Government spending, this was by no means the case even in the recent past. Among the opposers of this doctrine there were (and still are) prominent so called "economic experts" closely connected with banking and industry. This suggests that there is a political background in the opposition to the full employment doctrine even though the arguments advanced are economic. That is not to say that people who advance them do not believe in their economics, poor though these are. But obstinate ignorance is usually a manifestation of underlying political motives.

There are, however, even more direct indications that a first class political issue is at stake here. In the great depression in the thirties, big business opposed consistently experiments for increasing employment by Government spending in all countries, except Nazi Germany. This was to be clearly seen in the U.S.A. (opposition to the New Deal), in France (Blum experiment) and also in Germany before Hitler. The attitude is not easy to explain. Clearly higher output and employment benefits not only workers, but *entrepreneurs* as well, because their profits rise. And the policy of full employment outlined above does not encroach upon profits because it does not involve any additional taxation. The *entrepreneurs* in the slump are longing for a boom; why do not they accept gladly the "synthetic" boom which the Government is able to offer them? It is this difficult and fascinating question with which we intend to deal in this article.

The reasons for the opposition of the "industrial leaders" to full employment achieved by Government spending may be subdivided into three categories: (i) the dislike of Government interference in the problem of employment as such; (ii) the dislike of the direction of Government spending (public investment and subsidising consumption); (iii) dislike of the social and political changes resulting from the *maintenance* of full employment. We shall examine each of these three categories of objections to the Government expansion policy in detail.

2.—We shall deal first with the reluctance of the "captains of industry" to accept Government intervention in the matter of employment. Every widening of State activity is looked upon by "business" with suspicion, but the creation of employment by Government spending has a special aspect which makes the opposition particularly intense. Under a *laisser-faire* system the level of employment depends to a great extent on the so-called state of confidence. If this deteriorates, private investment declines, which results in a fall of output and employment (both directly and through the secondary effect of the fall in incomes upon consumption and investment). This gives to the capitalists a powerful indirect control over Government policy: everything which may shake the state of confidence must be carefully avoided because it would cause an economic crisis. But once the Government learns the trick of increasing employment by its own purchases, this powerful controlling device loses its effectiveness. Hence budget deficits necessary to carry out Government intervention must be regarded as perilous. The social function of the doctrine of "sound finance" is to make the level of employment dependent on the "state of confidence."

3.—The dislike of the business leaders of a Government spending policy grows even more acute when they come to consider the objects on which the money would be spent: public investment and subsidising mass consumption.

The economic principles of Government intervention require that public investment should be confined to objects which do not compete with the equipment of private business (e.g. hospitals, schools, highways, etc.). Otherwise the profitability of private investment might be impaired and the positive effect of public investment upon employment offset by the negative effect of the decline in private investment. This conception suits the business men very well. But the scope of public investment of this type is rather narrow, and there is a danger that the Government, in pursuing this policy, may eventually be tempted to nationalise transport or public utilities so as to gain a new sphere in which to carry out investment.[1]

One might therefore expect business leaders and their experts to be more in favour of subsidising mass consumption (by means

[1] It should be noticed here that investment in a nationalised industry can contribute to the solution of the problem of unemployment only if it is undertaken on principles different from these of private enterprise. The Government must be satisfied with a lower net rate of return than private enterprise, or it must deliberately time its investment so as to mitigate slumps.

of family allowances, subsidies to keep down the prices of necessities, etc.) than of public investment; for by subsidising consumption the Government would not be embarking on any sort of "enterprise." In practice, however, this is not the case. Indeed, subsidising mass consumption is much more violently opposed by these "experts" than public investment. For here a "moral" principle of the highest importance is at stake. The fundamentals of capitalist ethics require that "You shall earn your bread in sweat"—unless you happen to have private means.

4.—We have considered the political reasons for the opposition against the policy of creating employment by Government spending. But even if this opposition were overcome—as it may well be under the pressure of the masses—the *maintenance* of full employment would cause social and political changes which would give a new impetus to the opposition of the business leaders. Indeed, under a regime of permanent full employment, "the sack" would cease to play its role as a disciplinary measure. The social position of the boss would be undermined and the self assurance and class consciousness of the working class would grow. Strikes for wage increases and improvements in conditions of work would create political tension. It is true that profits would be higher under a regime of full employment than they are on the average under *laisser-faire*; and even the rise in wage rates resulting from the stronger bargaining power of the workers is less likely to reduce profits than to increase prices, and thus affects adversely only the *rentier* interests. But "discipline in the factories" and "political stability" are more appreciated by the business leaders than profits. Their class instinct tells them that lasting full employment is unsound from their point of view and that unemployment is an integral part of the "normal" capitalist system.

III

1.—One of the important functions of fascism, as typified by the Nazi system, was to remove the capitalist objections to full employment.

The dislike of Government spending policy as such is overcome under fascism by the fact that the State machinery is under the direct control of a partnership of big business with fascist upstarts. The necessity for the myth of "sound finance," which served to prevent the Government from offsetting a confidence crisis by spending, is removed. In a democracy one does not know what the next Government will be like. Under Fascism there is no next Government.

The dislike of Government spending, whether on public investment or consumption, is overcome by concentrating Government expenditure on armaments. Finally, "discipline in the factories" and "political stability" under full employment are maintained by the "new order," which ranges from the suppression of the trade unions to the concentration camp. Political pressure replaces the economic pressure of unemployment.

2.—The fact that armaments are the backbone of the policy of fascist full employment has a profound influence upon its economic character. Large-scale armaments are inseparable from the expansion of the armed forces and the preparation of plans for a war of conquest. They also induce competitive rearmament of other countries. This causes the main aim of the spending to shift gradually from full employment to securing the maximum effect of rearmament. As a result employment becomes "overfull"; not only is unemployment abolished but an acute scarcity of labour prevails. Bottlenecks arise in every sphere and these must be dealt with by creation of a number of controls. Such an economy has many features of a "planned economy," and is sometimes compared, rather ignorantly, with socialism. However, this type of "planning" is bound to appear whenever an economy puts itself a certain high target of production in a particular sphere, when it becomes a "target economy" of which the "armament economy" is a special case. An "armament economy" involves in particular the curtailment of consumption as compared with what it could have been under full employment.

The fascist system starts from the overcoming of unemployment, develops into an "armament economy" of scarcity, and ends inevitably in war.

IV

1.—What will be the practical outcome of the opposition to "full employment by Government spending" in a capitalist democracy? We shall try to answer this question on the basis of the analysis of the reasons for this opposition given in section II. We argued that we may expect the opposition of the "leaders of industry" on three planes: (i) the opposition on principle against Government spending based on a budget deficit; (ii) the opposition against this spending being directed either towards public investment—which may foreshadow the intrusion of the state into the new spheres of economic activity—or towards subsidising mass consumption; (iii) the opposition against *maintaining* full employment and not merely preventing deep and prolonged slumps.

Now, it must be recognised that the stage in which the "business leaders" could afford to be opposed to *any* kind of Government interventions to alleviate a slump is rather a matter of the past. Three factors have contributed to this: (*a*) very full employment during the present war; (*b*) the development of the economic doctrine of full employment; (*c*) partly as a result of these two factors the slogan "Unemployment never again" is now deeply rooted in the consciousness of the masses. This position is reflected in the recent pronouncements of the "captains of industry" and their experts. The necessity that "something must be done in the slump" is agreed to; but the fight continues, firstly, as to "*what* should be done in the slump" (i.e. what should be the direction of Government intervention), and secondly, that "it should be done *only* in the slump" (i.e. merely to alleviate slumps rather than to secure permanent full employment).

2.—In the current discussions of these problems there emerges time and again the conception of counteracting the slump by stimulating *private* investment. This may be done by lowering the rate of interest, by the reduction of income tax, or by subsidising private investment directly in this or another form. That such a scheme should be attractive to "business" is not surprising. The *entrepreneur* remains the medium through which the intervention is conducted. If he does not feel confidence in the political situation he will not be bribed into investment. And the intervention does not involve the Government either in "playing with" (public) investment or "wasting money" on subsidising consumption.

It may be shown, however, that the stimulation of private investment does not provide an adequate method for preventing mass unemployment. There are two alternatives to be considered here. (*a*) The rate of interest or income tax (or both) is reduced sharply in the slump and increased in the boom. In this case both the period and the amplitude of the business cycle will be reduced, but employment not only in the slump but even in the boom may be far from full, i.e. the average unemployment may be considerable, although its fluctuations will be less marked. (*b*) The rate of interest or income tax is reduced in a slump but *not* increased in the subsequent boom. In this case the boom will last longer but it must end in a new slump: one reduction in the rate of interest or income tax does not, of course, eliminate the forces which cause cyclical fluctuations in a capitalist economy. In the new slump it will be necessary to reduce the rate of interest or income tax again and so on. Thus in not too remote a time the rate of interest would have to be negative and income tax would have to be replaced by an income subsidy. The same would arise if it were attempted to *maintain* full employment by stimulating private investment: the rate of interest and income tax would have to be reduced continuously.[1]

In addition to this fundamental weakness of combating unemployment by stimulating private investment, there is a practical difficulty. The reaction of the *entrepreneurs* to the measures described is uncertain. If the down-swing is sharp they may take a very pessimistic view of the future, and the reduction of the rate of interest or income tax may then for a long time have little or no effect upon investment, and thus upon the level of output and employment.

3.—Even those who advocate stimulating private investment to counteract the slump frequently do not rely on it exclusively but envisage that it should be associated with public investment. It looks at present as if " business leaders " and their experts (at least part of them) would tend to accept as a *pis aller* public investment financed by borrowing as a means of alleviating slumps. They seem, however, still to be consistently opposed to creating employment by subsidising consumption and to *maintaining* full employment.

This state of affairs is perhaps symptomatic of the future economic regime of capitalist democracies. In the slump, either under the pressure of the masses, or even without it, public investment financed by borrowing will be undertaken to prevent large scale unemployment. But if attempts are made to apply this method in order to maintain the high level of employment reached in the subsequent boom a strong opposition of "business leaders " is likely to be encountered. As has already been argued, lasting full employment is not at all to their liking. The workers would " get out of hand " and the " captains of industry " would be anxious to " teach them a lesson." Moreover, the price increase in the up-swing is to the disadvantage of small and big *rentiers* and makes them " boom tired."

[1] A rigorous demonstration of this is given in my article to be published in *Oxford Economic Papers*

In this situation a powerful block is likely to be formed between big business and the *rentier* interests, and they would probably find more than one economist to declare that the situation was manifestly unsound. The pressure of all these forces, and in particular of big business—as a rule influential in Government departments—would most probably induce the Government to return to the orthodox policy of cutting down the budget deficit. A slump would follow in which Government spending policy would come again into its own.

This pattern of a "political business cycle" is not entirely conjectural; something very much like that happened in the U.S.A. in 1937-1938. The breakdown of the boom in the second half of 1937 was actually due to the drastic reduction of the budget deficit. On the other hand, in the acute slump that followed the Government promptly reverted to a spending policy.

The regime of the "political business cycle" would be an artificial restoration of the position as it existed in nineteenth century capitalism. Full employment would be reached only at the top of the boom, but slumps would be relatively mild and short lived.

V

1.—Should a progressive be satisfied with a regime of the "political business cycle" as described in the preceding section? I think he should oppose it on two grounds: (i) that it does not assure lasting full employment; (ii) that Government intervention is tied down to public investment and does not embrace subsidising consumption. What the masses now ask for is not the mitigation of slumps but their total abolition. Nor should the resulting fuller utilisation of resources be applied to unwanted public investment merely in order to provide work. The Government spending programme should be devoted to public investment only to the extent to which such investment is *actually needed*. The rest of Government spending necessary to maintain full employment should be used to subsidise consumption (through family allowances, old age pensions, reduction in indirect taxation, subsidising of prices of necessities). The opposers of such Government spending say that the Government will then have nothing to show for their money. The reply is that the counterpart of this spending will be the higher standard of living of the masses. Is not this the purpose of all economic activity?

2.—" Full employment capitalism " will have, of course, to develop new social and political institutions which will reflect the increased power of the working class. If capitalism can adjust itself to full employment a fundamental reform will have been incorporated in it. If not, it will show itself an outmoded system which must be scrapped.

But perhaps the fight for full employment may lead to fascism? Perhaps capitalism will adjust itself to full employment in *this* way? This seems extremely unlikely. Fascism sprang up in Germany against a background of tremendous unemployment and maintained itself in power through securing full employment while capitalist democracy failed to do so. The fight of the progressive forces for full employment is at the same time a way of *preventing* the recurrence of fascism..

For Product Safety Concerns and Information please contact our EU representative GPSR@taylorandfrancis.com
Taylor & Francis Verlag GmbH, Kaufingerstraße 24, 80331 München, Germany

www.ingramcontent.com/pod-product-compliance
Lightning Source LLC
LaVergne TN
LVHW020626300926
849161LV00004B/619
9780415249348